Growing
Older,
Growing
Better

OTHER BOOKS BY AMY E. DEAN

Facing Life's Challenges
Pleasant Dreams
LifeGoals
Caring for the Family Soul
Daybreak: 52 Things Nature Teaches Us
Natural Acts
Night Light
Peace of Mind
Proud to Be
Letters to My Birthmother
Making Changes
Once Upon a Time

Visit the Hay House Website at:
http://www.hayhouse.com

Growing Older, Growing Better

Daily Meditations for Celebrating Aging

❧   ❧   ❧

Amy E. Dean

Hay House, Inc.
Carlsbad, CA

Published and distributed in the United States by:
Hay House, Inc., P.O. Box 5100, Carlsbad, CA 92018-5100 • (800) 654-5126
(800) 650-5115 (fax)

Edited by: Jill Kramer   Designed by: Jenny Richards

The author of this book does not dispense medical advice or prescribe the use of any technique as a form of treatment for physical or medical problems without the advice of a physician, either directly or indirectly. The intent of the author is only to offer information of a general nature to help you in your quest for emotional well-being and good health. In the event you use any of the information in this book for yourself, which is your constitutional right, the author and the publisher assume no responsibility for your actions.

Library of Congress Cataloging-in-Publication Data

Dean, Amy.
     Growing older, growing better : daily meditations for celebrating aging / Amy E. Dean.
        p.   cm.
     Includes index.
     ISBN 1-56170-353-2 (trade paper)
     1. Affirmations. 2. Aging—Psychological aspects. 3. Middle aged persons—Psychology. 4. Aged—Psychology. I. Title.
     BF697.5.S47D424   1997
     305.26—dc21   96-46161
                                                      CIP

ISBN 1-56170-353-2

00 99 98 97   4 3 2 1
First Printing, January 1997

Printed in the United States of America

To Kim Parker,
an "old" friend, who just keeps getting better and better.

INTRODUCTION

When America was founded a little over two centuries ago, the median age of the citizens of the Republic was 16, with an average life expectancy of 35 years. A century later, little had changed: the median age was 21, and the average life expectancy was 40. As a result, little thought went into how to handle growing older. People lived less than a few decades and then died, most often from diseases such as smallpox, cholera, tuberculosis, measles, pneumonia, influenza, whooping cough, and syphilis. Epidemics, poor sanitation, limited medical knowledge, the lack of disease-controlling drugs, nutritionally unsound diets, harsh living conditions, and many other factors contributed to the high mortality rates that kept this nation young.

As a result, adult children rarely had to deal with taking care of their aging parents, and couples didn't have to deal with relationship issues after their children left home since "empty nests" weren't empty for too long. People weren't concerned with Social Security, Medicare, and other financial transfers between generations. There was no need for retirement housing and nursing homes for older people.

But in the second century, significant breakthroughs in medical care brought under control many of the diseases that once spread unchecked. Living conditions improved. Sanitation guidelines were established. Nutrition needs were addressed. As a result, the median age steadily began to climb, reaching today's all-time high of 35 years. Also, the life expectancy of the entire American population has doubled since the country was founded. Whereas in the past, only one in ten people could have expected to live to the age of 65, today nearly 80 percent of Americans will live well past that age.

You may be one of the more than 75 million "baby boomers" in the United States who have living parents or who are blessed with the presence of at least one living grandparent in your life. Or, you may be a member of the growing population of "senior boomers" who have an average life expectancy of 75 years for men and 83 years for women. Yet no matter which population you're a part of, you're in the midst of a life-span migration. That means that you'll probably live longer than you might expect, as each year medical science slows the aging process through new drugs, therapies, health programs, foods, and lifestyle changes. You'll probably discover that your concept of marriage may change over time; a "till-death-do-us-part" union may not adequately address your needs over the decades you share with one person. This means that you may find yourself falling in love later in life (or many times in your life), gravitating toward serial monogamy relationships, or exploring your sexuality well beyond childbearing years. You'll most likely change the physical environment in which you live, opting—as you grow older—to move to communities that offer a population and lifestyle more geared to what you need. You may never retire, or you may "retire" many times after reentering the work force at a variety of levels. Or, you may return to school, start your own business, begin a family with a new partner, work flexible hours, and explore many other post-retirement options for personal and professional stimulation.

In short, you'll most likely challenge—and change—the myths of aging and the perceptions of older people that younger people (and many older people) have. In freeing yourself from such ageist stereotypes of older people, you'll most likely discover that you can be a productive, active, alert, sexual, creative, energetic, healthy, and joyous member of a population of social pioneers who not only welcome growing older, but grow better in the process.

Growing Older, Growing Better is a book for anyone over 50 years old who is convinced that the decades after the forties can be rich and fulfilling, a time in which to celebrate the potentials and possibilities in the second half of life.

JANUARY 1

"It is always important to create one's unique being in the world, and in midlife, it is imperative. If Nature has prolonged our lives 25–40 years...it is vitally important to create/discover our purpose in the large picture, and to use our living, developing wisdom for the good of ourselves and those with whom we share life."

— nurse practitioner Maura Kelsea

MIDLIFE ATTITUDE

Midlife can be a frightening time. It can be a period in which you're forced to confront the many choices that you've made thus far in your life—choices that have guided you down certain paths. It can be an intensely disconcerting time of emotional reckoning in which you recognize unfinished emotional business you may have with family members, friends, co-workers, or an intimate partner. It can be a disheartening time in which you begin to feel your physical limitations caused by the onset of aging.

Yet, midlife can also be a challenging time of growth, for you can reconsider choices that you've made and make new ones, bring closure to leftover emotions, discover or rediscover your spirituality or belief in God or a Higher Power, explore and strengthen your ties of intimacy with others, and learn more about relating to, as well as healing, your body. The difference between being *frightened* by midlife and being *challenged* by it comes from the attitude you bring into midlife, as well as the attitude you choose to foster.

Today, resolve to approach midlife not as the point in your life from which everything now goes downhill, but rather as the point from which an entirely new possibility of living and relating to yourself and to others can begin.

I SEE MYSELF AS A NEW PERSON WHO HAS A
POSITIVE ATTITUDE IN MIDLIFE.

JANUARY 2

"You squat on a piece of ground nobody but the buffalo ever occupied. No money, and you wonder how you're going to feed your family. You're 65 miles by horse and buggy from a doctor, and the kids get smallpox. Nobody can imagine how hard it was."
— centenarian Audrey Stubbart, talking about life in Wyoming in 1916

SURVIVING A CENTURY

Today there are more than 52,000 men and women in America who live up to and even beyond the age of 100. Over half of the country's centenarians are in good health—physically, mentally, and spiritually. The option of "triple-digit survival" can challenge you to rethink your definition of old and what being old means in terms of chronological years as well as human abilities. For, if you're not really old or "washed up" at 65, 70, or 80, but instead have the potential to live for two or more decades, then what does that mean in terms of how you're going to live the rest of your life?

Beatrice Wood still creates works of art displayed in galleries and museums around the world; Levy Washington checks on the two houses he built in his three-wheeled motor cart. Both are 102 years old. And centenarian Audrey Stubbart, who lived through the days of horse-and-buggy transportation and the scourge of smallpox in the early 1900s, works a 40-hour week as a proofreader and columnist at a Missouri newspaper.

Today there are many other centenarians who use their independent spirit, sense of pride, sharp minds, and positive attitudes to live each day to the fullest. They care more for the *quality* of their lives than the *quantity* of their years.

I RETHINK MY IDEAS ABOUT AGE AND WHO
REALLY IS OLD.

JANUARY 3

"Well, it finally happened. I hit 40....How many 40-year-olds do you know who are barely out of school, have no family, either live in athletic dorms or share apartments with younger runners, spend their summers hopping from one running camp to the next, still do 130-mile training weeks, and are healthy?"

— runner/writer Andy Palmer, Ph.D.

AGING AND RUNNING

Just as aging is inevitable, so too is it inevitable that as you get older, your athletic performance level drops. Also, your recovery from vigorous exercise slows down with age. This is why you may think that you should start "taking it easy"—that is, back off from rigorous training and make concessions to your age.

However, former NBA star Kareem Abdul-Jabbar once said, "Make concessions to age, and age will win every time." His belief is supported by a well-known study on aging and exercise that concluded that regular, intense training often postpones the performance declines associated with aging. What that means is that if you are able to, you can feel free to continue to run the way you always have—or even more intensely. Also, the study added that while moderate exercise is better than none, it's the exercise that "pushes the envelope," which adds intensity and challenge—that most effectively delays the effects of aging.

So, do your speed work, increase distances, run on varied surfaces, train on hills, and enter road races so you can compete against your peers. Even though you may have to make age-related adjustments in order to continue running—that is, you may have to ice sore muscles longer, stretch more slowly and carefully, alter your stride, or take some time off after a hard workout, you can still run and run well, no matter what your age.

I USE RIGOROUS RUNNING TO RACE AGAINST
THE AGING CLOCK.

JANUARY 4

*"If you cannot find the kind of work you have done in the past, try
something new. It need not be something that appeals to you at
first sight....Look for something you can do; the chances are, you
will begin to enjoy it as soon as you do it well."*

— psychologist B. F. Skinner

TO WORK OR NOT TO WORK

Have you begun to question when you'd like to retire as well as
whether retirement makes any sense to you at all? Maybe you
like the security of going to your job. Perhaps you don't want to
stop working altogether, but just don't want to work as hard as you
have been. Maybe you still have the option to earn more, learn
more, or advance to higher levels. Or perhaps you'd simply like to
be doing something.

Whatever the reason for your hesitancy about retirement, with
the work options available today such as semi-retirement, flex- and
part-time hours, phased retirement, sabbaticals, retraining programs, and self-employment, as well as more humanized work-
places and mentoring programs, you really have a lifelong option
of working. Gone are the days of yesterday's retirement, where
gold watches were given out and naps were interrupted by sojourns
to a local fishing hole or games of checkers on the front porch.
Today's retirement has a more interesting mixture of work and
leisure, with long-time homemakers returning to universities to
complete master's programs and former corporate managers
enrolling in cooking classes, taking flying lessons, or opening up
bicycle repair shops in the garage.

The age of retirement can become a time in which you shift
gears and mix productivity with leisure, learning, community service, travel, and time with friends and family. It can become a time
in which you can find new ways to work and new ways to live.

I SEE RETIREMENT AS A TIME FOR NEW OPPORTUNITIES.

JANUARY 5

"I think my present age, although it is very advanced, is my pleasantest and the finest of my life. I would not exchange my age and my life for the most flourishing youthfulness."
— 16th-century Venetian nobleman Cornaro

AGING WITH A FLOURISH

If you feel that you lived your life a lot differently when you were younger, and if you look back on those yesteryears with wistful longing, then you're not aging well. Even though growing old really happens in your body—you may not be able to bound up and down the stairs the way you used to, you may not be sexually active, you may be retired from work, and you may not be able to keep your eyes open past 8:00 P.M.—aging actually happens in your mind when you think that your present life can't be as satisfying and fulfilling as life was when you were younger.

You can take better care of yourself now than you ever did when you were younger and discover a reservoir of energy you never knew you had. Rather than overindulging in alcohol and food, not getting enough rest, and letting trivial issues bother you, you can make the choice to eat and sleep well and let go of the little things. Not only that, you can take pleasure from your daily activities, think of your life as meaningful, regard yourself as worthwhile, set goals you'd like to achieve, live each day optimistically, and stay healthy. Living a balanced, sane, and healthy life now that you're older can help you to appreciate those people, places, and things that have always meant a great deal to you, but which you've never been fully able to appreciate until now.

Today, remember that aging well psychologically—keeping your pleasures simple and your satisfaction level high—helps you to age well physiologically.

❀   ❀   ❀

I ACCEPT MY AGE AND AM SATISFIED WITH MY LIFE.

JANUARY 6

"I wish I knew what people mean when they say they find 'emptiness' in this wonderful adventure of living, which seems to me to pile up its glories like an horizon-wide sunset as the light declines. I'm afraid I'm an incorrigible life-lover & life-wonderer & adventurer."

— writer Edith Wharton

WOMEN ADVENTURERS

For many women, age has never been a factor in preventing them from living life to the fullest. Louie Dingwall, a grandmother and trainer of winning racehorses, was 79 when she applied for a license to ride in women's races; when she was 82, two of her horses won the first and second races in the English National Hunt season. Pilot Marian Hart, in her single-engine Beechcraft Bonanza, completed a second solo transatlantic flight at the age of 84. Josephine Baker gave four concerts in Carnegie Hall when she was 66. Dr. Malley Kachel of Munich was the oldest practicing woman physician in Germany, who continued to care for her patients at the age of 94. And Maggie Kuhn was a "young" 64 when she organized the Gray Panthers, a highly vocal group of older people who are dedicated to fighting ageism.

Sometimes the greatest achievements an older woman can make in her life are those that are sought out later in life—sometimes after years of honing a skill or polishing a craft, sometimes by stepping out of the role of wife or grandmother, or by simply working up the courage to take the first step. For an older woman, actively filling the glass of life with love, wonder, and a sense of adventure, rather than passively watching it be drained of all the wonderful things it has to offer, keeps the glass from ever becoming empty.

❊   ❊   ❊

I AM A LIFE-LOVER, LIFE-WONDERER,
AND LIFE-ADVENTURER.

JANUARY 7

"From what we get, we can make a living; what we give, however, makes a life."

— tennis great/author Arthur Ashe

YOUR HELPING HAND

Do you realize that as an older person, you are one of the country's most valuable national resources? You, as well as many others your age, have so much to contribute to society, to your community, to social and political causes, to charities, to churches and day care centers, to corporate-sponsored volunteer corps, and to younger people who could learn skills that they may need for future vocations, to name but a few areas. Volunteer work can be one of the most significant ways for you to make meaningful use of your life as you grow older.

How can you extend a helping hand to others? You can think about making a serious commitment to an organization such as the Peace Corps, which has a ten-week training period followed by an unforgettable two-year experience in the field. You can become a volunteer instructor in your community's adult education program and design an interesting course that falls within your knowledge or expertise—from making quilts to making the best investments. You can deliver nutritious lunches and dinners to homebound people through your local "Meals on Wheels" program. You can volunteer at your local library for the children's reading hour.

When you can see yourself as a valuable and untapped resource who has much to contribute, rather than a drain on society, then you'll be surprised by the amount of time, energy, and compassion you have to give to others.

ᘓᑟᘒ   ᘓᑟᘒ   ᘓᑟᘒ

I AM READY TO EXTEND A HELPING HAND TO OTHERS.

JANUARY 8

"I love every thing that's old: old friends, old times, old manners, old books, old wines..."

— playwright Oliver Goldsmith

FINDING JOYFUL MEMORIES

As you grow older, you may find yourself looking back with fondness at some of the things you remember from the past. You may go to flea markets and church bazaars and delight in finding copies of games you used to play, old radios and televisions like the ones you used to listen to and watch, and books you used to read when you were growing up. You may flip through a high school or college yearbook or browse through a photo album and smile as you remember all the people you knew, all the places you traveled to, and all the good times you shared. You may reread special cards and letters you saved over the years and be touched by them once again. You may go through boxes or trunks in the attic and laugh at the style of clothes you used to wear. Or you may open a book and come across a pressed flower that propels you back to a special time in your life when you placed the living flower within the pages of the book.

Finding joyful memories can be especially important as you age, for they serve as reminders of all the good you've had in your life. Such reminders can ease some of the unhappiness or blue feelings you may experience from time to time in the present, when you find it hard to remember that there have been pleasant things and helpful people in your life.

While it's never wise to *live* in the past, there's nothing wrong with *reliving* it from time to time. By re-experiencing feelings of joy and happiness, you revitalize your sense of well-being in the present.

❀   ❀   ❀

I REVIEW THE PAST SO I CAN BRING JOY INTO MY LIFE.

JANUARY 9

"These days I am reluctant to make love, but when I do,
everything else—children, money, work, gravity—drifts away.
My body draws all of my thoughts, the space between my toes, my
mouth, nipples, thighs, into one keen place, trembles there, trills.
This is wonderful, I think.
I must be mad not to do this every night."

— writer Jill Jeffery Ginghofer

SEXUAL LONGEVITY

Has your sexual activity diminished or even disappeared as you've grown older? Maybe it's difficult to find available partners who are also divorced or widowed. Perhaps you'd rather snuggle with someone than have sex. Maybe you're troubled by a physical disability or muscle aches that make sexual activity difficult or even painful. Perhaps you're embarrassed by changes in your body that you feel take away from your sensual appeal. Maybe hormonal changes have left you with a waning libido. Or perhaps you're simply no longer interested in sex.

However, remaining sexually active throughout your life—when you're young, as you progress through midlife, and into your later years—not only provides you with the best chance of remaining sexually active in old age, but also improves the overall quality of your health. Sexual activity with a long-term partner—whether you make love once a week or three or four times a year—deepens intimacy and strengthens the bonds of love you have for one another. And the desire for sexual activity with a new man or woman encourages you to socialize, travel, try new things, and helps you meet new and interesting people.

Rather than believing that you'll be less likely to have sexual relationships as you age, envision yourself as sexually deserving now and in future years. You can still have sex and enjoy it!

❀ ❀ ❀

I LOVE SEX AND ENJOY IT MORE THE OLDER I GET.

JANUARY 10

"There are parts of a ship which taken by themselves would sink. The engine would sink. The propeller would sink. But when the parts of a ship are built together, they float. So with the events of my life. Some have been tragic. Some have been happy. But when they are built together, they form a craft that floats and is going someplace. And I am comforted."
— clergyman Ralph Washington Sockman

SPIRITUAL STRENGTH

The science of longevity involves the study of groups of aging people and usually focuses on each group's physical and psychological characteristics in order to come up with answers as to why some individuals live longer than others. More often than not, the studies reveal that those who live longer eat good foods, exercise, stay rested, enjoy life, drink or smoke in moderation, and avoid stress, anxiety, and worry.

But what the studies often ignore are the spiritual beliefs that each person holds dear—beliefs that go beyond a particular religious affiliation or involvement in church functions. Such convictions are strengthened by the power of faith that allows each person to feel whole and to stay afloat, even through tough times like the Depression. Such faith helps each person to sustain trust in life's arbitrary distribution of tragedies and triumphs. And such beliefs help each person to feel spiritually strong in order to continue to live with satisfaction from day to day without being ripped apart or discouraged by any one event in life.

Thus, while your longevity requires that you pay attention to your physical as well as your emotional health, living long and living well also relies upon the healing power of your faith.

BECAUSE I AM SPIRITUALLY STRONG, I AM WHOLE.

January 11

*"Underneath the anguish of death and pain and ugliness are the
facts of hunger and unquenchable life."*

— essayist/food connoisseur M.F.K. Fisher

STAYING NUTRITIONALLY HEALTHY

For older people, getting enough calories and nutrition can be a challenge. Physical impairments such as digestive or chewing problems can restrict a diet to a narrow range of choices. Problems with mobility may make shopping for and cooking nutritious, full-course meals impossible. Medications can block the body's ability to absorb much-needed nutrients, curb the appetite, or even make food taste funny. And because aging can sometimes diminish the ability to appreciate smells and tastes, the once-pleasurable experience of dining can become dulled.

As you get older, you need a more nutrition-dense diet, high in nutrients such as calcium, and vitamins such as D and B-12. But instead, you may find yourself gravitating toward "easy" meals such as tea and toast, oatmeal, or sweets. Because of this, you run the risk of lowering your immune system and endangering your health. Also, you put yourself at risk of becoming malnourished.

To stay nutritionally healthy, you can ask family members or neighbors to help you prepare large quantities of nutritious meals that you can freeze and thaw for later use, such as soups, casseroles, and stews. If you live alone and dislike eating in solitude, ask others to join you for meals, or make it known that you're available for lunch or dinner invitations. Enlist help when shopping for food, or sign up for an inexpensive meal-delivery program. And talk to your doctor about vitamin supplements you may need or how medications you take may impact your diet.

I AM ABLE TO SATISFY MY HUNGER IN
NUTRITIONALLY SOUND WAYS.

JANUARY 12

"Old age is similarly a waiting-room, where you go after life's over and wait for cancer or a stroke."

— writer Ursula K. LeGuin

ELIMINATING EMOTIONAL DEBT

Large numbers of aging people often find themselves in emotional debt—a condition in which they're pessimistic about their future years, plagued by uncertainty and doubt, and fearful of change, loss, and death. Living each day in this fashion, depressed about the future and unhappy in the present, can take its toll; the result is often infirmity, sickness, and death.

One of the best ways to ascertain whether you suffer from emotional debt is to pay attention to the conversations you have with people. Do you prefer to talk about the problems and hassles in your life, or do you focus on personal achievements and light-hearted, entertaining anecdotes? Do you find yourself drawn to listen to those who discuss tragic events and personal crises, or do you prefer to listen to those who make you laugh or who have something interesting and exciting to share?

Noted psychiatrist Dr. David Viscott writes about emotional debt, "Sorrow ages you prematurely....The present is for action, for doing, for becoming, and for growing." Today, remember that you have a choice. You can view aging as a waiting room, where you choose to passively sit around doing nothing until your number is called, or as a jumping-off point where you choose to actively explore a variety of people, places, and things. Even though life's uncertainty will often make demands upon your emotions, how you deal with such uncertainty can influence a positive and optimistic emotional outlook.

❊   ❊   ❊

I ACCEPT UNCERTAINTY WITH A POSITIVE
EMOTIONAL ATTITUDE.

JANUARY 13

"As a well-spent day brings happy sleep, so life well used brings happy death."

— Leonardo da Vinci

FAMOUS LAST WORDS

Can death ever be a happy experience? For those who have seen a loved one suffer, there may be a certain level of relief and joy that's experienced in knowing that the beloved one is no longer in any pain. For those who can only focus on their material benefit after the demise of a wealthy relative, there may be some degree of satisfaction mixed in with the greed. For those who have suffered at the hands of an enemy or abuser, there may be joy at the realization that no further interactions with the villain will ever take place.

But what about your own death? Can you view this as a positive experience?

The last words of many famous people have revealed a high level of happiness—and even humor—when faced with death. On his deathbed, founding father John Quincy Adams purportedly said, "This is the last of earth! I am content!" Dame Edith Louisa Sitwell, English poet, writer, editor, and literary critic, was heard to remark, "I'm dying, but otherwise I'm in very good health." Naturalist Henry David Thoreau cried out, "Moose!...Indians!" And witty playwright Oscar Wilde, upon looking at his new bedroom curtains, said, "Either they go, or I do."

Being able to let go of a long life with a smile on your face or, at the very least, willing acceptance, reflects satisfaction with the completeness of your life. If you feel that you've not yet lived life well enough to have a "happy death," there's still time to spend your days well—starting now!

I VIEW MY LIFE AS A WONDERFUL JOURNEY THAT
HAS A BEGINNING, MIDDLE, AND END.

"You've been cranky since your last birthday.
Didn't you know it's in to be over forty now?...
They call it middle-age zest."

— writer Linda Morley

AGING ZESTFULLY

Finding yourself with physical limitations due to aging can bring frustration, sadness, and a strong sense of loss. You may miss things that you're no longer able to do. You may resent health problems when they're painful, make you feel weak and tired, and restrict your movement and your life. You may even get angry at your body because you want to do everything the way you used to—and you can't. As one middle-aged woman commented, "I have reached the stage in my life that I had not given much thought to. Somehow I thought that I would continue being as active as I had been in the past. This is not so."

But just because you feel "over the hill" doesn't mean you can't pedal up it in lots of different ways. Regular physical activity and exercise can help improve energy and increase stamina and endurance—as long as you don't assume you have to continue these activities at the same pace. Try walking, gardening, swimming, and exercising at a slower pace or for shorter periods of time. You may find that you enjoy these activities more when you ignore any feelings of haste or the need for achievement.

Thinking, meditating, watching, and listening are also as worthwhile as more strenuous activities. In your younger years, you may have been too busy and rushed for such reflection. But now that you can't rush, you can turn to these quieter pursuits if you wish.

❀   ❀   ❀

I CONSERVE MY ENERGY BUT STILL EXERT EFFORT.

JANUARY 15

THOSE OLDIES BUT GOODIES

The proliferation of oldies radio stations, cable stations that program reruns of television shows from the past, classic movie offerings in video stores, re-releases of music from the forties, fifties, and sixties on CDs, and "reunion" tours of music groups from the past have allowed you the opportunity today to relive the culture in which you grew up. Some of the memories they bring back may be pleasant—a song may return you to your high school prom, to thoughts about a first love, or to an enjoyable summer vacation. But some of the memories may force you to take stock of where you are today as compared to yesterday. For example, you may say to yourself, "When I was watching this television show, I was captain of the basketball team. Now I can't even dribble the ball and run at the same time." Not only that, but listening to current music, watching today's television shows, and viewing some of the movies that are now showing may make you feel even older.

Today, remember that you can still enjoy the culture that influenced you when you were growing up as long as you maintain the perspective that there's a whole new culture today that can influence you. Rather than look back with regret over what used to be, remember the milestones you've achieved and how far you've progressed.

❄   ❄   ❄

I AM AN AGING BABY BOOMER WHO IS STILL
HAPPILY GROWING UP.

JANUARY 16

*"I certainly don't regret becoming a writer later because
I know a lot more about life than I did 20 years ago, 10 years
ago. I think it's important to know how the water's gone
over the dam before you start to describe it. It helps to
have been over the dam yourself."*

— writer Annie Proulx

AGING GAY MEN AND LESBIANS

In some countries and cultures, the elderly are revered more than any other people. They are sought out for their opinions, wisdom, and sage advice. They are treated at all times with courtesy and respect. They are thought to be blessed with psychic, magical, or spiritual powers. Younger household members will even live in cramped quarters just so their older relatives can enjoy more space and comfort.

You may find that in your gay or lesbian community, however, you and other older members are not treated as kindly and respectfully. Some younger gay men and women may become impatient with you when you can't keep up with their pace or the times. Others may view you as a stepping-stone on the way to something bigger or better. Still others may ignore you if your physical appearance is not as attractive as it once was, or if you no longer put a great deal of time and effort into maintaining a finely tuned physique.

Yet, rather than feeling excluded by such snubbing, remember what it took to get you to where you are today. You've had to face far greater challenges and clear far more difficult hurdles to achieve acceptance than many of the young people in your community have. So, be happy with who you are at this age and what you have accomplished. Being the best you can be at any particular time in your life is something to be proud of.

I ACCEPT THE FACT THAT YOUNGER PEOPLE IN MY COMMUNITY MIGHT NOT APPRECIATE ME...BUT I **DO** APPRECIATE ME!

JANUARY 17

"We need to discuss these issues before we get sick. But, realistically speaking, it's when someone gets sick that it really creates what I call 'the teachable moment,' the prime opportunity to share feelings and attitudes about death."
— medical ethicist Joan McGiver Gibson

TALKING ABOUT HEALTH CARE

Do you talk about death? While you may not like to talk about this subject at all, concerns about such topics as debilitating injuries, cancer, and aging in a long-term relationship have made dying an issue that affects you, your partner, your family, and your extended family members. Right now, the opportunity to talk about death is greater than ever before.

If you're exploring the scenario of your own death or the death of a loved one, you need to discuss health-care alternatives, living wills and durable power of attorney, and the goals of medical treatment. For example, what kind of life-sustaining care do you want if you're unable to make or express such decisions? What will be the goals of your medical treatment: relief from pain, prolonging life, or remaining independent? Would you prefer to die at home, in a hospice, or in a hospital? While you don't have to make a decision on every last clinical procedure you may face, you need to at least explore some of the possibilities.

Today, start to explore such options as a living will or a durable power of attorney for health care. Appoint an attorney to help you work on a will that would recognize the people who have been important to you in your life. If you take care of such business while you're alive, it can ease your worries and fears and thus lessen your pain and suffering at the end.

I DISCUSS HEALTH-CARE ALTERNATIVES AND RELATED
ISSUES WITH OTHERS.

JANUARY 18

"I only went out for a walk, and finally concluded to stay out till sundown, for going out, I found, was really going in."
— naturalist John Muir

CONNECTING WITH NATURE

When your mind, body, or spirit is troubled, going out into nature can help you to work through some of the difficulties in your life, broaden the boundaries of your existence, and reconnect with yourself in meaningful ways. Recognizing your relationship with nature can expand your vision of the present and the future, as well as give you a more profound sense of your worth and the value of your life. Also, connecting with nature can remind you that sometimes all you have to do is hear the sounds of the great outdoors in order to forget some of your own troubles.

There are many ways to connect with nature, from walking in the woods to starting seedlings for spring planting in your garden. The best way to begin is to take a slow, meditative walk around your neighborhood. Notice how different the month of January looks from the month of June. Feel the ground beneath your feet. Breathe in deeply, and savor the air as it fills your lungs. Hear the sound your shoes make as they make contact with the earth. Look closely at all the colors around you. Hear how the birds talk to you. Feel how the rhythms of your body interact with the natural rhythms around you.

Then, turn around and retrace your steps, reexperiencing all the sights you've just seen and also noticing those you missed the first time. Say out loud, "I am one with the sun. I am one with the trees. I am one with the wind. I am one with the birds. I am one with nature. I am one with myself."

I CONNECT WITH NATURE SO I CAN BETTER
CONNECT WITH MYSELF.

JANUARY 19

"You stay young as long as you can learn, acquire new habits and suffer contradiction."
— novelist Baroness Marie von Ebner-Eschenbach

BACK TO SCHOOL

Returning to school for more education at 30, 40, 50, 60, 70—even 94—years old is no longer considered an oddity but a common practice. Education is not just preparation for lifework for teenagers, or job advancement for workers in their late twenties and early thirties. Rather, education is now looked upon by older people as a way to achieve goals that may have been abandoned years ago, to make life richer by expanding their horizons, and to further intellectual growth.

Fordham University in New York is one of the many institutions of higher learning to offer programs for older people. "College at 60" places students in regular, credit-bearing academic seminars with their peers. Harvard University's Institute for Learning in Retirement enrolls older people both as professors and as students. Eckerd College's Academy of Senior Professionals in St. Petersburg, Florida, has retirees serving as advisors, career counselors, and mentors in the student body. And the Boston-based Elderhostel program is a self-supporting, nonprofit program for older Americans over 60 that allows them to travel to college campuses during semester breaks and live together in dormitories, eat together in dining halls, and take courses.

You may feel challenged by becoming part of a college or university community. Or you may be interested in finding out more about organizations that combine learning with a leisure activity such as travel, hiking, golfing, or sailing.

I SEARCH FOR NEW AWARENESS THROUGH LEARNING.

JANUARY 20

*"The real sadness of fifty is not that you change so much
but that you change so little."*

— author/columnist Max Lerner

REMODELING YOUR IDENTITY

Your personal identity, made up of such things as your personality, your habits, your mannerisms, your way of thinking, your way of behaving, and your belief system, to name but a few, will persist throughout your life if you'd like it to. That doesn't mean, however, that identity is stronger than age and that if you try to change any part of your personal identity, you can't.

The ability to change is one of the most wonderful aspects of living and growing as an individual. Change can break stereotypes, debunk myths, overcome limitations, improve health, increase vitality, offer choices, lift prejudices, release tension, and build inner strength. Change can keep you fully alive, active, and as vigorous as the young. And change can offer new perspectives that expand your horizons in ways that help you learn more about yourself.

So, if you think that simply because you're a certain age and you've been doing things a certain way for so many years that you have to continue doing them that way, then you're wrong. You can change any aspect of your personal identity that you'd like. Just because you've never done anything remotely "out of the ordinary" doesn't mean that today you can't try something new. Now is the time to sleep late, go out to a movie, telephone someone you haven't spoken to for a long time, sign up for a sky-diving lesson, eat crackers in bed, stop drinking, adopt an animal—or even tell someone your real age!

❀   ❀   ❀

I CHANGE AN ASPECT OF MY IDENTITY
AND ENJOY THE NEW ME.

JANUARY 21

"The older you get, the stronger the wind gets—
and it's always in your face."

— golf great Jack Nicklaus

WINDS OF CHANGE

Since 1900, the average American life span has increased by 50 percent; Americans are living well into their seventies and eighties rather than their fifties or sixties. Yet, there are some things that haven't changed. For example, modern medicine has still not been able to prevent cancer or heart disease or do more than ease the pain and slow the progression of degenerative disorders such as arthritis, diabetes, multiple sclerosis, and osteoporosis. Also, loss of muscle tissue from most complex organs is still one of the main reasons older people slow down. And, mental functions still decline with age.

Even though everyone is different, and some people are more physically capable and mentally alert than others of the same age, the effects of time on the mind and the body are inevitable. What was once easy may be hard; where the wind was once at your back, now you must strive to move against it.

However, if you start to live by the adage, "Use it, or lose it," you can slow down your physical and mental deterioration. Researchers at Tufts University discovered that older bodies benefited as much from exercise as did younger ones. In fact, the gain in muscle mass measured from 12 weeks of weight-lifting in a group of 60-year-olds was the same as that in a much younger group!

So starting today, begin to regularly exercise your mind as well as your body. This will help you to slow the effects of aging so you can shift the wind.

❦   ❦   ❦

I EXERCISE MY MIND AND BODY.

JANUARY 22

"Science has salvaged scrap metal and even found vitamins and valuable oils in refuse, but old people are extravagantly wasted."
— novelist Anzia Yezierska

THE MATURING MARKETPLACE

Do you feel excluded in today's advertising? When you look through a magazine or watch a television commercial, do you feel that companies are even remotely interested in selling their product or services to you and others in your same age group?

Even though nearly one-fourth of the U.S. population is over the age of 50, advertising is clearly biased against older men and women. Only recently have older models been used to deliver messages to a maturing population that controls nearly 70 percent of the total net worth of U.S. households.

You can become more involved in how products are marketed to you by playing a more active role as a consumer. If you have a "brand loyalty," write to the company that markets the particular product and offer your comments about the company's advertising. If you enjoy certain magazines but are put off by advertisements that are geared toward younger people, make the magazine's publisher aware of your feelings. When you do see or hear an ad that's geared toward the mature consumer, voice your approval.

According to Carol Allen, an expert in the 50-plus marketplace and director of a marketing consulting firm, advertisers have been slow to market to older people because "people in advertising are still so young themselves. They can't imagine how 50- and 60-year-olds can even be alive!" Let the advertisers know you're alive, and ready to support their products.

I SUPPORT THE PRODUCTS OF COMPANIES
THAT SUPPORT ME.

JANUARY 23

"Age puzzles me. I thought it was a quiet time. My seventies were interesting and fairly serene, but my eighties are passionate. I grow more intense as I age."

— writer Florida Scott-Maxwell

RECREATIONAL RETIREMENT COMMUNITIES

Did you ever think that you could be well into your seventies and eighties and be more active than you were when you were working full-time or raising a family? Could you ever imagine that you would grow old but have so many activities you could enjoy— dancing, attending lectures, going to concerts, swimming, golfing, joining clubs, jogging, painting, hiking, lifting weights, or writing poetry—and that there wouldn't be enough hours in the day to accomplish everything? Did you ever consider that as a single older person you would have many opportunities for love and romance?

Such things are not the stuff of some old-age fantasy, but are the reality for the thousands of residents of Sun City and Sun City West, located near Phoenix. These recreation-focused retirement living communities, like so many other retirement villages that have been built in California, Florida, and other locations in Arizona, provide residents with morning, noon, and nighttime opportunities for socializing, learning, and recreating. In such supportive atmospheres that draw like-minded individuals together, it's only natural that there are always things to do and people with whom to do them.

Rather than spending your remaining years stuck all alone in an apartment in the city or a house in the suburbs until you can no longer care for yourself, why not consider the option of living in a retirement community?

❀   ❀   ❀

I INVESTIGATE THE POSSIBILITY OF LIVING IN A
RETIREMENT COMMUNITY.

JANUARY 24

"I have never wanted to live to be old, so old I'd run out
of friends or money."
— prima ballerina Margot Fonteyn

FUTURE FINANCIAL PLANNING

Government estimates predict that the first of the baby boomers will hit traditional retirement age around the year 2011. A little over a decade later, estimates also predict that the Social Security program will start to run into huge deficits. What this means is that growing older may also mean growing poorer.

What can you do about this now? If you haven't already retired, some companies offer participation in a phased retirement program. What this allows you to do is reduce the number of hours per day, per week, or per year that you work. By tapering off your hours before full retirement, you have a chance to explore other activities—perhaps train part-time for a new line of work, explore starting an at-home business, form a consulting partnership with other retired workers in your field, or devote more time to making crafts that you can sell at fairs. If you have retired, you might consider reentering the labor force in one of many available service positions—as a security guard, exercise instructor, tour guide, adult-education teacher, or a fast-food service worker, to name a few.

At this point in your life, you might like to consider continuing to work as long as you can, not only for the psychological satisfaction it can give you in helping you build your self-worth as a valued and valuable worker, but also in helping you contribute to your financial worth by drawing a salary, collecting from billable hours, or earning money from a side business for your future financial security.

❧ ❧ ❧

I CONTRIBUTE TO MY SELF-WORTH AND MY
FINANCIAL WORTH BY WORKING.

JANUARY 25

*"Life is like a great jazz riff. You sense the end the very moment
you were wanting it to go on forever. "*

— writer Sheila Ballantyne

FACING DEATH

Is today another day you fear because you're facing death—not
the death of someone close to you, but your own? Perhaps you
have a heart condition, have been diagnosed with cancer, are suffering from a debilitating medical condition, or have simply
become worn out. Are you saying to yourself now, "I hurt. I'm
tired. I'm scared. How can I find the strength, hope, and courage to
get through another day"?

Well, today is not just another day to get through. Living while
you're dying doesn't mean you have to continuously swim against
the current of life until you're too weak to fight anymore. Death
should never be thought of as such a battle—for no matter what you
do, you'll never win.

Rather, seek to discover that the greatest reward in living with
the presence of death is to become one with the current of the river
of life. Let go, and go with the flow. Surrender and become part of
the river. Trust that you'll be safe, secure, and never alone. Trust,
too, that you will always see something new on your journey, for it
has been said that "one cannot step twice in the same river, for fresh
waters are forever flowing round us."

Even though the river of life may lead you toward still waters,
you can enjoy the journey. Today, let go and simply let this day happen. Relax your emotional and physical tension and tightness;
become one with the waters of life. Let your spirit flow, and you
will be strong and fearless.

I AM COMFORTED WHEN I FLOW WITH THE RIVER OF LIFE.

JANUARY 26

"Perhaps with full-span lives the norm, people may need to learn how to be aged as they once had to learn to be adult. It may soon be necessary and legitimate to criticize the long years of vapidity in which a healthy elderly person does little more than eat and play bingo....To fall into purposelessness is to fall out of all real consideration."

— writer Robert Blythe

PHYSICAL FITNESS GOALS

What are the first activities that come to mind when you think about what old people who are still active are supposed to do? Play bingo? Golf? Travel? Play shuffleboard? Dance to bands that play swing music?

What about pumping iron? A man won in his 65-and-over age bracket by power lifting a combined 870 pounds; an 84-year-old woman once competed in the men's 35-and-over age category because no one other women had signed up to compete—and she beat her male competitors!

What about running a marathon? Fitness guru Noel Johnson, who died in his nineties, took up exercise during retirement, and at 80 years old was the oldest New York City marathon finisher; he ran 21 marathons after turning 70 and set world records at the mile and half-mile in his age group.

How about hang gliding? Sky diving? Training for the grueling Iron Man Triathlon in Hawaii? White-water rafting? Hiking all day across rugged wilderness terrain with 80-pound backpacks? Downhill skiing?

You can be one of millions of people who are well into their seventh, eighth, and even ninth decades who live an active, purposeful life by setting challenging physical fitness goals—to hone an ability or even train for a difficult contest. Getting serious about your physical activity can happen at any age.

❁   ❁   ❁

I SET PHYSICAL FITNESS GOALS THAT CHALLENGE ME.

JANUARY 27

"I have always had a dread of becoming a passenger in life."
— Princess Margrethe of Denmark

OVERCOMING BOREDOM

How often are you bored with the people, places, or things in your life, but do little or nothing about it? Too often you may complain that you're bored, but you stay in the same rut. Or maybe you're a creature of habit—someone who does the same things in the same ways at the same time —and you realize now that you've become bored living this way. Rather than being bored with any aspect of your life, it's up to you to take the initiative and explore what you can do to make your life more interesting.

The best way to overcome boredom either with yourself or your life is to change the scenery from time to time. This doesn't mean that you have to pack your bags and move elsewhere; sometimes very simple changes can really stimulate your mind and give you the sense that you've "gone" somewhere new. For example, if you usually read biographies, read a mystery. If you find yourself sitting every evening in the front of the television, turn off the TV and go out to a movie. If you always walk the same route every day, find a new one. If you're tired of spending time with the same individuals, volunteer your time to an organization or join a club so you can meet new people. If you like to travel but find it financially burdensome, go away for a weekend to a bed-and-breakfast inn. Plan a dinner party. Set up an aquarium. Learn a new language. Sign up for an adult-education course. Change the scenery of your life in just a small way so you can get a whole new outlook on your life.

I MAKE AN EFFORT TO LIVE A MORE INTERESTING LIFE.

JANUARY 28

"There have always been hard times. There have always been wars and troubles—famine, disease, and such-like—and some folks are born with money, some with none. In the end it is up to the man what he becomes, and none of those other things matters. It is character that counts."

— writer Louis L'Amour

ACCEPTING THE PAST

Have you ever thought, If I only knew back then what I know now? Imagine how you would now handle the difficult situations you endured back in high school, college, during the first decade of your marriage, and during middle age. Now you might say to yourself, "So what if I wasn't the greatest athlete or the brightest student, the best communicator or the smartest parent, the most dedicated employee or the most mature decision-maker? Those things might have mattered then, but look at me now. I guess I did okay." Think about where you might be in your life right now if you could have used today's knowledge to help you years ago. Would you still have wanted to marry when you did? Would you have opted for a degree instead of a job? How might your life be different today?

There may be some things you'd like to do that you've never had a chance to do before. Well, *now* is the time to do them. You can make up your mind that such opportunities can happen to you *this* year.

Today you don't have to despair or harbor regrets over yesterday's experiences or decisions. What has happened, has happened. Although the past is gone, you have the power now to change your life whenever you'd like. Even though time marches on, you can determine what direction you'll take.

I BEGIN MY LIFE ANEW EVERY DAY BY LOOKING
FORWARD, NOT BACKWARD.

January 29

"Twenty can't be expected to tolerate sixty in all things, and sixty gets bored stiff with twenty's eternal love affairs."

— artist Emily Carr

THE IMAGE OF AGING

Today's old people have little in common with yesterday's. A whole new image of aging is being created as more and more people in their later years become part of a very powerful "elder-culture"—one that prides itself on its ability to stay young, to travel extensively, to live through incredible technological and world changes, and to maintain productivity or even increase it in ways that past generations never have. Today, fewer older people are willing to step aside and let younger people take their place on the work force, in colleges and universities, in social settings, in politics, and in competitive events. Also, more and more older people are challenging the myths of aging that contrast the young with the old.

Being over a certain age no longer equates to being unappealing or unattractive. For example, many of today's most engaging and successful actors and actresses—Goldie Hawn, Lauren Hutton, Paul Newman, Robert Redford, Shirley MacLaine, and Lauren Bacall—are in their forties, fifties, sixties, or even their seventies. No longer are the young considered to be full of passion and the old devoid of such intimate expression. Romance is alive and well at all ages, with a greater willingness for sexual and lifestyle experimentation being exhibited by older generations. No longer are the young considered to have it all and the old devoid of hope and a future. Today's older generation has wealth, power, creativity, vigor, and the ability to enjoy everything they have.

Today, see yourself as part of a new, positive image of aging!

I VIEW AGING AS A POSITIVE STAGE IN LIFE.

JANUARY 30

*"Life appears to me too short to be spent in nursing
animosity or registering wrongs."*

— writer Charlotte Brontë

FORGIVING THE PAST

Do you have a propensity for dwelling on old hurts and past
mistakes? You probably can't practice forgiveness when
grudges stand in your way; you certainly can't look forward to the
future with any sort of positive outlook when you get an almost
perverse pleasure from hanging on to transgressions made by yourself or others. As Charles E. Jinks observed, "The main difference
between optimism and pessimism resides in the notion of memory.
The pessimist aptly recalls the hurts and failures of yesterday, but
simply cannot remember the plentiful possibilities of a new tomorrow. The optimist has a hopeful future already memorized."

According to American Indian tradition, "enemies" such as
failure and hurt are sacred because they can make you strong. The
unfortunate things that have happened in your past can teach you
how to become stronger in the present and how to succeed in the
future. But if you can't forgive what's gone on in the past, then
you're going to remain an angry, vengeful, negative, perpetually
pessimistic person.

How can you change this propensity? Take a moment to recall
a hurt or failure from the past. Ask, "How has it made me stronger
or wiser? How has it provided me with lessons that have helped me
grow? How has it brought new opportunities into my life?" Focus
on the positive aspects of yesterday's hurts and failures, and then
say, "I can let this go now. I forgive." With each act of forgiveness,
you create a positive foundation on which to build a successful
future.

ᘐᕒᕳ   ᘐᕒᕳ   ᘐᕒᕳ

I IMPROVE MY ATTITUDE THROUGH THE
ACT OF FORGIVENESS.

JANUARY 31

"Maturity: Among other things, not to hide one's strength out of fear and, consequently, live below one's best."
— Swedish statesman Dag Hammarskjöld

VOICE OF FEAR, VOICE OF STRENGTH

There's a parable about a group of older congregants who were asked by their pastor to share what they often prayed for. One who had just retired said "financial security." Another who had medical problems said "health." And another who was moving into a nursing home said "friends."

But one congregant shook his head at the responses. When his turn came, he said, "I don't pray to escape the things that frighten me. Instead, I pray for the ability to trust that no matter what happens to me each day, it is the *right* thing."

It has been said that there are two voices you can listen to. One is the voice of fear, and the other is the voice of strength. The voice of fear is high-pitched and frantic; it whines and warns and whispers messages designed to scare you. But the voice of strength sounds soft, confident, and soothing; it tells you not to worry, assures you that all is well, and sometimes grows silent so you can listen to your Higher Power.

Today, still your voice of fear, and let your voice of confidence grow louder. Pray for the wisdom to be able to live each moment to the fullest. A reassuring prayer you can recite is, "No matter what happens each day between sunrise and sunset, I will never be surrounded by darkness." Know that you have nothing to fear and nothing to pray for besides the ability to trust in yesterday, today, and tomorrow.

I LET MY VOICE OF STRENGTH SPEAK FOR ME.

FEBRUARY 1

*"What if a demon were to creep after you one night, in your
loneliest aloneness, and say, 'This life which you live must be
lived by you once again and innumerable times more; and every
pain and joy and thought and sigh must come again to you, all in
the same sequence....Would you throw yourself down and gnash
your teeth and curse that demon? Or would you answer,
'Never have I heard anything more divine'?"*

— philosopher Friedrich Nietzsche

POTENTIAL IN THE SECOND HALF

Has your life so far been rich and fulfilling—all that you would
like it to be—or has it fallen short of your expectations?
Perhaps you've spent much of your life as a caregiver, putting the
needs of others before your own. Maybe you've had low self-
esteem that has prevented you from exploring your capabilities and
realizing your potentials. Or perhaps you've followed the path others have made for you and never deviated from what you thought
was the "right" and only way.

If the thought of reliving your life today fills you with dread,
then it's time to look at the potential you can develop in the second
of your life. Becoming so habituated to caring for others and helping others achieve, ignoring who you are and what you can do, and
allowing others to make your choices for you may have left you
blind to your own goals. Starting today, you can regain sight of
your own dreams and take steps to achieve them. You can learn
new skills, travel with your own itinerary, make the time to build
on old friendships or meet new people, and create an entirely new
supportive community for yourself.

If you think of the coming years as a time in which to create a
better life for yourself, you can look forward to a future filled with
confidence and enthusiasm.

❧   ❧   ❧

I SEE GREAT POTENTIAL FOR MYSELF IN THE
SECOND HALF OF MY LIFE.

FEBRUARY 2

*"I've aged, Sidney. There are new lines in my face.
I look like a brand-new, steel-belted radial tire."*

—Maggie Smith's character,
scrutinizing her face in the mirror in the film *California Suite*

THE ATTRACTIVENESS OF AGE

What does looking older mean to you? Does it make you feel distinguished or diminished? When you look in the mirror and notice gray hairs or a receding hairline, weight changes or redistribution of folds and rolls, and wrinkling skin or age spots, how do such things affect not only the way you see your body, but also the way you see yourself?

According to recent studies, most middle-aged men are considered more attractive than younger men because they are thought to be at the peak of their social, financial, and career success. On the other hand, most middle-aged women are considered past their prime and viewed as less attractive than those younger than they are.

However, if looks are associated with power and usefulness, then the more powerful you are and the more useful you become, the less likely you'll view looking older in negative ways. Also, the less value you place on appearances and the more value you place on who you are and how you've lived, the less likely you'll be to let your changing appearance influence how you feel about yourself. As a 48-year-old woman commented, "Sometimes I think of the alternatives to looking older, and I wonder what it would be like to have my face frozen the way it was in my 30s. But that would be ridiculous! That's not me—that doesn't reflect the years I've lived and all the things I've experienced. I don't want to deny my experiences, and I feel that if I dislike my aging looks, I'm denying all the wonderful parts of my life."

I RESPOND TO LOOKING OLDER IN POSITIVE WAYS.

FEBRUARY 3

"Fear not that thy life shall come to an end, but rather fear that it shall never have a beginning."
— Cardinal John Newman

OVERTURNING AGEIST BELIEFS

Your beliefs about aging may be based on a simple rule that one must grow progressively older, then progressively weaker, and finally one must eventually die. Yet even though in terms of chronological years, this is true, the reality about aging is that your mind, body, and spirit can be in a continual state of renewal throughout your life. That means that you don't really have to grow old unless you want to. For, as one 81-year-old remarked, "People don't grow old. When they stop growing, they become old."

You can start today to think about aging in a different way—in a way that allows more time for beginnings rather than time for just endings. To do so, you need to be willing to engage in new pursuits, develop new skills, and explore new ways of looking at the world on a daily basis in order to keep your mind and body growing. Not only that, you need to be ready to strengthen or rekindle your faith in a Higher Power through prayer, meditation, and connection with nature in order to keep your spirit growing.

Aging can become a time in which you overturn beliefs that have been formed or supported by fear, that hinge on ageist stereotypes, and that are based on the premise that mind, body, and spirit decay with time. You can experience the joy of life through a mind, body, and spirit that are willing, each day, to begin anew.

EVERY DAY I CREATE A NEW MIND, BODY, AND SPIRIT.

FEBRUARY 4

"With men who have taken risks all their lives, it often happens that their boldness shines out with particular brilliance in their last years. [Writer Bertrand] Russell...showed it...when he was eighty-nine. At this time he was a member of the Committee of a Hundred against nuclear weapons: he called upon the public to join in a non-violent manifestation, and in spite of the police prohibition, he sat down on the ground among the others... in fact he spent a week in prison."

— writer Simone de Beauvoir

ADVOCACY WORK

It may take a lot of your strength to cope with being alone, having limited finances, suffering from chronic pain, or being dependent upon others. But will such difficulties make you retreat into a self-focused shell, where you think only of yourself and your needs, or will such matters make you look outside yourself and do things that have an impact on other people—or even on the world at large?

Many older people who have become advocates find the work they do can not only can be rewarding for those they help, but also for themselves, for their own personal growth. You can become an advocate simply by spotting an injustice and striving to do something about it. For example, if you experience age discrimination on the job, you can file a complaint with the Equal Employment Opportunity Commission to protect your interests as well as safeguard the interests of others who might find themselves in a similar situation. You can start an advocacy organization such as the Older Women's League or the Gray Panthers, which began as support groups for the aging population. You can volunteer at a homeless shelter or provide pro bono services for a charitable group. Because advocacy work represents cooperative caring and personal action, you'll see as well as feel the importance of what you're doing.

I ACTIVELY MAKE CHANGES FOR MYSELF AND OTHERS.

FEBRUARY 5

*"I refuse as I age to deny my years. When asked at 30, I'll be 30.
When the question comes up at 45, I'll take 45. For what year
could I subtract? The one in which my son or daughter was born?
Or the year I first fell in love? How about one less favorable?
Like the year I came down with pneumonia. Or one of those grief-
filled years spent saying good-bye to someone close?...
No, I think I'll keep them all, the good years, the bad, and the
even not so memorable."*

— writer Sheila B. Cabrera

EMBRACING YOUR ELDER YEARS

For some, it can be very depressing to grow older. As you age, you may find that you're not as strong, agile, attractive, lean, or as motivated as you were in your twenties or thirties. Although you may want to live a long and meaningful life, you may have difficulty dealing with your emotional and physical changes and fear the infirmities or disabilities that come with advancing age.

But there's a difference between aging and getting old. Aging encompasses all the biological changes that naturally occur over time—hearing loss or decreased hormone activity, for example. Getting old, on the other hand, is a social and personal concept. In a society that has a strong prejudice and apathy towards its elderly population, it's only natural to pick up on some of that stigma yourself. Your image of being a "wise old woman" or "jolly old man" may often be at odds with how you really feel.

Yet the decades after 50 can be rich and fulfilling. You can enjoy your later years and make the most of this precious season of your life. Taking control of your life, like taking control of your depression, is a matter of embracing every year that you've lived through and every one you've yet to live.

ￜￜￜ ￜￜￜ ￜￜￜ

I EMBRACE ALL THE YEARS OF MY LIFE—
THE GOOD AND THE BAD.

FEBRUARY 6

"We Americans, with our terrific emphasis on youth, action, and material success, certainly tend to belittle the afternoon of life and even to pretend it never comes. We push the clock back and try to prolong the morning, over-reaching and over-straining ourselves in the unnatural effort....In our breathless attempts we often miss the flowering that waits for afternoon."

— writer Anne Morrow Lindbergh

THE GARDEN OF LIFE

Years ago, Sigmund Freud didn't believe much in adult development. Rather, he thought of childhood as the essential shaper of the psyche. But then Erik Erikson, dubbed the "father of adult development," suggested that human development takes place in each of eight significant life stages. To move successfully through each life stage, the "task" that marked the life stage needed to be resolved.

However, too many people prefer to stay in the life stage of young adulthood or even puberty and adolescence rather than move on to the two remaining life stages: adulthood and maturity. Perhaps that's because the tasks in the earlier stages are more self-focused—concerned with the identity, the ego, and satisfying physical and emotional needs—as opposed to the later stages, which are concerned with what to pass on to future generations and how to attain a sense of personal fulfillment, or wholeness, in the final years of life. The stages of youth are more centered on the rewards that can be received, while the stages of adulthood revolve around what can be given to others and the self.

Yet the reward for successful movement through each stage of life is a blossoming of self— an experiential learning that grants you wisdom and a profound understanding of life that lets you see the garden of life in all its glory.

❀   ❀   ❀

I GRACEFULLY GROW INTO ADULTHOOD WITH MATURITY.

FEBRUARY 7

"To be seventy years old is like climbing the Alps. You reach a snow-crowned summit and see behind you the deep valley stretching miles and miles away, and before you other summits higher and whiter, which you may have strength to climb, or may not. Then you sit down and meditate which it will be."
— Henry Wadsworth Longfellow

STRETCHING AND STRENGTHENING

As you grow older, you may experience aches and pains in your muscles and joints that make movement difficult. As a result, you may tend to move around less, even though one of the best ways to prevent joint and muscle pain is to strengthen the muscles and increase their flexibility with exercise and gentle stretching.

But until you feel as if you can get back on your feet to begin a prevention program, it's best to treat aches and pains immediately. Use ice if there's swelling and heat if you're stiff and there's no evidence of swelling. Although it's wise to rest after any injury, too much rest can result in the loss of muscle strength.

The best recovery program combines rest with muscle relaxation in order to reduce muscle tension. To relax your muscles, lie down on your bed or sit in a comfortable chair. Close your eyes, then systematically tense and then relax groups of muscles. Start at your head and slowly work your way to your toes. Focus on one small group of muscles at a time. For example, tense and then relax your hands, then each forearm, then each upper arm, then each shoulder. Slowly take a deep breath as you tense each muscle group for a few seconds. Visualize the muscle group as a closed clam shell. Then, as you relax, slowly release your breath and imagine the clam shell opening wide.

I VISUALIZE RELAXED, PAIN-FREE MUSCLES AND JOINTS.

FEBRUARY 8

"It is surprising that stories about old people should make bright reading."

— writer Carol Bly

YOUR BOOK OF LIFE

It used to be that some of the greatest inspiration came from the achievements of youth. To be young and talented, to be young and intelligent, to be young and gifted, or to be young and successful were signs of greatness. American culture cooperated with the adulation of youth by marketing to its youth. The American spirit of competitiveness deemed it only fitting that parents should push their children as much as possible to discover any hidden talents that would give their kids "the edge" over others.

But today, American culture has shifted from being youthful to more mature, with a greater emphasis being placed upon the needs, problems, and dreams of a middle-aged and older population. Athletes are competing longer against much younger opponents and remaining active in their sports by coaching or training for senior events. Politics is dominated by older men and women. Movie stars and music groups you grew up with are making great comebacks or are still performing. Young, rising talents are citing older role models as some of their greatest influences.

You're part of this incredible phenomenon in which older people are rewriting the later years of their lives with lively prose that makes for great reading. You create for yourself a true page-turner when you envision that anything is possible for you. No longer is there a division between generations but, instead, a bridge that links the old with the new so that anything and everything is possible.

❀   ❀   ❀

THE LIFE SAGA I'M CREATING IS SURE TO BE A BESTSELLER!

FEBRUARY 9

"I am one of those people who just can't help getting a kick out of life—even when it's a kick in the teeth."

— "madam" Polly Adler

THE IMPORTANCE OF LAUGHTER

Sometimes you may not see the importance of laughter as you grow older because you're blinded by your fears, immobilized by blue moods, or incapable of feeling anything other than physical or emotional pain. But being able to laugh in the face of incredible tragedies such as illness, death, and loss can provide you with the same much-needed physical and psychological benefits that laughter can give you at other times, including helping keep things in perspective and keeping you in balance when life seems totally out of kilter.

In addition, remaining open to levity in even the most solemn situations can help you, if you're a survivor, stay both mentally and physically healthy. Being overly serious in the grieving process can actually be unhealthy, as a study of the immune systems of grieving spouses showed: the spouses had lower activity levels of T cells—one of the body's most important defense mechanisms against illness.

From this moment on, how can you maintain your perspective through the difficulties you experience while aging? Rabbi Harold Kushner, in his book *When Bad Things Happen to Good People*, recommends changing your focus from the past or the pain. Instead of asking, "Why did this happen to me?" you can instead ask, "Now that this has happened, what shall I do about it?" And then keep in mind the ancient Chinese proverb that says, "You cannot prevent the birds of sorrow from flying over your head, but you can prevent them from building nests in your hair."

I SEE THE LIGHT SIDE EVEN IN MY DARKNESS.

FEBRUARY 10

"There must be more to life than just eating and getting bigger."
— writer Trina Paulus

WEIGHTY ISSUES

As you grow older, some of your lean muscle tissues are replaced with fatty tissue. So even if you stay the same weight, you'll have more body fat than you did when you were younger. Also, it takes less energy to maintain fatty tissue than it does lean muscle tissues, so you'll gain weight even if you eat the same amount and type of foods as you did when you were younger.

How can you avoid some of the weight gain that naturally occurs with age? Achieving a balance of activity and healthful eating can help you to focus less on what the scale is telling you and more on how you feel. This is important because weight loss as you grow older isn't as critical as maintaining your weight while building muscle and reducing fat. You do this by beginning to slowly increase your activity level until you can do at least 20 minutes of activity each day. At the same time, you need to make your meals nutritious by cutting down on high-fat foods and replacing them with whole grains, vegetables, fruits, and legumes. This doesn't mean that you can't indulge a sweet tooth or fried food craving every once in a while, but you might think about keeping a daily log so you can track your eating habits.

In addition, you may find it helpful to set goals that give you the proper motivation for creating a healthy food-and-activity balance in your life. Sometimes setting just one small goal — such as eating a piece of fruit each day — can help you to develop the confidence and take the next steps to achieving other, more challenging goals.

❄   ❄   ❄

I FEEL WELL BECAUSE I EAT WELL.

FEBRUARY 11

"If we lived on a planet with no cycle of seasons, we would miss the beauty and wonder of spring's renewal, of summer's bounty and fall's glowing moments. Winter's time of healing and sleep and preparation for regeneration is also necessary to the human heart, if in more subtle ways."

— writer Jane L. Mickelson

BODY CYCLES

Cyclical patterns occur throughout nature: an orchard tree blossoms in springtime, bears fruit in the summer, drops its leaves in the fall, and remains dormant in the winter so prolonged periods of cold temperatures can enable the tree to spring forth with new life.

Like the seasons, you undergo daily cycles that dominate your emotions as well as your physical energies. For example, you may be aware that there are times during the day when your energy flows the strongest. Maybe you're a morning person who arises feeling alert and ready to exercise or begin other activities. But then you may notice that your energy cycle slows down during the day, perhaps in mid-afternoon or early evening, and you may feel tired and withdrawn.

Your body has its own cycles which, as you age, change from year to year and decade to decade. Women may feel this through a most significant body change—menopause. But as they age, men may also be aware of changes to their bodies that are influenced by the inevitable pull of gravity and time.

By respecting the cycles around you as well as the cycles within you, you can learn to accept the changes that are part of life's natural process of birth, growth, and decline.

I HARMONIZE WITH NATURE'S CYCLES AND MY OWN.

FEBRUARY 12

"Those who have the strength and the love to sit with a dying patient in the silence that goes beyond words will know that this moment is neither frightening nor painful, but a peaceful cessation of the functioning of the body."

— psychologist/author Elisabeth Kübler-Ross

SELF-SUPPORTIVE CAREGIVING

B ecause so many of the people in your life may be living to older ages, you may find that you need to provide caregiving to elderly parents, a partner, a sibling, or a long-time friend. Also, if your partner becomes disabled or chronically ill, but is well enough to be cared for in the home, you may become the primary caregiver.

Caregiving can be emotionally, physically, and even financially stressful. As a caregiver, you may feel frustrated at seeing someone you love so debilitated; you may also feel lonely in your isolation from the companionship of the relationship, as well as from social contacts you have little or no time to maintain. You may have physical limitations that are challenged in taking care of yourself as well as caring for another. And, you may find that holding a job outside the home in addition to caregiving can affect your work productivity.

That's why it's important to take care of yourself. No one can be a full-time or even part-time caregiver without help. Think about friends and relatives who can sometimes fill in for you. Explore the possibility of in-home care, transportation services, Meals on Wheels, senior centers, telephone reassurance programs, mental health and counseling services, hospice services, and adult day-care health centers. You may also wish to contact a support group for caregivers so you can share your experiences and receive comfort, advice, and understanding.

I GIVE CARE TO MY LOVED ONE AND TO MYSELF.

"At sixteen I was stupid, confused, insecure, and indecisive. At twenty-five I was wise, self-confident, prepossessing, and assertive. At forty-five I am stupid, confused, insecure, and indecisive. Who would have supposed that maturity is only a short break in adolescence?"

— cartoonist Jules Feiffer

THE AGING OF THE BRAIN

Although over time the structure of the brain changes—it grows lighter and shrinks slightly— there's no medical explanation for why one older person's brain stays creative and alert while another's starts to deteriorate. Arthur Rubinstein, for example, was 89 years old when he gave one of his most remarkable piano recitals. Even though a serious eye condition restricted his ability to read a note of music or to even see the piano keys beneath his fingers, he played magnificently at Carnegie Hall—and entirely from his memory.

One possible explanation for an older person's capacity to remain mentally lively was based on an experiment with rats that showed the effect of socialization on mental alertness. Rats that were confined to small cages and deprived of social interaction with other rats began to develop shrinking cortexes and to lose the filaments that connected brain cells. But when the same rats were returned to "rat society," their brains expanded, and new filaments replaced the ones that were lost.

What this means is that if you're isolated from others, it's more likely you'll be confused, disoriented, and dull. To maintain mental alertness and stimulation, become actively involved with others— with family members, neighbors, friends, a support group, and clubs. Even talking on the telephone on a regular basis can help you re-enter "people society."

☙ ☙ ☙

I STAY MENTALLY ALERT BY INTERACTING WITH OTHERS.

"Whether you call it cuddling, companionship or outright passion, love can—and does—flourish in nursing homes and other geriatric facilities."

— writer Judy Foreman

ROMANCE AMONG THE ELDERLY

Not too long ago at the Hebrew Home for the Aged at Riverdale in the Bronx, the staff was required to separate two people if they were sexually involved. Now, however, social workers look upon intimacy as a genuine need rather than as a behavior problem. The center now has a policy that spells out "the right to seek out and engage in sexual expression."

For many of those who are living in nursing homes, assisted living facilities, and retirement communities, special friendships between women and men, men and men, and women and women are being formed that satisfy human needs for warmth, tenderness, kindness, physical intimacy, sexual satisfaction, and love.

Although many older people have no desire to start a relationship late in life, especially if they were happily married and prefer to remain "true" to a deceased partner, romance can—and does — flourish among the elderly. For some, romance means cuddling together on a couch but sleeping in separate apartments; for others, it means taking advantage of private rooms with locks on the doors.

This Valentine's Day, you can romance someone you already love or show your affection to a new, special friend. Or, if you haven't yet found a new love, take heart in knowing that the odds of your rekindling love in your seventies, eighties, or even nineties run pretty high. Make yourself available, and you'll discover how easy it is to bond with another!

I BELIEVE IN ROMANCE AND LOVE AT ANY AGE.

"When I was 40, my doctor advised me that a man in his forties shouldn't play tennis. I heeded his advice carefully and could hardly wait until I reached 50 to start again."

— politician/jurist Hugo Lafayette Black

HEALTHFUL MOVEMENTS

Age is not the crucial factor in determining and improving your level of fitness. Rather, the patterns of activity you established in the past have determined how well you're able to stay active for your good health today. If you've been consistently exercising, chances are you're in good shape today. You probably suffer less from headaches, chronic back pain, stiffness, painful joints, irregularity, and insomnia. And, as you may know, when you exercise as hard as your body lets you, you have more energy for living, learning, and loving.

But if you haven't been consistently exercising, you need to start off slowly and gradually. Have a complete medical analysis, and get your doctor's okay first. Then explore all the opportunities for being physically active by designing your own program or setting your own goals of walking, jogging, running, biking, hiking, swimming, or skiing. Or, you can get active with others by joining a health club, the YWCA or YMCA, a group of like-minded individuals, or even by starting a group that brings people together in the pursuit of adventurous outdoor activities such as camping, backpacking, canoeing, or mountain biking.

Regardless of what you've done in the past, now's the time to start living a healthier, more active life!

❀   ❀   ❀

EVERY DAY, I GET ACTIVE AND STAY ACTIVE
FOR GOOD HEALTH.

FEBRUARY 16

*"The misery of a child is interesting to a mother, the misery of
a young man is interesting to a young woman, the misery of
an old man is interesting to nobody."*

— author Victor Hugo

SHORT-TERM SELF-PITY

Self-pity is an emotion that you can sometimes indulge in when
you've just experienced one of life's major trials, such as the
death of a loved one, the loss of financial security, relocation,
retirement, or a grave medical diagnosis—not simply because your
children haven't stopped by to visit you lately or you just had
another birthday. But engaging in self-pity for any reason for any
extended period of time can have serious consequences.

When you're in the throes of self-pity, you have a limited perspective. All you can see is what you don't have and how it affects
you. Too much self-pity can cut you off from supportive people
who can share in your difficulty—or can even damage your relationship with them. Self-pity can sometimes exacerbate the loss in
ways that make it seem far worse than it is. Self-pity can focus your
energy on the problem rather than the solution, keeping you stuck
in a negative cycle in which recovery and healing become impossible. And self-pity can offer you a convenient excuse to do nothing
so you're not able to get past the point of crisis, or have the desire
to take action to help yourself.

Willingness to let go of your self-pity is all it takes to process
your hardship in effective ways. Although you may stand still from
time to time, you'll be able to make progress if you release the need
to feel sorry for yourself.

I RELEASE MY MISERY IN ORDER TO MOVE
FORWARD WITH MY LIFE.

"Life is precious to the old person. He is not interested
merely in thoughts of yesterday's good life and tomorrow's path
to the grave. He does not want his later years to be a sentence of
solitary confinement in society. Nor does he want them
to be a death watch."

— surgeon David Bacharach Allman

FOLLOWING YOUR ELDER HERO

Do you have an elder hero—an older person you consider to be a role model, someone who has challenged social conventions, fought ageist stereotypes, rejected generational myths, and turned deaf ears on what others thought was best, and instead created a new vision of what life could be? Perhaps your elder hero is someone you know who continues to evolve professionally after retiring from one career and embarking on another. Maybe your elder hero is someone you learned about in a magazine article or interview, someone who found great personal satisfaction and happiness in the pursuit of a life-long dream. Or perhaps your elder hero is someone famous who embarked on a path in their middle years that led them toward fame—Mother Teresa, Mahatma Gandhi, Albert Schweitzer, or Henri Matisse.

You can follow in the footsteps of your elder hero and also set off on a journey that will lead you to new possibilities for yourself, new challenges, and new visions of what to expect from the later years of your life. Reflect on what your elder hero needed to do to make his or her dream for the future come true. Close your eyes and see yourself achieving one of your dreams for the future. Then open your eyes and say, "Today is the day in which I'll take the first step toward realizing my dream."

I AM INSPIRED BY MY ELDER HERO TO
PURSUE MY DREAMS.

FEBRUARY 18

*"There is an art to wandering. If I have a destination, a plan—
an objective—I've lost the ability to find serendipity. I've become
too focused, too single-minded. I am on a quest, not a ramble. I
search for the Holy Grail of particularity and miss the chalice
freely offered, filled and overflowing."*

— naturalist/writer Cathy Johnson

THE SPIRITUALITY OF NATURE

Each day you may pay attention to your goals—you eat, you exercise, you rest, you read the paper, you do your chores. But do you also pay attention to your spiritual goal of needing some time each day for spiritual renewal? If you neglect taking care of your body, it will eventually break down in some way. So, too, can you become emotionally imbalanced and find your world filled with continual conflict if you avoid meeting your spiritual goals.

Setting aside time for moments of reflection is the best way to pay attention to your spiritual goals. Taking time for reflection may seem like self-indulgence when you feel there are so many other things you need to do or that there are "better" uses of your time. Yet, it's one of the most responsible things you can do for yourself.

When you find yourself more focused on your intellectual or physical goals, say out loud the words of this Navajo song: "Walk on a rainbow trail; walk on a trail of song, and about you will be beauty." Then go outside and make contact with nature. Take a walk on a nature trail near your home. Look for the prints of animals' paws on the ground. Listen to the sound of the birds. When you're spiritually centered, you can see things more clearly, act more effectively, and feel healthier. Today, set a goal to balance your intellectual and physical needs with your spiritual ones in order to achieve peace and harmony in your life.

MY GOAL IS TO REFLECT UPON THE NATURAL
WORLD AROUND ME.

FEBRUARY 19

*"If I hadn't had children, I probably would have had more
money and material things. I probably would have gone more
places, gotten more sleep, pampered myself more. My life would
have been much more boring and predictable. As a result of being
a parent, I have laughed harder, cried more often. I have worried
more and hurried more. I've had less sleep, but somehow I've
had more fun. I've learned more, grown more. My heart
has ached harder, and I've loved to a capacity beyond my
imagination. I've given more of myself, but I've derived
more meaning from life."*

— Dr. Marianne Neifert

CHILDBEARING IN MIDLIFE

More and more women are choosing to have children in their
middle years after concentrating on other areas of their lives
in their young adult years. Despite some of the added pressures of
the middle years, men and women are discovering the joys of parenting and often make capable parents because they've had experience in balancing life's demands.

There are many worries, however, that middle-aged parents-to-be have. For instance, how will a child handle having older parents during college years? Will there be enough money in retirement to support the parents as well as the child? What kind of support network will be available to the parents? And, of utmost consideration, how great a risk will the pregnancy place on the older woman?

While most of the questions regarding parent-child interactions and support networks can be resolved over time, if you're a candidate for a high-risk pregnancy you might want to consider midlife childbearing alternatives such as adoption and foster parenthood.

❋　　❋　　❋

I EXPERIENCE THE JOY OF BEING A PARENT
IN MANY WAYS.

FEBRUARY 20

"The best mirror is an old friend."

— English proverb

PRECIOUS FRIENDS

Your friends are some of your greatest possessions. With them you're always free to be yourself. With them you have an established base of mutual trust and honesty. With them you always want the best for one another and, to this end, are always willing to provide support and guidance. With them you can ask for and receive sound advice. With them you can learn more about yourself. With them you can share hopes and dreams. With them you can be joyful and playful. With them you can simply be.

Even during those times when you dislike yourself, grow impatient with yourself, feel ill, grow weary, lose sight of where you're going, forget even the simplest things, or feel lonely or blue, your friends still like you. Your friends will always be there to cheer you up, make you feel comfortable, provide you with gentle reminders, and lend a helping hand. Also, your friends will always be able to see the things that you can't—your beauty, your wisdom, your strength, your wit, the progress you're making, and the positive changes you're making in your life.

Today, remind yourself that you're truly blessed by the wonderful friends you have in your life. Then think of something nice you can do for one of your precious friends with whom you've lost touch. Pick up the telephone, make a special gift to mail, or create a greeting card with a collage that depicts all the wonderful memories you've made with your friend.

I REMEMBER A VERY PRECIOUS FRIEND TODAY.

FEBRUARY 21

"Travel has a way of stretching the mind. The stretch comes not from travel's immediate rewards, the inevitable myriad new sights, smells and sounds, but with experiencing firsthand how others do differently what we have believed to be the right and only way."
— writer Ralph Crawshaw

LIVING ON THE ROAD

Do you want to travel but feel restricted by a limited budget? Do you feel that you'd like a change of scenery but want to be with people who speak the same language, share your interests, and have similar backgrounds? Then perhaps you'd like to "live" on the road in America with other retired people.

When you combine retirement living with travel, you get a moving residence—a mobile home that you can set up in a "town" with other retired folks for any length of time. You can live in such a mobile-home community year-round. You can be a "snowbird" and "fly" south to such a community in the winter. Or you can stop there for a while until you're ready to get back on the road again.

Many mobile-home communities attract a large number of retirees who like to travel, yet want to avoid hassles such as making reservations, sitting on long airplane flights, maintaining special diets, budgeting for numerous expenses, boarding beloved pets, depending on others to take in mail and newspapers, and being far away from home. In some communities, such as one in Yuma, Arizona, the summer population reaches nearly 50,000 people, with an additional 30,000 or more who "fly down" in the winter from the north.

Rather than be talked into taking a trip, consider investing in a moving residence that can take you to all the places you've always wanted to see.

I LIKE THE ADVENTURE OF LIVING ON THE ROAD.

FEBRUARY 22

"You die as you've lived. If you were paranoid in life, you'll probably be paranoid when you're dying."

— film director James Cimino

REPLACING PANICKY FEELINGS

Anytime you experience an anxious, panicky, or paranoid feeling, that's a signal that needs your attention. Perhaps your palms are sweaty, you feel edgy and restless, your breathing is rapid and shallow, you can't seem to stop shaking, or you feel as if you're not thinking very clearly. Such symptoms are physical signs that your body's trying to communicate with you, to tell you that you need to pay attention to what you're thinking or feeling.

If you ask yourself what's going on, you might hear answers such as, "I'm really scared to be alone," "I'm afraid of what the doctor might tell me," "I think my children don't really care about me—they're just after my money," "I feel so helpless and dependent on other people," or "I don't know how I'm going to make ends meet." You may be feeling frustrated, scared, angry, sad, or fearful about growing older and what that means for you.

One of the best ways to get through times like this, when you're feeling edgy and panicky, is to try to place yourself in the present. You can do this by remembering such things as the date, the time, and the temperature. Then identify objects about you. Look at what you're wearing. This simple exercise helps to bring you back to the present and calm you down in a way that removes you from the space you were in that contributed to your anxiety. It will then be easier for you to work through your feelings by thinking about them when you're in a less agitated, more relaxed state.

I CALM MY ANXIOUS FEELINGS BY STAYING IN THE
PRESENT MOMENT.

*"The spiritual eyesight improves as the physical
eyesight declines."*

— Plato

FINDING YOUR CENTER

While modern life emphasizes the surface of things—how things look and what they are— spirituality teaches you that without a center, a deep-rooted belief, and an inner sense of peace and calm, the surface really means nothing. For it's not what you look like, how old you are, what you do, how much money you have in the bank, or where you live that matters—but what you think, feel, and believe in your heart. Externals are fleeting; what is internal becomes eternal.

To find this spiritual place inside your heart requires that you let go of the externals that rule your life. Perhaps you struggle to please others. Maybe you work hard for social causes. Perhaps your calendar is cluttered with commitments and obligations. Maybe your focus is more on your possessions than on your blessings. Or perhaps you've become overly concerned with your health or the health of someone close to you.

Now imagine that you're an ocean. On your surface are all the externals of your life. Sometimes they sway in gentle swells, sometimes they swirl about in turbulent motion. Yet below the surface are the quiet depths; herein lies your deep source of peace and spiritual inspiration. To get below the surface, think of the externals as things that flow through you; they are part of you, but they're really separate from you. Enjoy these externals, be committed to them, but keep them from ruling your life. What really matters is finding your center so you feel peaceful and harmonious no matter what is happening outside you.

I AM CENTERED, WHOLE, AND COMPLETE.

FEBRUARY 24

*"Youth is happy because it has the ability to see beauty.
Anyone who keeps the ability to see beauty never grows old.*

— writer Franz Kafka

BEAUTIFUL WONDERS OF LIFE

How often do you take time to notice the beauty of the natural world—the way the snow clings to trees after a snowfall, the glorious colors of the birds that frolic around your bird feeder, or the silvery brilliance of a full moon? How often do you pay attention to the softness of your cat's fur, the shine of your dog's coat after you brush it, and the melodiousness of your caged bird's songs? How often do you take time to look at friends or loved ones and appreciate their beauty—what you see on the outside as well as what you know is on the inside? How often do you look in the mirror and see the beauty of your own eyes, face, and smile?

When you're caught up in the web of grief, defeat, despair, dejection, or depression over things you can't control, you can easily forget that there's a world around you that's teeming with beauty. But those beautiful wonders won't come to you; you have to take time to notice them.

At this moment, no matter how you feel, take time to notice the beauty that surrounds you. As Maya Angelou once wrote, "I'm looking out a large window and I see about forty dogwood and maple and oak and locust trees and the light is on some of the leaves and it's so beautiful. Sometimes I'm overcome with gratitude at such sights and feel that each of us has a responsibility for being alive...." Today, open your eyes to the world, look out on all of its beauty, and thank God that you're alive to experience this beauty for another day.

❁ ❁ ❁

I NOTICE THE BEAUTY AROUND ME AND WITHIN ME.

"The evening of life brings with it its lamp."
— essayist/moralist Joseph Joubert

THE LIGHT OF EXPERIENCE

Think about what it would be like to walk through the woods at night without a flashlight. You'd be at the mercy of every root, stump, rock, and hole. Although you may be so familiar with the woods that you could take the same path in daylight without a problem, without the guidance of a light at night it would be like walking the path blindfolded—and for the very first time.

But if you rely upon the wealth of your life experience, which is based upon those things you've learned from and which you've come to trust, you'll most certainly be able find the right paths so you have fewer problems getting to where you need to go. For, as Patrick Henry once said, "I have but one lamp by which my feet are guided, and that is the lamp of experience."

Just as you know the best places to eat lunch, the greatest places to shop for bargains, and the right people to call to get a job done quickly and efficiently, so too do you know the right paths to take when you're going through a period of darkness in your life. You may learn some valuable lessons by heeding sayings such as: "One day at a time," or "And this, too, shall pass." Some of your friends or family members may show you how reliable they can be or what sound advice and support they can offer; they can provide you with a light so you can see your way without stumbling. Some of your prayers may be answered, also, as your Higher Power illuminates your way.

I KNOW AND TRUST IN ALL OF MY EXPERIENCES
TO GUIDE ME.

FEBRUARY 26

*"There is nothing more remarkable in the life of Socrates than
that he found time in his old age to learn to dance and play on
instruments and thought it time well spent."*
— essayist Michel de Montaigne

TIME TO DANCE AND SING

Have you danced today? Have you taken a moment yet to sing a song or listen to music? If you haven't, then it's time now to add the joy of movement and the stimulation of music to your life.

Dancing is perhaps second only to walking as an extremely beneficial form of exercise. Dance develops flexibility and strength and also gives you a natural "high," whether you dance alone in the privacy of your own home, in an instructional class with others, or socially with a dance partner. Dance can help you to get moving at your own pace so you can loosen stiff muscles, breathe deeply, and stir the air around you.

Music can help you to unwind or help you to get wound up. Soothing music by itself can calm the nerves; used in conjunction with visualization and meditation, music and the mind can combine to heal stress-related illnesses, relax painful muscles, heighten awareness and insight, lower blood pressure, and calm anxiety and tension. Uplifting music such as Dixieland jazz, swing, or reggae can provide you with the energy to start the day, give you an extra push to get you through your chores, or perk you up when you're tired.

Combining dance with music you create—for example, moving to the rhythm of tambourines, castanets, or drums—can give you such a great feeling of well-being that you won't be able to get through any day without dance or song!

I MOVE AND GROOVE TO SOME MUSIC TODAY.

FEBRUARY 27

"The young man who has not wept is a savage, and the old man who will not laugh is a fool."

— philosopher/poet George Santayana

LAUGHING AT THE PROGRESSION OF LIFE

How easy it is to be extremely serious about growing older! You may be able to think of a dozen things you can get serious about—your health and all the diseases and infirmities you can look forward to, retirement and money matters, increasing dependency upon others and, of course, the most serious downside of aging—dying and death. Is it any wonder, then, that even though you may be decades away from the end of your life, you're already depressed about what's to come? Rather than seeing life as an enjoyable, pleasurable adventure, you're only able to focus on what you fear is going to happen.

But have you ever noticed how much better you feel after a good laugh? That's because laughter stimulates the production of endorphins, the body's natural painkillers. Laughter also improves respiration, activates your immune system, relaxes your muscles, and relieves stress. With laughter comes a lighter attitude towards life; with a lighter attitude comes the realization that all things will come to pass and everything and everybody evolves through the cycle of aging.

Today, you have a choice. You can either look forward to the cycles of life and get the most out of them, or you can fear and resist them. Enjoying the cycles can bring joy; resistance brings despair. Can you find something to enjoy? Laugh at life's ironies, chuckle at a comedian's sense of humor or a funny television sitcom, or laugh at yourself. Resolve not to take the progression of life too seriously. After all, as it has been said, "You'll never get out of it alive!"

I PUT ON A HAPPY FACE AND REDISCOVER MY
SENSE OF HUMOR.

FEBRUARY 28

"There is a wicked inclination in most people to suppose an old man decayed in his intellect. If a young or middle-aged man, when leaving a company, does not recollect where he laid his hat, it is nothing; but if the same inattention is discovered in an old man, people will shrug their shoulders and say, 'His memory is going.'"

— author/lexicographer Samuel Johnson

MEMORY LAPSES AND LOSSES

As you grow older, you may find yourself becoming more and more forgetful. You may not be able to remember names and telephone numbers, you may misplace keys or other household items, and you may forget important dates or appointments. You may have always had such memory lapses, but since you're growing older, you may interpret them as signs of aging or the onset of senility, Alzheimer's disease, or dementia.

Not all lapses or losses of memory are a result of aging, although the loss of nerve cells in the brain—cells that aren't regenerated after the age of 50—can impact the memory. But fatigue, anxiety, stress, and depression can also cause moments of memory loss or periods of memory decline.

There are things you can do to help yourself to remember, though. You can write lists or notes to yourself instead of relying upon your memory. Before attending a social function, recall the names of people who are expected to be there and other information about them. Keep areas in your home organized, and set aside particular places for easily misplaced items such as car keys, your purse or wallet, address books, bills to be paid, and so on. Wear a watch with an alarm, or set an alarm clock to remind you when to leave for an appointment.

If you do have difficulty, try not to get upset. Take a deep breath, clear your mind, and chances are this will be enough to jog your memory.

❀   ❀   ❀

I REMEMBER TO HELP MYSELF REMEMBER!

FEBRUARY 29

*"As for me, except for an occasional heart attack,
I feel as young as I ever did."*

— humorist Robert Benchley

STRAIGHT FROM THE HEART

While cardiovascular disease is the leading cause of death in the United States, more often than not, it's a disease that develops over time. This makes it a disease that can be prevented. You can decrease the probability of serious illness or premature death from heart disease by reducing the risk factors associated with the disease. Quit smoking, cut down on foods that are rich in saturated fats and cholesterol, reduce your level of stress, maintain a healthy weight, and exercise regularly. Also, have your blood pressure checked regularly, and become familiar with the early warning signs of heart attack and stroke.

How do you know you're having a stroke? You have temporary weakness or numbness in the face, arm, or leg on one side of the body; a severe, persistent headache; a temporary loss of speech or difficulty speaking or understanding speech; temporary dimness or loss of vision; and dizziness or unsteadiness on your feet.

How do you know when you're having a heart attack? You'll have uncomfortable pressure, tightness, squeezing, or pain in the center of your chest that lasts two minutes or more; pain that spreads to your arms, shoulders, neck, jaw, or stomach; dizziness, fainting, sweating, or nausea; and shortness of breath.

Even if any of these warning signs fades away, do not ignore them. Remain calm, but get help right away. Call an emergency telephone number, or ask someone to drive you to the emergency room at a nearby hospital.

I DO ALL I CAN TO MAINTAIN A HEALTHY HEART.

MARCH 1

"To know how to grow old is the master work of wisdom, and one of the most difficult chapters in the great art of living."

— philosopher/poet Henri Frédéric Amiel

CREATING GREATER JOY

Have you lived most of your life by placing your happiness outside yourself? If you have, then you've been straining, competing, and living with stress. You've been caught up in the drama of life, unable to detach from the problems, conflicts, resentments, and negative emotions that have swirled within you and around you. You've felt as equally exposed to ridicule and criticism as you have to flattery and attention. And you've had difficulty maintaining a balance between purpose and detachment, discipline and adventure, and intensity and play.

How can you create greater joy in your life as you age? You can use the wisdom that has guided you through the years to change the patterns of how you've lived. To do this, start to enjoy the drama of life without getting caught up in it; you can still do for others and offer them your support, but do so while you remain independent of them. Be unaffected by the praise as well as the criticism of others; trust more in what you think of yourself. Slow down your pace of living; eliminate excessive haste, and take time to consider whether what you're doing is really what you want to do. Remove yourself from the "trap" of retirement or "ought-to's"; do things that you love or that give you a sense of purpose. Let go of feelings of self-pity, resentment, anger, or other negative emotions that can drag you into a quagmire of unhealthy, joyless living. Live in the present moment, and find the value in every moment of the day.

❀   ❀   ❀

I CREATE JOY AND HAPPINESS IN MY LIFE.

"Life is not living, but living in health."

— poet Marcus Valerius Martialis

LIVING IN HEALTH

Ancient Indian sages define healthy life energy as *prana;* the Chinese know it as *chi.* Other cultures and religions have different names for this life energy. But no matter what name it goes by, what it encompasses are the ways of attaining and maintaining a level of physical, emotional, and spiritual balance that result in physical vitality, enthusiasm, strong disease immunity, mental alertness, balanced body rhythms, a strong spiritual connection, and a sense of exhilaration.

A healthy life demands that you eat well; a diet that includes lots of fresh fruits and vegetables, complex carbohydrates, easily digestible proteins, plenty of water, and few processed or fried foods is the best. Physical exercise is also important because such activity helps bring energy to the body. Regular meditation clears the mind of negative emotions and eases stress; meditating for at least 20 minutes each day prompts the development of slow, deep breathing techniques and also promotes balance of the senses. Conscious contact with a Higher Power through meditation, prayer, attendance at self-help groups, connecting with nature, or weekly church services releases negative emotions and restores faith, hope, and trust. And, avoiding all nonviolent activity— actions such as expressing rage, entering into conflict with others, maintaining grudges, harboring resentments, engaging in self-pity, focusing on guilt or shame, looking for revenge, and sabotaging relationships— promotes refined behavior, self-acceptance, and serenity.

Today, begin to live a healthy life so you can increase your physical, emotional, and spiritual vitality.

I LIVE IN HEALTH SO I STRENGTHEN MY LIFE ENERGY.

MARCH 3

"Let it be a source of consolation, if not of triumph, in a long, studious life of true genius, to know that the imagination may not decline with the vigour of the frame which holds it; there has been no old age for many men of genius."

— author Isaac D'Israeli

MATURITY AND PRODUCTIVITY

It's truly remarkable that some of the greatest achievements have been accomplished by those in their mature years. Chaucer wrote *The Canterbury Tales* at quite an advanced age. Jomo Kenyatta was purportedly in his seventies when, in 1964, he became the first President of the Republic of Kenya. Charles Darwin wrote *On the Origin of Species* when he was 50; he completed *The Descent of Man* at the age of 62 and *The Power of Movement in Plants* at 71. Charles de Gaulle was 68 years old when he returned to power in France. Benjamin Franklin served on the committee that drafted the Declaration of Independence and was one of its original signers at the age of 70; at 81, he effected the compromise that made the Constitution of the United States a reality. Golda Meir resigned as Israel's Prime Minister at the age of 75. George Bernard Shaw wrote his first play when he was 36 years old and his last produced play when he was in his late eighties. John Wayne won an Oscar at the age of 62 for his starring role in *True Grit.* Cecil B. DeMille produced and directed the academy-award winning *The Greatest Show on Earth* when he was 71. And Duncan MacLean won a silver medal at the 1975 World Veterans' Olympics in Canada when he ran 200 meters in 44 seconds. He was 90 years old.

So, you, too, can accomplish great things—no matter how old you are!

I VIEW MY AGE AS A TIME IN WHICH I INCREASE
MY PRODUCTIVITY.

March 4

*"Fathers of three wear tank tops and mesh shorts on plane trips.
Forty-ish women strap on helmets and pads to go Rollerblading.
A New York teacher motel-hops across the country with a ninth-
grade girl and wonders why everyone's mad at him. Whatever
happened to grown-ups?...America is turning into a Doonesbury
cartoon, with millions of adults behaving as if they're still one
year out of college, working in a semi-flexi-job, eating happy-
hour food, and hoping that Mom and Dad
don't rent out their bedroom."*

— writer John Powers

ACTING YOUR AGE

There was a time in American history when there were numerous role models who showed us how to "act" like an adult.
These people wore suits and ties to work, or dresses, pearls, and
heels while baking cookies at home. They listened to grown-up
music, often singing along because they knew all the words. They
attended community functions and were active in the school and
church. They didn't smoke and had never used drugs, even in college. They gave sound advice to their children and commanded
respect. They were serious. They were Ward and June Cleaver, Ike
and Mamie Eisenhower, Bob and Dolores Hope. And they behaved
like adults.

But nowadays the age-related composition of American culture
has changed. Americans are living longer than ever before, the continuing birth dearth is keeping the population of children low, and
baby boomers are reaching their forties and fifties healthier, more
active, more vigorous, and more influential than any other middle
generation in American history.

So, in reality, you're just a youngster in the midst of a large
aging population. Why not just act the age you feel?

ॐ   ॐ   ॐ

I ACT AS GROWN UP AS I WANT TO.

March 5

"We ask for long life, but 'tis deep life, or noble moments that signify. Let the measure of time be spiritual, not mechanical."

— Ralph Waldo Emerson

PRAYER FOR THE MIDDLE-AGED

*L*ord, thou knowest better than I know myself that I am growing older and will someday be old. Keep me from the fatal habit of thinking I must say something on every subject and on every occasion. Release me from the craving to straighten out everybody's affairs. Make me thoughtful but not moody; helpful but not bossy. With my vast store of wisdom, it seems a pity not to use it all, but Thou knowest Lord that I want a few friends at the end.

Keep my mind free from the recital of endless details; give me wings to get to the point. Seal my lips on my aches and pains. They are increasing, and love of rehearsing them is becoming sweeter as the years go by. I dare not ask for grace enough to enjoy the tales of others' pains, but help me to endure them with patience.

I dare not ask for improved memory, but for a growing humility, and a lessening cocksureness when my memory seems to clash with the memories of others. Teach me the glorious lesson that occasionally I may be mistaken.

Keep me reasonably sweet; I do not want to be a Saint—some of them are hard to live with—but a sour old person is one of the crowning works of the devil. Give me the ability to see good things in unexpected places, and talents in unexpected people. And give me, O Lord, the grace to tell them so. Amen.

— Anonymous

❊   ❊   ❊

I RECITE THIS PRAYER ON EACH NEW YEAR OF MY LIFE.

MARCH 6

*"A medical revolution has extended the life of our elder
citizens without providing the dignity and security those
later years deserve."*
— President John F. Kennedy

AGING IS NOT A DISEASE

Ageism manifests itself first and foremost in the attitude that
aging is a disease. When this happens in the medical profession, caregivers can be slow or even reluctant to distinguish between the signs of aging and the symptoms of a disease. In fact, more often than not, if you cite an ache, pain, or new condition during a medical exam, your practitioner may dismiss such complaints with ageist comments such as, "What do you expect at your age?" or "You are getting older, you know."

But if you and your health-care provider view a particular problem you're having as separate from your age, then you both will be more inclined to actively and aggressively seek solutions to it. Since statistics reveal that the majority of people over the age of 65 have at least one chronic health problem, you need to begin today to pay attention to how your caregivers pay attention to you. Refuse to accept any ageist put-down in response to a medical complaint; in fact, change practitioners if you feel that you're being treated differently—or diffidently—because of your age. Ask for medical alternatives to taking pain medication or explore other nonmedically accepted alternatives on your own, such as acupuncture, chiropractic adjustments, homeopathic or herbal preparations, or diet and environmental adjustments.

Today, believe that with proper treatment, you may be able to live more comfortably or even eventually eliminate a particular medical problem.

֍   ֍   ֍

I PAY PERSONAL ATTENTION TO THE QUALITY
OF MY MEDICAL CARE.

MARCH 7

"It is day by day that we go forward; today we are as we were
yesterday and tomorrow we shall be like ourselves today.
So we go on without being aware of it, and this is one of the
miracles of Providence that I so love."
— Marie de Rabutin-Chantal, Marquise de Sévigné

LIVING ONE DAY AT A TIME

Those who belong to self-help groups such as Alcoholics Anonymous, Smokenders, and Weight Watchers know the value of the saying, "One day at a time." The slogan makes it much easier to say, "I won't have a drink this afternoon," "I won't smoke for the next hour," or "I won't have dessert with dinner," so the focus is on the moment rather than on tomorrow, next week, or next month.

"Live for today" is another slogan you can use to help you focus on the present. It can prevent your mind from veering into worry, anxiety, and fears about tomorrow and all the tomorrows after tomorrow, and it can keep you in the place in time where you can do the most good—the present.

Because life is so unpredictable—it can only be experienced one day at a time—refrain from trying to write the events of tomorrow until after they've happened. Instead, see today's sunrise and sunset. Be free to experience all that's in store for you now, all that's fresh and new and exciting, right now. Whenever you feel like you're getting way ahead of yourself, repeat the slogans "One day at a time" or "Live for today" to keep your mind focused in the present. And keep in mind the words of Dean Acheson, who said, "I try to be as philosophical as the old lady from Vermont who said that the best thing about the future is that it comes only one day at a time."

I LIVE FOR TODAY—ONE DAY AT A TIME.

MARCH 8

"It is not strange that that early love of the heart should come back, as it so often does when the dim eye is brightening with its last light. It is not strange that the freshest fountains the heart has ever known in its wastes should bubble up anew when the life-blood is growing stagnant."

— Nathaniel Hawthorne

LOVING PEOPLE

What makes life worth living to you? Is it your health? Your work? Your home? Your personal possessions? While such things may rate highly with you, perhaps you would say that the people you love—a life partner, your children, friends, neighbors, co-workers, and family members— make life worth living.

Intimate relationships can make a profound difference in your life. They can take you outside yourself, encouraging you to think about and give to others. They can make the less enjoyable aspects of life more enjoyable by providing companionship and communication. They can bring you shared experiences and laughter. They can offer romance and passion. They can provide stability and security. They can strengthen and deepen love.

Yet, in the later years of life, forming and maintaining relationships can be difficult. Retirement from the workplace can sever a wide social circle. Your own relocation, or that of friends and neighbors, can be a traumatic experience. Children who grow up and move away from home can leave behind an "empty nest." And, the death of a close friend, parent, or life partner can be so devastating that it may seem as if the void can never be filled.

But new relationships can be formed in middle and late life by thinking of friends as family, by dating, and by exploring unique housing situations that will bring you in contact with others.

❁   ❁   ❁

I SEEK OUT PEOPLE TO LOVE.

MARCH 9

"Old age is an island surrounded by death."

— writer Juan Montalvo

HOPEFUL GRIEF

Visitors to the Fiji Islands learn about a strange custom among its native people known as "Calling to the Dead." A mourner climbs high up into a tree or scales a cliff and, after calling out the name of the deceased, cries out, "Come back! Come back!" The cry is made even more heartrending by the echoes that reverberate in "reply."

When you're filled with grief over the loss of another beloved person in your life, you may feel as if you're on an island that's surrounded by death. Your grief over yet another loss may make your present so unbearable that you may think that the future holds more of the same. You may feel hopeless, and you may even blame God for your losses and cry out, "Why did You do this to me?" or "Why don't You help me? Can't You see I'm in pain?"

Deep grief, combined with an estrangement from a Higher Power, can leave you with an intense spiritual emptiness. But even though you may feel as if you stand alone and are exposed to the elements of a cruel, heartless world that have been personally directed at you by some all-powerful unkind Being, that's just not the case. Every event in your life has been experienced by millions of others. You're not the recipient of a vengeful act that's been inflicted upon you from above.

Rather than dwell in hopelessness and despair, reach out hopefully. Cry out your pain, let your tears fall, get on your knees, or simply close your eyes and silently ask for spiritual guidance. You will get an answer.

❧   ❧   ❧

I PRAY IN MY GRIEF AND KNOW MY PRAYERS ARE HEARD.

March 10

"Only yesterday waistbands fit perfectly, you shifted into higher gear without a creak, and middle age seemed as remote as the stars. Start exercising now—whatever your age. Hitch your wagon to that bodybuilding star and discover a new lifelong vitality."
— writer/bodybuilder Armand Tanny

BUILD UP WITH BODYBUILDING

Regardless of your age, you can still fight the ticking clock of time that brings you deeper into your middle years by engaging in regular exercise. One of the best exercises to hold back aging is bodybuilding.

To be a bodybuilder, you need to participate in three kinds of workouts so you can build strong muscles, improve cardiovascular fitness, and increase stamina. The first is resistance training, which involves pushing and pulling against the resistance provided by dumbbells or health-club machines. The second is regular aerobic exercise, such as walking, running, cycling, swimming, and other activities that get the heart beating faster for a minimum of 15 minutes. The third is flexibility training, which incorporates muscle stretches that help overcome stiffness and keep the muscles pliable.

Be sure to get your physicians' approval before beginning any bodybuilding program. Also, learn from a qualified instructor how to use either machines or dumbbells properly. This person can demonstrate how to perform a particular exercise, as well as personalize a program for you according to your ability and level of fitness.

Working out with weights doesn't mean you have to want to look like Mr. or Ms. America. Rather, a regular program of bodybuilding builds attractive, strong, supple muscles that lift your energy level and help you to look and feel great.

I BUILD MY BODY FOR LIFELONG VITALITY.

MARCH 11

"A classic is something that everybody wants to have read and nobody wants to read."

— Mark Twain

A WHOLE NEW WAY OF LIFE

If you're willing, a wide array of interesting opportunities can open up as you grow older and find that you may not be as mobile as you were before. There's more time to share with a life partner, for instance, as well as the chance to renew the one-to-one relationship you may have had before your children were born. Volunteer work can be done out of the home; preparing newsletters and flyers, stuffing envelopes, or making telephone calls can provide a much-needed service.

Although there may not have been much time before, there's plenty of time now to pursue a craft such as quilting, painting, sculpting, and writing. For the first time in your life, you may have more time to focus on yourself, to get in touch with who you are. You now have the time to digest literary classics you've always wanted to read but never had the time or inclination for in the past. There are movie classics you can watch. There are letters you can write. You can learn a new language. You can enjoy a new hobby. You can even start a business out of your home.

Being housebound, confined to a wheelchair or bed, losing your driver's license, or simply being too tired to be as active as you once were doesn't necessarily mean that you have to stop living. A whole new way of life can open up to you, if you're willing to explore it.

I MAKE GOOD USE OF THE TIME I NOW HAVE AVAILABLE.

March 12

"My father told me, 'You gotta keep progressing or you decay.'
So rather than atrophy mentally and physically,
I just keep forging ahead."

— actor/director Clint Eastwood

RE-ENTERING THE WORK FORCE

Even though he's in his sixties, Clint Eastwood shows no signs of slowing down. "Some people long for retirement," he says. "I don't. I look forward to doing my best work in the present or future."

Because you need the sense of achievement and accomplishment that comes from satisfying and valued social work, work outside the home can happen at any age. You can enter the world of paid work in your middle or later years after your children are gone, following a divorce or the loss of your life partner, for economic survival, or simply out of choice.

If you're entering or re-entering the work force, it's important to assess your strengths and skills. You may have used or developed administrative, fundraising, writing and editing, or marketing and advertising skills in nonpaying jobs in your community or through service in organizations and charities. Also, you may be quite surprised to discover that the decades you spent running a household and raising children has made you a competent organizer and manager and given you the ability to deal with a variety of problematic situations.

You may also find it helpful to contact the National Displaced Homemakers Network, a support group for unemployed older women. Their programs can help you make the transition from the home to the workplace through sessions on career counseling, résumé preparation, job skills assessment, and job referral and placement.

I AM PROUD OF MY WORK SKILLS AND EXPERIENCE.

MARCH 13

"Some lucky souls sleep like babies, no matter what their age."
— writer Judy Foreman

RESTING IN PEACE

For over 40 million American men and women, sleep disorders such as insomnia are a chronic misery; for 20 to 30 million, they're an occasional problem. It would be wonderful to think that, over time, such problems might work themselves out. But studies show that the older you get, the harder it becomes to sleep.

The underlying biological cause of increasingly poor sleep as you mature is believed to be a result of the deterioration of the "clock" in your brain that controls when you sleep and when you wake up. This "aging clock" actually speeds up as you get older, pushing your body rhythms so you want to go to sleep earlier in the evening but then wake up much earlier in the morning.

How can you resolve this? Try not to nap on and off throughout the day; if you need a nap, take one that's no more than 45 minutes long—preferably before three in the afternoon. Avoid going to bed early in the evening simply because you feel lonely or bored. Become more involved and interested in life. Of all the recommendations by sleep researchers, psychologist Peter Hauri says, "...the most important one is to have a reason for living....If I can get that person involved in reading to the blind, or going traveling, or learning a new hobby, he or she will sleep better." Rather than sitting around during the day waiting for the evening to come, or lying awake in bed at night waiting for the morning to dawn, make your life interesting and exciting so you can go to sleep when you're good and tired.

I ALWAYS SLEEP WELL AFTER A DAY WELL SPENT.

"I suppose everyone continues to be interested in the quest for self, but what you feel when you're older, I think, is that...you really must make the self. It is absolutely useless to look for it, you won't find it, but it's possible in some sense to make it."

— writer Mary McCarthy

CHANGING YOUR CAREER

Do you wish you could change your career or feel the need to leave a company you've worked for during most of your working years? While there may be nothing wrong with what you're doing right now, you may sense that your time and energy could be put to better use with another employer or by doing something else. You may long to try something new but aren't sure what you'd like to do. You may feel bored, "stuck," or dissatisfied, and believe that more meaningful and interesting work would make you feel more content. You may want more money, a greater opportunity for advancement, or simply desire a new challenge.

Before making a decision at this time of your life, it's wise to assess what's available to you. Don't burn any bridges until you've crossed over safely. What this means is that you first need to take a hard look at the job you now have. Think about what you would gain by leaving the job, as well as what you would miss. Analyzing what you dislike about what you're doing, as well as what you like, can provide valuable information when deciding on a new situation.

Then start exploring the alternatives. Consider ways to work within the framework of your current job or occupation—take a job that's closer to home or transfer to a different department. Talk to people in a field you're considering about what they do, how they got into that occupation, and why. By looking at all your options, you can ease into an appropriate transition without regrets.

I MAKE CHANGES IN MY CAREER TO ACHIEVE
GREATER JOB SATISFACTION.

MARCH 15

"A light heart lives long."

— William Shakespeare

DIET AND THE HEALTHY HEART

As you age, the eating patterns you've established in your younger years tend to stay with you. But because you often exercise less, this increases the fat in your body. Accumulating fat around the waist and abdomen can place you at a higher risk of heart attack, stroke, and hypertension. Additionally, salt contributes to weight gain through fluid retention, and this too places the heart at risk by increasing the amount of energy that the heart needs to exert.

You can reduce the risk of heart disease by making some simple changes in your diet. Replace salt with herbal seasonings, and avoid canned and packaged foods, which are often high in sodium, as well as common condiments such as ketchup, mustard, and relishes. Eat poultry and fish rather than pork or beef. Studies have shown that eating fish two or three times a week reduces the risk of atherosclerosis. If you do have a taste for red meat, select the leanest cuts and trim all visible fat. Replace butter and shortenings with vegetable oils. To maintain your intake of calcium, which prevents both hypertension and osteoporosis, choose low-fat milk and cheeses. Reduce consumption of egg yolks to no more than three a week.

A program of regular aerobic exercise, combined with healthy weight-maintenance practices that concentrate less on dieting and more on healthy dietary changes, can be as effective as weight loss and drugs in controlling hypertension and preventing cardiovascular diseases.

I EAT WELL TO TREAT MY HEART WELL.

"Old age has a great sense of calm and freedom. When the passions have relaxed their hold, you have escaped, not from one master, but from many."

— Plato

CREATING PATTERNS OF STABILITY

Do you have rituals that help you to start each day clear and focused, to move through the events of the day at a pace that allows you to make unhurried decisions and go with the flow, and to end each day with a sense of personal satisfaction, balance, and peace? Maybe you start your day with meditation or exercise. Perhaps you take your dog for a walk at noon, or you take a nap. Maybe you take a bath or write in a journal in the evening.

Peace and harmony are the benefits of living a balanced life— one that's free from chaos, stress, and agitation. But living with balance means *creating* balance, and that takes discipline. One component of such discipline includes using rituals to create patterns of stability in your life that help you to clear your vision, to leave you free to meet your needs and pursue your desires, to simplify the overload in your life, to guide you on the path to happiness and contentment, and to encourage you to see great beauty in your life.

It's time now to add a ritual to your life. Think about something that leaves you feeling calm, relaxed, and at peace with yourself. Maybe it's running through the neighborhood at sunrise or sitting in your favorite chair sipping a hot cup of tea after dinner. Name this as your ritual, then resolve to do it every day at the same time. Then, no matter what happens, you'll have created one enduring pattern of stability in your life.

I CREATE A RITUAL THAT BRINGS ME STABILITY
IN MY LIFE.

MARCH 17

"As I look over my life, I find no disappointment and no sorrow I could afford to lose; the cloudy morning turned out the fairer day; the wounds of my enemies have done me good. So wondrous is this human life, not ruled by Fate, but Providence, which is Wisdom married unto Love, each infinite! What has been, may be. If I recover wholly, or but in part, I see new sources of power beside these waters of affliction I have stooped at."

— theologian/essayist Theodore Parker

SEEING THE GOOD

Do you have a propensity for remembering old hurts? It may be hard to see the good in your life when grudges stand in your way, when you remember more cloudy days than sunny ones, when past sorrows are as painful as they were yesterday, and when you see only failure and defeat rather than success and victory.

According to American Indian tradition, "enemies" such as disappointment, sorrow, failure, and hurt are sacred because they can make you strong. The unfortunate things that have happened in your past can teach you how to become stronger in the present and how to succeed in the future, but only when you can let them go, release the negative hold they have on you, and forgive them. Then, and only then, can you move on with your life. For it's then that you can see the good you've gained from such things.

Naturalist Henry David Thoreau learned how to see such good one rainy day at Walden Pond. He wrote: "The gentle rain which waters my beans and keeps me in the house today is not dreary and melancholy, but good for me, too. Though it prevents my hoeing them, it is of far more worth than my hoeing. If it should continue so long as to cause the seeds to rot in the ground...it would still be good for the grass in the uplands, and being good for the grass, it would be good for me."

WHEN I SEE THE GOOD IN MY LIFE, I SEE MY LIFE AS GOOD.

MARCH 18

᛫᛫᛫

"Probably the happiest period in life most frequently is in middle age, when the eager passions of youth are cooled, and the infirmities of age not yet begun; as we see that the shadows, which are at morning and evening so large, almost entirely disappear at mid-day."

— educator/scholar Thomas Arnold

THE BENEFITS OF AGING

In many ways, you couldn't have picked a better time to be approaching or passing through midlife. You're considered the "new kid" on the block; you belong to one of the largest groups of aging Americans in the country's history. That means that you and many others like you are generating a great deal of social, political, scientific, medical, marketing, and intellectual interest.

Gerontology—the study of aging—is becoming one of the fastest-growing areas of academic study. Thousands of men and women are employed in professional fields that serve the needs of older people. Newspapers, newsletters, and magazines are being launched that are geared to mature readers. Senior-advocacy groups have grown with such astonishing speed that one researcher determined that if the American Association of Retired Persons (AARP) were to become an independent nation, it would rank as the 30th largest nation in the world, with a population near that of Argentina! The "gray power" of older Americans is a growing concern that not only influences Congressional votes, but also sets the political agenda and dominates the outcome of elections.

So it's really the best of times for you. You're in the midst of incredible social, cultural, economic, and political change, which will be affected by your influence.

᛫᛫᛫   ᛫᛫᛫   ᛫᛫᛫

I USE MY AGE FOR SOCIAL, CULTURAL, AND
POLITICAL CLOUT.

MARCH 19

"If I did not keep telling myself my age over and over again, I am sure I should scarcely be aware of it. Although every hour of the day I tell myself, 'My poor old fellow, you are seventy-three and more,' I cannot really persuade myself of it."

— author Andre Gidé

NO BOUNDARIES, NO LIMITS

In 1982, mountain climber Hugh Herr and his partner Jeffrey Batzer reached the top of Odell's Gully on Mount Washington and decided to push for the summit. They immediately stumbled into a blinding blizzard. Herr and Batzer survived three nights in gale-force winds and below-freezing temperatures. Although they came out of the ordeal alive, Batzer ended up losing one leg; Herr lost both.

Doctors warned Herr about the limitations he would have to accept. Instead, Herr designed artificial limbs that enabled him to continue climbing. He invented a more comfortable socket for leg prostheses, and he became an advocate of technical solutions to physical disabilities, with a goal of designing legs to enable those who are physically challenged to run marathons.

Are you as determined as Herr to fight the disabilities you may have stemming from the aging process? Perhaps you've lost your hearing, or your eyesight has dimmed. Maybe you're not able to get around without the assistance of a cane, walker, or wheelchair. Perhaps you need help being cared for. While such things place limits on you, they aren't boundaries. Boundaries are walls you erect where walls have never existed.

Today, whether you realize it or not, there are no real boundaries—only those manifested in your imagination. It's up to you to define in your mind how you'll conquer your limitations so you can treat any boundary you've erected as an illusion.

I TEAR DOWN WALLS SO I CAN LIVE WITHOUT BOUNDARIES.

MARCH 20

"Lost, yesterday, somewhere between sunrise and sunset, two golden hours, each set with sixty diamond minutes. No reward is offered, for they are gone forever."

— publisher Horace Mann

OUTWITTING THE TIME BANDITS

Do you see time as an enemy—a heartless bandit that steals your valuable jewels of seconds, minutes, and hours and hides them so well that you can never retrieve them? "Where did the time go?" you may frantically question. "I can't believe the day's nearly over!"

And, when "time bandits" huddle together in a gang, are you horrified to realize that days, weeks, months—even years—have been swiped away from you? "I can't believe it's March already!" you may exclaim, and then realize you're yet another year older.

Time bandits have existed since the beginning of life. But their thefts may have only recently become more evident to you because you see the large accumulation of yesterdays and realize how quickly your todays are flying by. With each passing moment, time has become more precious to you. But trying to hold on to time, wishing there were more hours in a day, pushing yourself to do everything faster, or lamenting the things you can no longer do because of the passage of time can never get you more time or restore that which you once had. Time can't be protected, set aside for later, watched over, or hoarded.

But you can outwit the time bandits. From now on, cease agonizing over the passage of time; time's going to move on, and there's nothing you can do about it. Instead, make the most of the time you have. Spend your time enjoying your time!

I GET THE MOST OUT OF TIME AS IT PASSES BY.

MARCH 21

"I'm at an age where my back goes out more than I do."
— comedienne Phyllis Diller

LIMBERING UP YOUR JOINTS

Do you feel stiff and sore in the morning when you get out of bed, a couple of hours after a workout, or after sitting for a while? When you bend over, do your muscles feel tight? Is walking up and down stairs becoming a chore?

Even though muscle and joint stiffness, back pain, leg cramping, and arthritis are normal symptoms of aging, they can be eased by exercise. A good exercise plan concentrates on four areas—flexibility, cardiovascular endurance, muscular strength, and body composition, or the ratio of body fat to body mass. Flexibility is a key area; without it, joint stiffness can prevent free movement and even lock you into painful positions that keep you from moving in the ways you desire.

Flexibility involves gentle activity to warm the gel that surrounds the joint; this acts as a lubricant that eases movement. Upon arising and before any strenuous exercise, gently swing your arms and legs, march in place while doing shoulder shrugs and flexing your wrists, use a stationary bicycle, walk for about ten minutes, or take a warm shower. Once your body feels warmed up, stretch to increase the space between joints and to keep your spine flexible. Avoid bouncing while stretching, holding your breath, or performing any stretch that places too much stress on a particularly sore or weak area, such as arching your lower back if you have back problems.

Take as much time as you need to warm up before exercise. Then be sure to cool down after your workout with slow walking or other gentle movements to gradually ease your joints and muscles into a relaxed state.

ᕯᕯ   ᕯᕯ   ᕯᕯ

I FLEX AND STRETCH BEFORE ANY AEROBIC WORKOUT.

MARCH 22

"How unnatural the imposed view, imposed by a puritanical ethos, that passionate love belongs only to the young, that people are dead from the neck down by the time they are forty, and that any deep feeling, any passion after that age, is either ludicrous or revolting!"

— writer May Sarton

SATISFYING SEX

Are you amazed at the current of sexuality that runs through everyday life? Do you want pleasure, joy, fun, and passion during sex for many years to come? Or, do you think sex is naughty for older people and that you should be "over" sex at your age?

It seems only natural that if you combine the wisdom of your mind—what you emotionally and intellectually know and what you've learned—with the wisdom of your body—what you know brings you pleasure and what you've learned can be sensual and erotic—you can not only remain sexually active as you grow older, but you can also enhance your sexual satisfaction.

Although you may have grown up at a time when discussions about sex were avoided and attitudes toward sexuality and sexual expression were rigid, you're now living during a time in which people are more open and uninhibited about sex and sexual practices. And, while it may be true that as you age some physical changes can occur that may affect your sexual activity and responses, there are no age-based reasons why you can't continue to enjoy sex or begin to enjoy sex for as long as you live.

Myths about sex and the older person say that sex is for the young and that older people are no longer interested in sexual activity. The reality is that if you're interested in sex and want to act on that interest, you can have satisfying sex throughout your life.

❧ ❧ ❧

BEING SEXUAL FEELS RIGHT, COMFORTABLE, AND
JUST PLAIN SATISFYING.

MARCH 23

"The thermostat is off and I overheat like a stalled car."

— writer Judith Bishop

MANAGING HOT FLASHES

Although hot flashes are most commonly associated with the onset of menopause, a woman's "change of life," hot flashes can begin when menstrual cycles are still regular. Most commonly, they last for less than a year, but some persist for five, ten, or even more years, and some even begin years after menopause. Hot flashes can occur once a month, once an hour, or even several times in an hour, day, or night. Each woman has her own pattern.

Because it's not really known why hot flashes occur—some believe they're due to the decline in ovarian estrogen, while others speculate that the brain can trigger episodes—prescribed hormone treatments may not always be effective. However, some self-help techniques can make you more comfortable. Keep track of your hot flashes to see if you can discover a pattern; doing so can help you manage them better. Dress in layers so you can remove clothing when you become overheated. Avoid hot, spicy foods or caffeinated drinks, which may trigger hot flashes. Stay active. And don't suffer in silence. Talk to other people—particularly those close to you such as your partner and your children—so they understand how you're feeling. Explore acupuncture and herbal remedies such as ginseng and dong quai, which are often recommended for the discomfort of menopause. Meditate so you can ease stress, which can sometimes spark a hot flash. And, when you're in the middle of a hot flash, drink something cool, step outside, or stand in front of a fan, visualize yourself in a cool place, and relax until the moment passes.

ꗍ   ꗍ   ꗍ

I "CHILL OUT" MY MIND AND BODY DURING
A HOT FLASH.

"A family get-together was planned for my birthday. The first card I opened looked promising. The cover, in bold print, stated, 'Wine improves with age. Cheese improves with age.' And inside, 'It's not your fault you're not wine or cheese.' My daughter's Hallmark greeting suggested I have a snooze as soon as the day's festivities were over. My daughter-in-law's choice was a card...that read, 'Let's face it. At your age, sex isn't Fourth of July anymore,' and inside the cover, 'more like Thanksgiving.' "

— writer Doris Bircham

AGEIST HUMOR

Ageism is as much a part of American society as racism, sexism, and homophobia. People may express this ageism in unconscious ways, such as by talking louder when addressing an older person who, in reality, may not even be hard of hearing, or by choosing not to stand in a check-out line behind an older person.

However, there are also conscious ways in which you're disparaged because of your age. This is particularly evident in the greeting card industry. While some of the cards are certainly humorous, others can be downright insulting. You may have no problem making light of your own middle-age or late-in-life issues or sharing jokes and comments with friends and family who are around your age, but when those who don't know you well or who are younger than you seem to get a perpetual kick out of continually mocking your age—and that bothers you—then it's time to say how you feel.

Age is an important part of your identity as well as a measure of your wisdom and experience; ageist comments take away your individuality and also belittle your value, usefulness, and productivity. So, let others know that it's not okay to treat you in a disparaging manner.

🎗️   🎗️   🎗️

I SPEAK UP WHEN I'M TREATED WITH DISRESPECT.

"We grow accustomed to our parents over the years. Or we really take them for granted from infancy until the age when we begin to look at them as two human beings and not merely as part of our natural habitat. Then we grow accustomed to them anew, and really get to know them."

— business executive Joshua A. Davis

CHILDREN AS CAREGIVERS

Most likely your parents were there when you were a baby, when you were an adolescent, when you were a teenager, when you reached 30, and when you turned 40. And, chances are that your parents are still around; you're fortunate enough to live in a time when you'll probably see your parents live until they're quite old. Unfortunately, the challenge of such longevity is that older parents may need occasional help and, in years to come, they may require caregiving on a continual basis.

You may not want the burden of taking care of an aging, chronically ill, or infirm parent or parents. Yet because your mother and father were always there for you, you may feel caught between meeting your own needs and theirs. Should you defer your plans for the future to take care of them? Should you make every effort to help an older parent stay in his or her own home, care for the parent in your own home, or seek other solutions? Would your children benefit from having a grandparent living under the same roof, or would it cause frustration or resentment?

There are certainly no easy answers to these questions and a multitude of others that can arise when considering taking care of parents. The best first step you can take is to talk to others who have had or who are going through a similar experience for their advice.

I FIND OUT ALL I CAN ABOUT CAREGIVING
ARRANGEMENTS FOR AGING PARENTS.

MARCH 26

*"Dare. Go toward life. Take chances. Reach out to what you most
fear. Develop the habit of daring life so that you will not look
back with regret at what you have not done."*
— writer Donald M. Murray

LIVING ON THE EDGE

Imagine taking up the sport of snowboarding at the age of 72,
jumping out of a helicopter to land on a steep mountain peak in
Colorado for the downhill challenge of your life. Or think about
training for a 26.2-mile marathon at the age of 80. What about traveling to some exotic, faraway place, riding on thrilling roller coast-
ers or water slides, or gripping a paddle in your hands and churning down a river wild—the swift Susitna River in Alaska, the land
of the midnight sun—at one o'clock in the morning?

These adventures—and many more—are available to you now.
So are less thrilling, less frightening, less draining, and less challenging activities. But what do you want to reflect on when you're
no longer able to participate in such activities—all the activities
you wished you had done, but didn't do, or all the things you did
and all the risks you took?

There will come a time in your life when such activities will be
well out of your reach. You'll have no choice but to sit back and let
others participate. Right now, however, you can be a participant in
all the adventures that life has to offer. There's so much left to see,
to do, to experience, to savor. Are you up to the challenge? Dare to
do something different, something out of the ordinary, something
that you'll look back on years from now with pride and happiness.
Seek adventure, rather than retreat from it.

I SAMPLE ONE OF LIFE'S THRILLING ADVENTURES.

March 27

"Physically, the only serious problem I've noticed is that I can no longer read anything printed in letters smaller than Shaquille O'Neal. Also, to read a document, I have to hold it far from my face; more and more, I find myself holding documents—this is awkward on airplanes—with my feet. I can no longer read restaurant menus, so I fake it when the waiter comes around."

— humorist/writer Dave Barry

MAINTAINING HEALTHY EYES

Although you may retain good vision as you age, some changes in vision in your later years can be expected. Usually this is evidenced by presbyopia, or slowness in changing focus from far to near, which is correctable with reading glasses, bifocals, and contact lenses. Minor problems such as excess tearing or dry eyes are also easily corrected by frequent blinking and the use of artificial tear or lubricating drops. Various eye exercises, if done on a regular basis, can alleviate eye strain and improve eye focus, sometimes eliminating the need to read with glasses. And, regular eye exams that include a complete examination as well as tests for glaucoma and serious eye diseases can head off more major problems.

However, there are diseases of the eye that can impair vision and even lead to blindness. Glaucoma is one of the most common and severe disorders in people over 40, but with early detection and prompt treatment, it can usually be controlled. Cataracts, in which the lens of the eye become cloudy, and vision is hazy or blurred, can be corrected with outpatient surgery. Macular degeneration, or deterioration of sharp-color and fine-detail vision, can be helped with laser therapy as well as with a variety of low-vision aids such as magnifying glasses. And diabetic retinopathy can be controlled by early diagnosis and control of diabetes.

TO KEEP MY VISION ON THE FUTURE, I MAINTAIN
HEALTHY EYES.

MARCH 28

"I remember lunch. Not so many years ago, lunch happened to me in real restaurants, with menus you could actually hold in your hands. It used to last an hour or more, and sometimes— this is hard to believe—included a drink....
whatever happened to lunch?"

— writer Nathan Cobb

SLOWING DOWN YOUR PACE

How do you accelerate through each day? From the moment your alarm rings, you may taxi down the runway of your life and then become airborne at Mach 2 speeds like the Concorde jet.

You jump into your car, screech into traffic, hug tightly to the bumpers of the cars ahead of you, and frantically cut in and out of travel lanes, trying to better yesterday's drive-time record. You roar into the parking lot, jump out of the car, greet others with a rushed "Goodmorninghihowareyouhaveaniceday," and leap into your desk chair as the telephone rings and piles of work multiply before your eyes. At lunch you may dash to an express-style restaurant, load up piles of food on plastic plates, and sprint back to the office to take hurried bites in between meetings and the rest-of-the-day madness until it's time to get back in your car and begin the commute home.

After going through day after day at this frantic pace, stop for a moment and ask, "What am I really accomplishing by functioning at such a superhuman pace? What will all this mean years from now when I'm retired? Will I look back on this experience and think I really achieved something, or will I wonder, Why, oh why, didn't I take a time out every once in a while and treat myself to a nice, long, lingering lunch with my partner or a friend?

Maybe it's time to put yourself on Pause, instead of Fast Forward.

❀　❀　❀

I MOVE AT A SLOWER PACE, AND I ENJOY LIFE MORE.

MARCH 29

*"I don't like the idea of looking saggy and kinda sad. I'd be lying
if I said so. And I do find myself going to the gym more. But when
you're 20, everything that's fabulous about you is a total gift—
your personality, your looks, your promise....And the face
I have now I've really earned."*

— actress Susan Sarandon

FACING AGING, FACE-FIRST

Do you seek out creams, vitamins, and other products that remove wrinkles or claim to make your skin look younger? Do you hide your facial blemishes and lines with cosmetics? Have you considered plastic surgery so that a few nips here and a few tucks might give you a younger-looking face?

As the skin loses tone and elasticity with age (and gravity), it sags and wrinkles, particularly in areas where there's frequent movement, such as around the eyes, mouth, and neck. Because of the thinning of the skin surface, small blood vessels can become visible over time. Age spots, which result from exposure to the sun over the years, may appear. And, skin cells grow more slowly so the outer layer of the skin isn't shed and replaced at the same rate as when you were younger. As a result, the skin can become stiffer and drier.

While such things are part of the natural process of aging, they're often portrayed as unnatural—even terrifying—by those in the beauty industry who tell you that aging is unattractive and you should do everything you can to appear younger-looking. But the expensive cosmetics, creams, and risky surgical procedures they offer provide no guarantees of looking younger. There's really no miracle cream or sure-fire plastic surgery technique that can hold back the influence of time.

It's best to come to terms with your changing appearance and simply accept your evolving face.

❊   ❊   ❊

I LOVE MY ATTRACTIVE, WRINKLED FACE.

MARCH 30

"Rather than a degeneration, a running down, which is the old model, what we're talking about is that it's all been building up, adding to what a person is....For me, it seemed to be a time when I had to go through a lot of evaluation of who I was, what was important to me in life, what I wanted to do with my life. In so doing, I became involved with a spiritual path."

— therapist Joan Steinmetz

SEEKING SPIRITUAL COMFORT

It has been said that in order to feel that you're truly one with your spirituality, you need to study a dozen years under the guidance of a good spiritual teacher. But when you're in the midst of a time of evaluation or reevaluation—of taking a good, long look at yourself and your life—you may not want to take such a large amount of time.

The need to feel like you spiritually "belong"—that you're connected with a Higher Power, nature, or the universe—can sometimes become an obsession. When you're aging, whatever you're dealing with in your life such as stresses, emotional problems, or physical ailments can accelerate. If you feel that you don't have any way to handle such things yourself, you may feel so panicked that they'll get out of hand that you'll do anything to find your spiritual path. You may run off to spiritual workshops or retreats, carry a religious book with you at all times, restructure your life in order to accommodate a rigorous meditation schedule, or purchase numerous books, tapes, and guidance tools for fostering a relationship with a Higher Power.

But sometimes all you need to do is accept what's happening to you and be calm. You're safe because you're already connected with God.

☀ ☀ ☀

I FEEL A SPIRITUAL CONNECTION BETWEEN MYSELF
AND A HIGHER POWER.

*"Make it a rule of life never to regret and never to look back.
Regret is an appalling waste of energy; you can't build on it; it's
only good for wallowing in."*

— author Katherine Mansfield

JOURNEYING ON THE RIVER OF LIFE

Life is dynamic. Like a river, it constantly flows, its currents forming new patterns based on change. If you live your life as a dynamic person, then you're unafraid to travel on that river. You go where it takes you. You remain calm when its waters run calm; you race along when its waters rush; you make twists and turns as the water forges its path. As the river of life changes, so does the way you move through it.

But when you live your life holding onto the past—by remembering the pains of childhood or by reminiscing over "glory days" gone by—then you're not able to flow with the river. Instead, you watch the river go by or fight wherever the river wants to take you. Your regrets keep you from enjoying your travels down the river.

Many people resist enjoying their river journey or looking forward to where the waters of life take them. But there's an old Chinese adage that says, "Flowing water does not decay." When you go with the flow, you move. When you don't, you stagnate.

Life is a flow of energy. Each day, you can let the energy carry you with its strong, determined current. From now on, get into motion. Move your mind, body, and spirit. Do something new, different, exciting, and challenging. Be like Huck Finn. Build your raft, and journey to wherever the river of life takes you.

I SAIL BLISSFULLY DOWN THE RIVER OF LIFE.

APRIL 1

MEN AS CAREGIVERS

Although women are most often thrust into the role of caregivers for their children, in-laws, spouses, and aging parents, some men are thrust into the caregiving role as well. Forty-year-old John Delaney was single when he began caring for his 73-year-old mother, who had suffered a stroke. His household eventually expanded to include a wife and a baby girl. The challenge of balancing his work and taking care of his mother became compounded by the need to make time for his wife and family. But he made decisions that protected his role as primary caregiver, including turning down job opportunities that would have required travel and longer work hours, as well as discussing the situation in his household with his future wife in an honest and forthright manner.

"A lot of women couldn't handle it," John says. "[But] she has a close relationship with her mother, so she understands."

Even though family members of all ages often experience lifestyle transformations when making room for aging relatives, including tighter living quarters and a decrease in privacy and independence, there are many benefits to such living arrangements. Since elders would much rather be with family instead of in a senior facility, they are often happier and healthier. Grandchildren and great-grandchildren can form a close relationship with older family members. And the arrangement presents a golden opportunity for members of all generations to spend time together in a way that adds dimension to future memories.

❀   ❀   ❀

BEING A CAREGIVER IS ALL ABOUT FAMILY LOVE.

APRIL 2

"A sense of mortality should make us smarter. Life is short, so you do your work. You spend more time attending to music and art and literature, less time arguing politics. You plant trees. You cook spaghetti sauce. You talk to children. You don't let your life get eaten by salesmen and evangelists and the circuses of the media."

— humorist/writer Garrison Keillor

BEING MORE CHILDLIKE

No one has to teach a child how to relax, have fun, sing, dance, laugh, and play. They come into this world prepared to participate in everything as if it were new. Can you imagine a child saying, "I haven't taken time off from my schoolwork this week to go to the playground. Maybe I should set aside some time to have some fun."

As an adult, you may think play is too frivolous, or that choosing to do something you like to do—rather than something you feel you *ought* to do—is a waste of time. But how much time have you already wasted in your life doing all those serious, focused, goal-oriented, achievement-centered tasks? You may now be so caught up in ambitious career endeavors, in taking care of your family, in working on your intimate relationship, in attending to the priorities in your life—in short, doing all the "adult" things—that you've forgotten what it's like to be a child.

When was the last time you felt like a kid? Flying a kite, riding a bicycle, tossing a ball, or playing on the equipment on a playground are a few of the ways kids have fun. What can you do? Today, decide to do something playful, spontaneous, and nonadultlike. Read a children's book. Play a board game. Sing a silly song to yourself. Skip. Jump rope. Rediscover the fun in life by being a child.

☙ ☙ ☙

I LOOK AT THE WORLD THROUGH A CHILD'S EYES.

APRIL 3

"Once upon a time there was a mid-life woman. She was tired and she was discouraged, she thought it was the end of the world. She'd lost a job she loved; she'd had a nervous breakdown; and she was in the throes of a shattering divorce. She'd almost given up hope. She wanted to sit in the middle of the freeway and get squashed. By an eighteen-wheel semi. Brrmmm! Splat!"

— writer Marylou Hadditt

GETTING OVER DIFFICULTIES

You may often think how wonderful life would be if things were only easier. You may assume that since you've lived as long as you have, life should be easier—much more manageable.

But reflect for a moment on a particularly rough time you went through in the past. Maybe it was a difficult childhood or the loss of a parent at a young age. Perhaps it was a breakup from a steady boyfriend or being excluded from a friend's party. Maybe it was an injury or illness. Or perhaps it was taking a back seat to your spouse, your children, or a successful sibling. Would you be as strong as you are today if you hadn't had to go through that experience? Hasn't that event left a motivating influence on your way of thinking, feeling, acting, or believing?

German philosopher Arthur Schopenhauer once said, "There is no doubt that life is given us, not to be enjoyed, but to be overcome—to be got over." Each hard lesson you've had to face in your life has helped you to learn and grow in some way.

Today, remember that you've had to climb a lot of fences in your life to get over troubles and traumas. Some were hard to get over; others not so hard. Face your difficulties in the present by asking, "What will getting through this experience teach me? How will this make me a stronger person now and in the future?"

I CLIMB THE FENCES IN MY LIFE TO LEARN AND GROW.

APRIL 4

"There is something infinitely healing in the repeated refrains of nature—the assurance that dawn comes after night, and spring after the winter."
— naturalist/writer Rachel Carson

THE PASSAGE OF TIME

Time brings summer to a close, and brings winter to an end as well. Time ages the brilliant petals of flowers and also prepares new buds. Time advances moments to bring about change. Time signals the end of a life, as well as the beginning of another. Because of this continuum, you can trust that time always brings new experiences.

As you age, you may become aware of this passage of time on a more personal level. For example, you may remember a time when you could play a friendly game of tackle football with friends on a Sunday afternoon, race up and down a field and roll around on the ground, then go out afterwards for pitchers of beer and pizza. But at this time in your life, you may think that you couldn't possibly dash more than a few yards without getting out of breath, and that if you were tackled you'd lie on the ground for several moments in order to collect yourself and get your bearings, then arise slowly and painfully and know that a long hot bath and pain medication will provide some relief, and refuse to go out for pizza because it's not on your low-fat, no-sodium, no-spicy-foods diet, and trust that after drinking one beer you'll surely fall asleep!

You may wish you could slam shut the doors on each day to prevent time from moving on. Just as time signals beginnings, so too does it signal endings. But time is, in reality, always on your side. Time will always be taking you to new moments and new experiences—times that are fresh and untouched. As a Swedish proverb states, "The afternoon knows what the morning never suspected."

I REVEL IN WHAT I DISCOVER IN THE PASSAGE OF TIME.

APRIL 5

ARCHITECTURE OF AGING

No one and nothing escapes the ravages of time. The force of nature dictates that all things wear out, run down, weaken, slowly decay, and eventually die. Even buildings with the firmest foundations and highly reinforced structures age; they slowly sink and shift, mortar cracks and crumbles, floors buckle, pipes leak.

But the nature of human aging is fluid and changeable; it can speed up, slow down—even stop for a time—and sometimes even reverse itself. That means that aging is dependent upon the individual. You're not a victim of aging, sickness, and death; those things are simply part of the process. And because of this, you have the ability to make an impact on the process.

An old lion or a tiger does not realize what is happening when its teeth decay or break, when it can no longer chew food without pain, and when prey prove too elusive. Human beings are aware of this fact of aging. But when you can change your perception of the phenomenon, you change the experience of aging on your body, mind, and spirit.

Think of yourself as a glorious building that you lovingly maintain for the preciousness of its architecture and the strength upon which it was built, which has enabled it to last through the lapse of seasons and time. Each day, repair, remodel, and refurbish this building so you may live comfortably in it for years to come.

❧ ❧ ❧

I FEEL AS IMPRESSIVE AS A MAJESTIC BUILDING.

APRIL 6

"Mental activity increases throughout adult life—
if the mind is kept active, interested, and useful. It will
decrease by inactivity, not by aging."
— biologist Hardin B. Jones

MENTAL REJUVENATION

Over seven decades, Helena Rubinstein created and built a beauty empire that stretched across six continents. She composed her memoir, called *My Life for Beauty,* when she was in her nineties. In this book she wrote: "But work has indeed been my beauty treatment. I believe in hard work. It keeps the wrinkles out of the mind and the spirit. It helps to keep a woman young. It certainly keeps a woman alive."

Thomas Alva Edison, who attended school for only three months, patented a total of 1,033 inventions—the first at the age of 21, the last at 81. He was 70 years old during World War I when he directed research in torpedo and submarine devices; at the age of 73, he pushed hard for Congress to create the Naval Research Laboratory.

What Ms. Rubinstein and Mr. Edison shared in common was an ongoing desire throughout their lives—and long into their later years—to keep their minds active. Even though they may not have been blessed with the physical stamina they had when they were younger, their minds were just as spry late in life as in their youth because they kept their brain cells limber by thinking, planning, scheming, and creating.

Because the mind influences every cell in your body, mental activity sends impulses into your body like jolts of energy, which can rejuvenate you by creating new cells. So, staying mentally active benefits both the mind and the body.

I "EXERCISE" MY MIND EVERY DAY.

*"I had not loved enough. I'd been busy, busy, so busy, preparing
for life, while life floated by me, quiet and swift as a regatta."*
— writer Lorene Cary

LOVE IS AN ACTIVE PROCESS

Everyone wants love; everyone needs love. But which is more important to you, to love or to be loved?

You can spend a great deal of your time trying to make yourself lovable, and searching for love—in effect, waiting for fulfillment—instead of extending yourself so you experience love. Love is an active process that requires you to do something. You need to reach out, to act, to speak, and to give of yourself in order to love and be loved.

Expressing love takes you out of the course of life and into exciting, uncharted territories. In this way, love is like the waters of a mountain stream that rush down the mountainside each spring, fresh and clean and pure, to replenish ponds that have filled with dead leaves and rotted tree branches over the winter.

Love transcends ego, materialism, anger, self-defeating situations, and the hustle and bustle of daily living. Love brings compassion, tolerance, strength, and harmony with nature into your life. But such things can happen only when you actively extend yourself by taking time to be tender, attentive, kind, thoughtful, considerate, and focused on the needs of another or others.

Today, believe that you have not loved enough in your life. Then take the time to give love to another human being, no matter how busy your day is. Compliment a stranger. Listen to a friend. Extend an invitation to a family member. Plant seeds and bulbs. Make a donation. Smile.

꿔   꿔   꿔

I ACTIVELY LOVE TODAY.

APRIL 8

"Being over seventy is like being engaged in a war. All our friends are going or gone and we survive amongst the dead and the dying on a battlefield."

— novelist Muriel Spark

ACCEPTING DEATH

Any loss of human life is tragic. Even when death is expected, loss can be extremely painful. Part of this painful process is the necessary grief work you must do in order to be able to eventually move on with your life. Accepting the loss of a spouse, your friends, and family members means you need to slowly work through the numbness and shock, the sadness, the pain, the anger, and the grief. Acceptance of death can come only after a full experience of mourning, which may last for months or even years.

Even if you're unable to fully grieve at the time of loss—perhaps you're feeling too numb to cry, are incapable of expressing your feelings, or need to pull yourself together so you can go to work or keep the family going—you still need time to mourn. As one 78-year-old woman realized, her life was, in many ways, in a holding pattern for decades until she accepted the loss of her daughter: "My daughter died almost 40 years ago, when she was 10. I'm still angry, and I still miss her. But for years after she died, I couldn't quite believe that it had really happened—I kept thinking I heard her in the house. Now I can accept what happened, even if I don't like it."

Rather than putting off the grieving process, write down your feelings in a journal, discuss how you feel in a self-help group, meditate, pray, seek spiritual counsel from a member of the clergy, or ask for help from a bereavement counselor.

I ACCEPT AND DEAL WITH ALL OF THE LOSSES
IN MY LIFE.

"Old men are only walking hospitals."

— Horace, Roman poet

CARING FOR YOURSELF

In reality, neither hospitals nor medicine have been or are responsible for improving the health of old people or even extending their lives. Successful aging is centered more on your ability to avoid disease than your ability to fight it. This means that you need to make a lifelong commitment to caring for yourself, not to maintaining an ongoing relationship with a medical professional, in order to stay in good health throughout your life.

For example, the two leading surgeries for heart patients—the bypass graft and balloon angioplasty—are effective in alleviating the pain of angina. However, neither eliminates coronary artery disease; the combination of regular exercise and a healthy diet lower the risk of heart attack.

Yet, medical professionals want you to see them as heroes who win life-and-death battles. But where is such heroism in the treatment of cancer? The age-adjusted death rate from cancer hasn't changed in over 50 years, and the overall mortality rate of 20 percent of all deaths has remained constant since the 1940s. In fact, the 1990s has seen a rise in lung cancer, not because of what the medical profession is or isn't doing, but due to cigarette smoking in blacks and women.

Rather than be treated like you're a walking hospital, with kitchen counters and drawers filled with medications, and calendars booked with doctors' appointments, begin today to live a healthier life. Take charge of caring for your health instead of handing over this care to another.

I TAKE FULL RESPONSIBILITY FOR THE STATE
OF MY HEALTH.

APRIL 10

"O, great blue sky, see my roaming here.
I trust in you, protect me!"

— Pawnee saying

PRAYING FOR PROTECTION

There will always come a time in your life when you need to make a significant change, follow a new way of doing things, take a different path, or learn a different lifestyle. The outcome will not always be certain or even to your liking. But if you can trust that your every step is being guided by a spiritual source that can give you unending strength, then you can believe that you are always lovingly protected.

Whether you realize it or not, the protection of God is always near. All you need to do is open your eyes in faith, belief, and trust, and let yourself be carried through your particular difficulty. For, as the Indian saying goes, "Sometimes I go about pitying myself, and all the time I am being carried on great winds across the sky."

Relying upon a spiritual source through prayer and meditation can help you realize that there isn't a problem that can't be solved, a teardrop that won't be dried, a weary body that won't be energized again, or a lost soul who can't be found. When you are unable to see through a troubling time, or when you find that your outer nature is weakened, look within. Strengthen your inner nature by reciting your favorite prayer or by reading a spiritual poem such as the following one by an unknown author:

My life is but a weaving between my Lord and me,
I cannot choose the colors, He weaveth steadily.
Sometimes He weaveth sorrow, and I in foolish pride,
Forget He sees the upper and I the underside.

I AM ALWAYS AWARE OF THE PROTECTION OF GOD.

APRIL 11

"I'm still trying to find my true fashion self. Cute no longer works, nor does sophisticated. Mysterious is out. I hope I find it soon, before that last permanent stage; before floral print polyester with three-quarter sleeves, an acrylic shawl and shoes with built-in bunion lumps."

— writer Gretchen Sentry

AN AWKWARD AGE

Do you feel that you're at an awkward age, an age in which you're struggling to find the right hair style to show off, the right clothes to wear, the right music to listen to, the right car to drive, the right way of expressing yourself, the right everything that will "fit" you, that will make you not look too old but still appear to be young? You've probably seen older men and women trying to "act hip," to be a part of the younger generation. Watching them striving to be something they aren't may make you feel uncomfortable. "I don't want to make a fool out of myself," you may conclude, "but I also don't want to be perceived as old in how I dress, look, or act."

Do you remember another time in your life when you were at an awkward age—perhaps you were 12 or 13—when you worried all the time about whether you'd fit in with others your age? You may have spent a great deal of time looking at your reflection in mirrors, experimenting with different ways of styling your hair, trying on different clothes, practicing dance moves and smiles, and critically assessing every blemish. You would have given anything to have looked older—to have appeared to others as a mature adult who had it "together."

Rather than spending time struggling with your appearance, remember that your comfort is most important. As Austrian novelist Marie von Ebner-Eschenbach once said, "Being young is beautiful, but being old is comfortable. "

❄️   ❄️   ❄️

I WEAR WHAT I WANT, AND I DO WHAT I WANT.

APRIL 12

*"I have enjoyed greatly the second blooming that comes when you
finish the life of the emotions and of personal relations; and
suddenly find—at the age of fifty, say—that a whole new life has
opened before you, filled with things you can think about, study,
or read about....It is as if a fresh sap of ideas and thoughts
was rising in you."*

— writer Agatha Christie

JOURNEYS OF DISCOVERY

An increasing amount of learning is taking place outside the traditional academic environment, and many of these programs
welcome or are even specifically geared toward middle-aged and
older men and women. For example, the University of Pittsburgh's
floating campus, the S.S. Universe, takes students of all ages on
cruises to such places as India and the Middle East. On one trip, 60
adult students in their sixties and seventies joined over 300 college
students.

Combining learning with travel is becoming quite popular.
The excitement of discovery is often enhanced by interaction with
anthropologists, ornithologists, historians, naturalists, and others in
specialized fields. Society Expeditions, for example, takes more
than 2,500 people on such exotic learning journeys a year.
According to Aaltje E. van Zoelen, the majority of the passengers
who are "jumping into the rubber Zodiac boats to examine the plant
life on some obscure atoll or to learn about the ecology of a river
on these vigorous expeditions, are over 50." Also, regular cruise
lines are including lectures and workshops on everything from
marine and bird life to financial planning.

The new experiences and knowledge you can attain from participating in such programs can make your journey into the future
exciting and challenging.

❀   ❀   ❀

I ARRANGE A TRIP THAT COMBINES LEARNING
WITH ADVENTURE.

"Women may be the one group that grows more radical with age."
— Gloria Steinem

RADICAL WOMAN

What kind of older woman do you want to be? Will you continue to be there for others—a spouse, your children, your co-workers, your friends—or will you decide to do some things that you've always wanted to do? Will you continue to judge your body and your appearance critically, trying to hide signs of aging or the special parts of you that make you who you are, or will you start to see yourself as strong and beautiful just as you are? Will you lie about your age and give in to disease and infirmity, or will you stand tall and take good care of yourself? Will you shift your family from the center of your life, and instead focus on the needs of others or on your own personal projects and passions?

"Too many women *endure* old age rather than *enjoy* it," say the authors of *Ourselves, Growing Older: Women Aging with Knowledge and Power.* The loss of a spouse can make many women retreat into a shell rather than open doors to freedoms they never had when they were taking care of their husbands and children. Reduced finances and increasing infirmities can make women dependent and weak, rather than motivate them to create some level of independence for themselves. Decades of living, loving, and learning can be viewed as wasted years, rather than as precious contributions to a wealth of experiences to be used to better themselves and society.

Know that you can become any kind of older woman you want to be. It's never too late to make an important change in yourself, to set a challenging goal, or to do things that will make you feel good about yourself.

❧   ❧   ❧

I AM A STRONG, VITAL WOMAN.

APRIL 14

"Life is something to do when you can't get to sleep."

— humorist/writer Fran Lebowitz

CURING SLEEPLESSNESS

What's the cause of your sleeplessness? Is it worry or depression? Are you eating dinner late at night or going to bed hungry? Do you consume sugary sweets before bedtime? Are you taking vitamins B or C before bed? Are you drinking caffeinated beverages such as coffee, soft drinks, cocoa, and tea? Do you smoke? Are you taking antihistamines or cold formulas? Do you use over-the-counter or prescription medications for such problems as asthma or high blood pressure, for relief from pain, or for heart rhythm and thyroid troubles? Have you changed your "internal clock" so your normal sleep pattern has been disrupted? Have you recently discontinued the use of sleeping pills, tranquilizers, or anti-anxiety drugs? Are you troubled by sleep apnea, which is the sudden cessation of breathing, while you sleep?

These are just a few of the causes of occasional or ongoing sleeplessness. In addition, life itself—all of its ups and downs—can prevent you from falling to sleep or rouse you to alertness after only a few hours of sleep.

To deal with your sleeplessness, try to stick to a set schedule. Go to bed at night at the same hour, and arise about the same time, even if you haven't had a lot of sleep the night before. Your body will eventually adapt to the time regimen so you'll be able to get to sleep quicker and stay asleep longer. Soak in a hot tub before bedtime. Drink decaffeinated beverages, warm milk, or herbal tea. Keep your bedroom free from distractions such as a television set or a project you're working on. Listen to soothing music or a relaxation tape. And, use medication to aid sleep only when prescribed by or discussed with a doctor.

❧ ❧ ❧

I CHANGE PRE-SLEEP ACTIVITIES SO I CURE SLEEPLESSNESS.

APRIL 15

"On Friday, Lendl played the tortoise to Edberg's hare.
He was always a step slow. And he was 30 years old.
He will not get quicker."
— news account of tennis star Ivan Lendl's defeat by
Stefan Edberg at the 1990 Wimbledon tournament

YOUTHFUL RETIREMENT

The concept of retirement takes on a whole new meaning when viewed through the eyes of some of the most gifted athletes. Young legs that once led a basketball team on fast breaks now trot down the court. Quick reflexes that once slammed tennis balls back at opponents during net play are now just a few seconds late to successfully return the ball. Youthful stamina that once earned Heisman Trophies, Rookie of the Year accolades, and Most Valuable Player Awards now wait for possible induction into Halls of Fame. Olympians who once stood proudly on the steps of the medal platforms now coach.

Retirement can take place at any time in your life, depending on your career or lifework. Athletes may retire from their sport at age 30; homemakers may retire from taking care of the family at age 40; entrepreneurs may sell their businesses and retire at the age of 50; workers may retire from jobs to work for themselves at the age of 60.

As writer and editor Alexandra Robbin once penned, "The aging aren't only the old; the aging are all of us." Because you're growing older every day, it's important to look at what you've been able to accomplish thus far in your life and what you'd still like to accomplish, as well as what you can realistically expect to accomplish. Even though you may not be able to win another Wimbledon, you still have a good chance of working with a future Wimbledon champion.

I KEEP MY SKILLS SHARP TO PREPARE FOR
FUTURE ACCOMPLISHMENTS.

APRIL 18

"Life is either a daring adventure or nothing. To keep our faces toward change and behave like free spirits in the presence of fate is strength undefeatable."

— Helen Keller

TRYING SOMETHING NEW

Think of everything you might have to fear as you grow older—urinary incontinence, osteoporosis, hypertension, cancer, diabetes, memory loss, rheumatic disorders, living in a nursing home; and vision, hearing, and other sensory loss. If you think about such things for too long, you may wonder why you'd ever want to live to an advanced age.

Now, imagine being a child and not being able to see, hear, speak, or even care for yourself. Would you want to participate in the world around you, even if that meant you might injure yourself or face incredibly difficult challenges, or would you want to be locked in a room for the rest of your life?

Helen Keller, who was blind, deaf, and mute from birth, has been an inspiration to so many people because she resolved to face her fears, overcome them, and then learn from them. So, too, can you. You can make your life into a daring adventure by refusing to be intimidated by the effects of time and, instead, being willing to try something new.

Such risk-taking can be frightening. The best risk-takers are the ones who know how difficult a risk can be, but who still take the risk anyway. From now on, resolve to take charge of your life by facing your fears and learning from them. Instead of asking, "What am I afraid of?" reassure yourself with the thought, "Whatever fears I have, I can always conquer them."

❃　❃　❃

I FEEL FEAR, BUT I FACE NEW CHALLENGES HEAD-ON.

APRIL 19

"...all humans are frightened of their own solitude. Yet only in solitude can we learn to know ourselves, learn to handle our own eternity of aloneness."

— unknown

ENJOYING YOUR SOLITUDE

Loneliness can attack you like a disease. Physically, it can drain you like a potent strain of a flu, wearing you down to a point of exhaustion. It can also drain you emotionally and spiritually, eating away at your ability to think positively and to trust that you're okay during the times in which you're alone.

You may think that the best antidote to loneliness is to ride a crowded subway or bus or to live in a place that's in close proximity to a lot of other people. But often what's best is to go within yourself in search of companionship. For, as theologian Paul Tillich has written, "Language has created the word *loneliness* to express the pain of being alone, and the word *solitude* to express the glory of being alone."

Strive not to depend upon others for your sole method of conquering loneliness; instead, look within yourself. Rather than saying to yourself, "Oh, I haven't a person in the world who cares to be with me right now," you can say, "I enjoy this time alone by finding out more about me. Who am I? What are my likes and dislikes? How do I feel? What's important to me in my life?" Having the opportunity to be quiet with yourself can let the inner voice within you be heard.

Today, in your times of solitude, find the serenity that's nestled within. Enjoy your own company for a change.

I REVEL IN MY MOMENTS OF SOLITUDE.

"There is only one solution if old age is not to be an absurd parody of our former life, and that is to go on pursuing ends that give our existence a meaning—devoting to individuals, to groups or to causes, social, political, and to intellectual or creative work...One's life has value so long as one attributes value to the life of others, by means of friendship, indignation, compassion."

— writer Simone de Beauvoir

PRESERVING THE ENVIRONMENT

The world's current ecological problems—pollution, acid rain, destruction of the rain forests, and the depletion of the ozone layer, to name a few—can remind you on a daily basis that you're part of a complex web of life. Major catastrophes such as oil spills or the release of harmful chemicals into the atmosphere can impact everyone and everything, from the bottom of the chain of life to the top.

Yet, you may question the impact that you, as one person, can make on healing the damages made by centuries of civilization. While you may never be able to recreate the ideal environment or even see it recreated in your lifetime, you can take positive action every day.

American naturalist John Muir wrote that "...most people are *on* the world, not in it—have no conscious sympathy or relationship to anything about them...." His sense of oneness with his environment led him to found the Sierra Club, to campaign in Congress to preserve the wilderness, and to establish Yosemite National Park.

What can *you* do? Plant a tree. Set up a recycling area in your home or health-care facility. Join an organization dedicated to the preservation of sand dunes, conservation land, or natural habitats. Make a lasting contribution!

❧ ❧ ❧

I PRESERVE THE ENVIRONMENT FOR THIS GENERATION AND FOR FUTURE ONES.

"Her life was like running on a treadmill or riding on a stationary bike; it was aerobic, it was healthy, but she wasn't going anywhere."

— writer Julia Phillips

CREATING BALANCE

Do you find that you get caught up in a succession of mundane activities each day with barely enough time to catch your breath? Too often the schedules you set for yourself or try to live by can keep you moving at such a frantic pace that you never have enough time for yourself, for the things you want to do, for making choices and thoughtful decisions, and for relaxation.

Whatever pace of living you maintain, the more you'll become accustomed to the same pace as time goes on. But if you establish a new, saner pace of living now, then you can create a more balanced way of living that you'll appreciate in years to come.

The best way to modify any stressful schedule is to become aware of it. For a week, monitor how you use your time. Determine how much time each day you spend doing the following activities: eating and preparing meals; sleeping and napping; working at a job or in your home (be sure to include commuting time); shopping/running errands; exercising; socializing; attending to family responsibilities (babysitting, going to a soccer game, and so on); doing routine household and yard chores; volunteering; engaging in recreational activities such as reading, playing games, and so on; and meditating and relaxing.

Look at the patterns and time imbalances that emerge. Then, slowly restructure your day and week so you can make time for the things you not only *want* to do, but *need* to do.

I BALANCE MY TIME SO I ENJOY LIFE MORE.

APRIL 22

"It is a bore, I admit, to be past seventy, for you are left for execution, and are daily expecting the death-warrant; but...it is not anything very capital we quit. We are, at the close of life, only hurried away from stomachaches, pains in the joints, from sleepless nights and unamusing days, from weakness, ugliness, and nervous tremors...."

— writer/clergyman Sydney Smith

SEARCHING FOR A NURSING HOME

You may react negatively to the thought of nursing homes, thinking that they're mere holding cells for the decrepit and dying. You may envision drab buildings with sterile-looking, fluorescent-lit corridors filled with unpleasant sounds and smells. You may recall newspaper articles about abusive treatment of helpless patients. You may believe that nursing homes are places to discard older people.

While a nursing home is one of many options for the care of an older person, sometimes it's the right choice. Staff that can offer round-the-clock care, a variety of planned activities, the availability of physical therapy, prepared meals, and constant contact with peers are just some of the benefits.

But since all nursing homes are different and each older person has individual needs, care ought to go into the selection of the right facility. Look through nursing-home directories or talk to the continuing-care coordinator at a local hospital. Check into the track record of any facilities you're interested in, including their financial status and survey reports. Establish criteria you're looking for in a home, and then visit the ones that meet your criteria. During your visit, talk to as many people as possible—administrators, staff and, most important, the residents with whom your loved one will interact.

❀　❀　❀

I LOOK FOR CLEANLINESS, FRIENDLINESS, AND
HAPPINESS IN A NURSING HOME.

APRIL 23

"It seems to me you can be awfully happy in this life if you stand aside and watch and mind your own business, and let other people do as they like...."

— writer Mary Stewart

BECOMING LESS CONTROLLING

Are you someone who just has to speak your mind or direct how something is done? Perhaps sometimes when you do so you impart valuable information, give sound advice, offer a different outlook, or point out an easier way of doing something. But there may be times when, in speaking out or directing, you push your point of view or way of doing things on people and come across as annoying, know-it-allish, and much too controlling.

There's a difference between being controlling and being in control. When you're controlling, you want people to do what you want them to do, when you want them to, and in the way you want them to. Being in control, however, is the feeling that you can get what you want without needing to dictate to others. When you're in control, you're more willing to accept that other people have their own direction and that it's not up to you to direct them.

Instead of managing everyone else, manage only yourself. Although many people share the stage of life with you—your children, your co-workers, your life partner, your housemates, fellow committee members, your parents, and so on—it's not up to you to direct them. They, like you, have their own direction. Today, strive to life by the words of Larry Eisenberg: "For peace of mind, resign as general manager of the universe." Discover what's best for you, not someone else, so that you assume a much more active role in determining what you can get from life.

❀   ❀   ❀

I MANAGE MY OWN AFFAIRS AND LET
OTHERS RUN THEIRS.

APRIL 24

"It's only when we truly know and understand that we have a limited time on earth—and that we have no way of knowing when our time is up—that we will begin to live each day to the fullest, as if it was the only one we had."

— psychiatrist/writer Elisabeth Kübler-Ross

LIVING EACH DAY TO THE FULLEST

Musician Quincy Jones survived a brain aneurysm and two brain operations in 1974. Since that time, the highly successful and driven record producer, composer, and musician has renewed his belief in the importance of having a balance in his life that allows him to live each day to the fullest, without devoting an inordinate amount of time to one task or activity to the detriment of others. He strives to live each day by these words: "God has given each of us approximately 25,000 to 26,000 days on this earth. I truly believe He (or She) has something very specific in mind: 8,300 days to sleep, 8,300 to work, and 8,300 to give, live, play, pray, and love one another."

Think of Quincy Jones's words as a daily checklist that can remind you of the brevity of life. You do have only a limited time on earth; you may have more or less time than others, but you're not immortal. At some point, you'll no longer see the beauty of a sunrise or a sunset, speak with and touch a loved one, hear the sounds of nature or your favorite music, laugh at the antics of a child or grandchild, enjoy walking barefoot on the beach, make a great business deal, eat a delicious meal, feel the wind on your face, cry, sing, dance, and make love in your bed.

Time is precious; every minute of this day is significant. Resolve to give, live, play, pray, and love another. Savor each moment you have in this life.

I RESOLVE TO APPRECIATE EVERY DAY OF MY LIFE.

APRIL 25

*"In the morning, we carry the world like Atlas; at noon,
we stoop and bend beneath it; and at night, it crushes
us flat to the ground."*
— clergyman/editor/writer Henry Ward Beecher

STRENGTHENING YOUR BONES

Osteoporosis is a "woman's condition" of thinning bones result-ing from calcium loss that usually takes years to reach the stage of detection. However, once you've reached this stage, you're more susceptible to bone compressions or fractures from a major (or minor) fall or accident, as well as from simple movements such as making a bed or opening a door. Other warning signs that you may have this condition include loss of height and muscle spasms, or pains in the neck while you're resting or doing routine work.

You can improve bone strength at any age by simply changing some of your daily habits. Since vitamin D aids in the absorption of calcium, eat a balanced diet with foods that are rich in it. Spend a half an hour in "nature's vitamin D"—the sun—but be sure to refrain from excessive exposure. Limit your intake of alcohol and caffeine, because they act as diuretics that can cause a loss of cal-cium and zinc. Quit smoking, due to the effect nicotine has on the body's metabolism of estrogen, which assists in the body's absorp-tion of calcium. Participate in weight-bearing exercises such as walking, jogging, jumping rope, and dancing, which make your bones work hard and strengthen the muscles and ligaments that support the skeleton. Finally, eliminate hazards from your home or property that can contribute to a fall. Wear shoes with nonskid heels around the house, and maintain a comfortable room temperature.

I MAKE LIFESTYLE CHANGES THAT PROTECT AND
STRENGTHEN MY BONES.

"Bernard Jupiter is having a hard time with the electronic cash register. As the machine beeps a warning, the sixtyish Jupiter, his watery blue eyes peering over half glasses, struggles to find the right key. 'I'm sorry, sir,' he says to the man on the other side of the counter, who appears to be waiting somewhat impatiently for a burger and fries, 'I just started working here.'"

— writer Jeffery C. Rubin

"McSENIORS"

Bernard Jupiter and his classmates, who are all 55 or older, are the first students in a training program begun in 1995 as a joint venture between New York City's Department for the Aging and the Riese Organization, a company that owns 200 chain-restaurant franchises. The goal of the program is to help the elderly rejoin today's service-oriented economy after years of unemployment or retirement, leaving them with skills that are no longer applicable in today's world. Comments Riese CEO Dennis Reise, "This ought to be a win-win situation. We're helping the seniors get jobs, helping employers expand their labor pool, and helping the city in the process." The training center is a full-scale mock-up of a fast-food restaurant; students learn everything from mastering the electronic registers to giving customers the right orders—while serving up a smile.

Rather than feeling that you're fading away in retirement, stay active by pursuing activities you never had a chance to do while you were working, or retrain for something new. As presidential candidate Bob Dole remarked on his 72nd birthday, "I think the records show that people who sometimes retire fade away pretty quickly. I remember my dad used to ask me, 'Boy, how many times can you sweep the walk and empty the trash?'"

I COME OUT OF RETIREMENT TO LEARN AND EARN IN AN EXCITING NEW CAREER.

APRIL 27

"When asked to define middle age, a comic once replied,
'Someone who is five years older than you are.' True, middle age
is constantly moving up, and it is not unusual to find the span
defined as covering the period from 45 to 65...a polite way of
characterizing the middle years, as has been pointed out by actor
David Niven. When someone mentioned a 55-year-old man as
being middle aged, Niven said, 'And how many 110-year-old
men do you know?'"

— writer Myra Waldo

THE AGE OF APPRECIATION

The middle years of life—between the ages of 40 and 65—can be strange ones for you. That's because younger ages seem to have a sense of purpose. The adolescent years are times for parental approval and conformity with peers. The teenage years are times for nonconformity and rebellion. The college years are times for self-focus, self-analysis, and self-fulfillment. The early adult years are times for establishing a foothold on the career ladder of success, for seeking a desirable partner, and for developing long-lasting security.

However, the middle years are times for coming to terms with yourself and your life. You may experience a sense of panic that life is passing you by. Even though you may recognize and appreciate your successes and achievements, you may brood over your failures and your lost opportunities. You may find it hard to accept whatever can't be changed in your life with good grace. You may go through times of introspection and depression; men may experience episodes of impotence and women difficulties with menopause.

But the middle years can be times for appreciating life without any interference from parents or the world—a time when you've *become* yourself.

❖　　❖　　❖

THE MIDDLE YEARS ARE MY TIME FOR
CHANGE AND EVALUATION.

APRIL 28

*"I never feel age....If you have creative work, you don't
have age or time."*

— sculptor Louise Nevelson

CREATIVE TIME

Henrik Ibsen, the great 19th-century Norwegian playwright, dramatically changed his style of writing when he was in his sixties; his later works are considered his finest and most imaginative. Giuseppe Verdi, Italy's greatest composer, wrote two of his finest operas—*Otello* and *Falstaff*—during his eighth decade. French poet, playwright, and novelist Victor Hugo published his last great work at the age of 81. American architect Frank Lloyd Wright began his most creative work at the age of 69; New York's circular Guggenheim Museum was completed when Wright was 91. Anna Mary Moses, better known as Grandma Moses, farmed in the Shenandoah Valley in New York State until her late seventies. When her fingers became too stiff to embroider on canvas, she began to paint in oils; her pictures of rural America were soon exhibited internationally. When she turned 100 years old, she illustrated an edition of *'Twas the Night Before Christmas.'*

Painting, writing, sculpting, singing, dancing, weaving, and quilting are just a few of the creative activities in which you can participate at any age and which you can learn at any time. Have you always wanted to learn to play the piano? It's not too late to take lessons. Would you like to see one of your poems published? Submit your poetry to publishers. Would you like to make a quilt for a grandchild? You can start today. It doesn't matter whether or not you've always been creative. What matters is that you simply *be* creative.

❀   ❀   ❀

I CREATE MY OWN "MASTERPIECE" TODAY.

April 29

*"Old age is like a plane flying through a storm. Once you're
aboard, there's nothing you can do."*

— Golda Meir

ACCEPTING WHAT YOU'VE BEEN GIVEN

What do you do to get through some of your upsets, difficulties, and disappointments? Learning how to accept life with a shrug and a smile instead of rigidly clinging to a desperate desire to change things is not always easy.

There's a story that Dr. Bernie Siegel, author of *Love, Medicine and Miracles,* tells that gives good advice on how to stop struggling with your circumstances, let go, and accept what you've been given:

A farmer who depends on his horse to plow his field is working the field one day when the horse drops dead. The people of the town say, "That's very unfortunate," but the farmer says, "We'll see." A few days later, somebody feels sorry for the man and gives him a horse as a gift. The people of the town say, "How fortunate," but the farmer says, "We'll see." A couple days later, the horse runs away. "How unfortunate," say the townspeople, but the farmer says, "We'll see." A few days later, the horse returns with a second horse. "How fortunate," say the townspeople, but the farmer says, "We'll see." One day, while out riding with his son, the boy falls and breaks his leg. "How unfortunate," say the townspeople, but the man says, "We'll see." A few days later, the army comes to the man's farm to draft young men for war, but they can't take the boy because he has a broken leg.

The story could go on and on. The point is: upsetting moments may decrease or even disappear completely without any input from you. So, rather than fret and fume, just sit back, relax, and enjoy the ride!

◌   ◌   ◌

I ACCEPT LIFE'S CHALLENGES WITH A "WE'LL SEE" ATTITUDE.

"Life was meant to be lived, and curiosity must be kept alive. One must never, for whatever reason, turn his back on life."

— Eleanor Roosevelt

BEING INTERESTED IN LIFE

"Dear World...I am leaving because I am bored," wrote George Sanders on April 25, 1972. The actor, who appeared in more than 90 films, won an Oscar for his performance as a cynical drama critic in *All About Eve* with Bette Davis, and who had the finances and time to travel the world, somehow found life too dull. So he swallowed five bottles of Nembutal and penned his infamous suicide note as a farewell to a world that bored him to death.

How often are you bored with your life? What do you do about it? Too often, people complain that they're bored, but they don't do anything more than that. That's why it's up to you to change your feelings of boredom into feelings of curiosity and interest in yourself, others, and the world around you.

If you're bored sitting in front of the television for hours, then turn it off and pick up a book or go for a walk. If you're bored with your work, then scan the classified ads for a more interesting job, or enlist the help of a career counselor. If you're bored in your intimate relationship, then do something out of the ordinary—make reservations at a bed-and-breakfast inn or prepare a special dinner. If you're bored in general, renew an interest in the arts—rent a classic film, enroll in a painting class, visit a museum, or listen to some old records or tapes.

It's your responsibility to overcome the boredom in your life. From this moment on, resolve to take the initiative and explore those interests and pursuits that can spark your interest.

❦   ❦   ❦

I TAKE AN ACTIVE INTEREST IN LIFE.

MAY 1

"Happy indeed are the men and women who age gracefully, gradually, and wisely, and who keep fit and vigorous in mind and body. These people have developed a way of life that is inwardly friendly and outwardly considerate, and they have a compassionate attitude toward time."

— writer Myra Waldo

SECRETS TO STAYING YOUNG

So much is now known about the aging process that you can use your middle years to make the best choices and take the most constructive steps to "postpone" aging—to extend your prime of life as far into the future as possible. While no "fountain of youth" or "age-erasing" cream exists that can magically wipe away the effects of time, there are practical actions you can take that will improve as well as preserve your emotional, physical, and spiritual health and well-being.

First, learn how to be at peace with yourself and the world. Enjoy the time you spend with friends and family, as well as the time you spend with yourself. Second, take control of daily activities. Learn how to organize your day, how to say no to others who demand more time than you have to give, and how to delegate responsibilities that others should rightly handle. Third, approach daily duties and tasks as if they're essential to your well-being. Regard even the most boring, routine, or mundane tasks—food shopping, vacuuming, reading a book—as having a significant impact on your life so that failing to do them will make you feel as if you've left something unfinished. Fourth, avoid food temptations that will create a pattern of poor eating habits by preparing at least three nutritious, home-cooked meals a week. Finally, get outside for fresh air and sunshine for at least 20 minutes each day.

I CREATE A WAY OF LIFE THAT KEEPS ME YOUNG.

MAY 2

"I used to dread getting older because I thought I would not be able to do all the things I wanted to do, but now that I am older I find that I don't want to do them."

— English politician Nancy Astor

SETTING NEW IDEALS

The dreams of youth are far different from the dreams of the middle-aged and elderly. Those ideals you may have set for yourself when you were younger—to scale mountains, to travel around the world, to write volumes, to build your own home, to heal the world—may have never been realized. But that doesn't mean that you've failed in your life or that you'll never be able to achieve any other milestone you set for yourself. Starting today, you can use your experience, capabilities, and determination to set achievable, practical, and rewarding goals for yourself.

You can aspire to do something unexpected—something that completely changes the direction of your life. Such a life-altering ideal may help you to change and grow more in the later stages of your life than dozens of dreams realized when you were younger. Jacob Landers, a 65-year-old man, listened to his daughter go on and on about her experiences in law school and felt so envious that he decided to go to law school himself. He had less than a week to prepare for the Law School Admission Test, but he studied hard and took the test as a walk-in candidate. To his surprise, he did well and then enrolled. "One of the proudest moments in my life was at graduation in Carnegie Hall," Landers recalled. "The dean had cautioned the audience not to applaud or do anything else that would disrupt the proceedings, but when my name was announced, *everybody* got up and applauded. I was so proud...."

I REACH TOWARD AN IDEAL THAT MAKES ME PROUD.

MAY 3

"What would you do if you were stuck in one place, and every day was the same, and nothing mattered?"
— Bill Murray's character in the film *Groundhog Day*

MAKING MIDLIFE MATTER

In the film *Groundhog Day*, an obnoxious and egocentric television weatherman, played by Bill Murray, gets stuck in a time-warp fantasy. While covering the Groundhog Day festivities in Punxsutawney, Pennsylvania, Murray discovers that there's no tomorrow. Instead, he keeps waking up the next morning to discover that it's still February 2nd. He's doomed to relive the day until he gets it right.

Is that how midlife feels to you? Midlife can be a time when you're through with studying, building your career, raising your family, and making a home. Thus, midlife becomes a "maintenance stage," where you direct your energy simply into getting through each day. Like Murray's character, you may feel trapped and depressed as you face each new day that looks just like the one before it. But today, think about this: you can change your world and each day in it, but only by first changing how you respond to your life. As Roman writer, philosopher, and statesman Seneca once remarked, "Life is a play! 'Tis not its length, but its performance that counts." When the outline of your life is pretty clear—as it is in midlife—then what you need to do is strive to make the most of what you have. Making the most of what you have means becoming a more active, lively participant in the performance of your life. It means learning how to look at your life with a different set of eyes so you can see that some of the commitments of midlife—the work you do, the family you've created, and the things that interest you—can be exciting.

❧   ❧   ❧

I GIVE RAVE REVIEWS TO THE PLAY OF MY LIFE.

MAY 4

"'Tis a maxim with me to be young as long as one can: there is nothing can pay one for that invaluable ignorance which is the companion of youth; those sanguine groundless hopes, and that lively vanity, which make all the happiness of life. To my extreme mortification, I grow wiser every day."

— poet Lady Mary Wortley Montagu

EVIDENCE OF WISDOM

Some people think that those who memorize a great deal and remember much of it are wise. Others—mostly the young, because they have a mania for information in the data-saturated world in which they live—believe that accumulation of facts and figures is evidence of their wisdom. Still others hold that a lifetime filled with adventure is what creates wisdom.

As you age, you may come to realize that wisdom is not simply a mental process, but the sum total of a human being. So, if you can mix what you know with what you've learned through your experiences, your adventures, your experimentations, your spiritual beliefs, the intimacies you've shared, and the insights you've gained during times of introspection and contemplation, then you can be said to be wise. Wisdom is the bridge that connects the facts you've accumulated with what you can intuit about yourself and life.

Also, wisdom is the ability to be able to live somewhat haphazardly from time to time—to accept that life isn't always clear-cut, that it doesn't always provide you with meaningful patterns or reassuring understandings, but often mixes the good with the bad, the ugly with the beautiful, the successes with the failures, the sweet with the bitter, the mistakes with the victories.

I GROW WISER BECAUSE I SEEK WISDOM.

MAY 5

"So much has been said and sung of beautiful young girls, why doesn't somebody wake up to the beauty of old women?"
— abolitionist/writer Harriet Beecher Stowe

SENIOR SENSUALITY

At the age of 61, actress and international superstar Sophia Loren is still beautiful, youthful, and sexy. She lives—and loves—by the motto that women are never too old to be perceived as beautiful and appealing. Although she claims to have no beauty secrets that help maintain her alluring looks and sensual appeal, she does stress the importance of being open to the pleasures of life. To this advice she adds, with a sensual smile, "I like to seduce—and be seduced."

You're never too old to feel beautiful and appealing or to be sexually active. In fact, the two often go hand-in-hand. The happiest older people, those who report that they're not only satisfied with their lives in general—their employment, their marital status, and their overall health and well-being—but also with the way their bodies look, are those who are also sexually active.

You may look at young and attractive girls and boys today and think they have it "all," but think back to when you were younger. Did you really know what beauty was all about? Did you really have a clear understanding of sex? Aging beautifully is less about appearances and more about what you feel inside.

I AM BEAUTIFUL BECAUSE I FEEL BEAUTIFUL.

MAY 6

"It is a mistake to regard age as a downhill grade toward dissolution. The reverse is true. As one grows older, one climbs with surprising strides."

— novelist George Sand

THE CHALLENGE OF THE CLIMB

Where youth may have the stamina, guts, and the desire to take incredible risks, those who are older have the need to seek out and respond to the challenges in life with a dogged determination, as well as a deep understanding. While a young person may look at a mountain and think, I'd like to climb that mountain someday, if the question is posed, "Why climb such a mountain?" the youth may not know the reason why or even see the prospect of any gains beyond personal satisfaction.

But the older person looks at a mountain and sees it as a challenge that must be responded to. Also, the older person knows that there is more to be gained than just the personal satisfaction of having scaled the mountain. The path taken up the mountain is one forged for others, for those who may wish to follow. And, after the struggle to climb forever upward is overcome, the view from the top is majestic.

Mountaineer George Leigh Mallory, who conquered Mount Everest, once said, "...if you cannot understand that there is something in man which responds to the challenge of the mountain and goes out to meet it, that the struggle is the struggle of life itself upward and forever upward, then you won't see why we go. What we get from this adventure is just sheer joy. And joy is, after all, the end of life."

I CLIMB UPWARD TO CONQUER THE MOUNTAINOUS
CHALLENGES OF MY LIFE.

MAY 7

*"I don't want to get to the end of my life and find that I lived just
the length of it. I want to have lived the width of it as well."*
— writer/poet Diane Ackerman

MAKING THE MOST OUT OF LIFE

On a clear spring day in 1952, Gertrude Lepine looked out of
the window of her one-room Stowe Hollow, Vermont, school-
house and had an illuminating thought: if she stopped teaching, she
could return to the farm where she grew up. That night, she called
the school superintendent and quit. Then she returned to the 670-
acre farm her father had purchased in Mud City, Vermont, during
the Depression.

Since 1952, Gertrude and two other sisters who later joined her
have run the family's rambling dairy farm, tending to the farmhouse,
sturdy barn, uneven fields, and their herd of Jerseys. Their day begins
at 3:30 A.M., feeding and milking the herd. After the first milking is
done, the sisters eat breakfast together—a hearty meal of eggs, cere-
al, milk, and thick slices of homemade bread slathered with butter
and jam. A variety of chores keeps them busy until the second milking, in the late afternoon or early evening. "[Mother] was 90 years
old and was still down here in the barn," boasts Gertrude.

The sisters, who are all in their late sixties, are realistic about
being able to run their farm for much longer; last year, the farm lost
several thousand dollars, and they've had no takers on the option of
renting the barn and continuing farming. Soon the cows will be sold
at auction. But despite the toll of time, the sisters have kept their
roots and lived the length of their lives as well as the breadth.
They've sold the development rights to the state, preserving their
land as farmland so their heritage as farmers will live on for future
generations.

❀   ❀   ❀

I CARRY ON TRADITIONS THAT ARE FULL OF
PURPOSE AND MEANING.

MAY 8

"The years teach much which the days never know."
— Ralph Waldo Emerson

THE "CLASSROOM" EXPERIENCE OF LIFE

In your mind is a multitude of stored memories, knowledge, and skills. Some of these are the result of living and learning, but most are made up of information that has been provided to you by others in the "classroom" called life. In your early years, for example, teachers may have given you much in the way of factual knowledge, religious teachers may have helped you to form your spiritual values, and your family may have offered you moral instruction. In your later years and even today, your friends may show you different personalities and lifestyles, your co-workers may share their professional expertise, and your children may reflect what you've taught them and give you their view of the world. People, therefore, are often the greatest sources for your storehouse of information even though, on a day-by-day basis, you may not realize this.

That's why writer Harry Emerson Fosdick once said: "Life is like a library owned by an author. In it are a few books which he wrote himself, but most of them were written for him." All the information you have been given up to this very minute has been and still is valuable to you. Every person you meet, each place you visit, and every thing you try contributes to your library of knowledge and experience. Even though, from time to time, others may borrow what's on your "shelves," you always need to keep them stocked with fresh material every day. In that way, you can be open to the lessons of life that are being given to you so you can value them today and in the years to come.

❈ ❈ ❈

I PAY ATTENTION TO ALL THE "TEACHERS" IN MY LIFE.

MAY 9

*"I understand nothing, feel everything. I am wise. I am silly,
often teary and goosebumpy over the most amazing things.
I want a lover. I want to be alone. I feel strong, yet afraid of
death. I don't put up with any crap. I am not sure where I am
going. Words from a blues song stick in my mind: 'My brain is
cloudy and my soul is upside down.'"*

— writer Dena Taylor

COMPLEMENTARY BALANCES

Growing older can be confusing and, at times, frightening as you wonder what each new stage of your life is going to bring. Menopausal women may throw open doors and windows in the middle of winter. Men may awaken frequently during the night, plagued by prostate problems. Men and women both may experience mental deterioration—frequently losing things or misplacing them—have a hearing loss, or go through vision difficulties that make it harder to see at night, to judge the speed of moving objects, or to read the fine print on the back of a bottle of aspirin.

Sometimes, as you grow older, you may feel as fragile as a mobile. Lose one object from the mobile, and the whole balance is destroyed. Replace the missing object with one that's too light or too heavy, and the mobile will hang crooked. To bring everything into balance, you need to hang each object so it perfectly complements the others. But how can you do this when so many things in your life are changing—sometimes even raging—out of your control?

At times like this, you need to remember when you were much younger and began to experience changes in your body that signaled that you were moving out of adolescence. After a time of adjustment, everything soon got back into balance. So, too, it will be with you. Your life will be restored to balance—in time.

I PATIENTLY ENDURE THE IMBALANCES OF MY LIFE.

MAY 10

"If you have known how to compose your life, you have accomplished a great deal more than the man who knows how to compose a book. Have you been able to take your stride? You have done more than the man who has taken cities and empires. The great and glorious masterpiece of man is to live to the point. All other things—to reign, to hoard, to build—are, at most, but inconsiderable props and appendages."

— essayist Michel de Montaigne

SEEKING SIMPLICITY

No other living entity collects things as obsessively as humans do. Your garage, kitchen, cabinets, linen closets, basement, dresser drawers, china closet, table tops, and counters may be filled with items that have been stacked and stockpiled, cast aside, broken, and that may be dusty with age or lack of use, accumulated over the years as part and parcel of the complexity of living. Rather than being content with the simple things life has to offer you—health, companionship, stability, beauty, wisdom, and comfort—living in the midst of so much clutter and chaos leaves little room for stability or balance in your life.

From this moment on, resolve to live your life more simply. Discard those things you no longer use by recycling what you can and donating other items to charities. Seek out periods of silence each day, times in which you shut out the sensory overload that often assails you from radios, television sets, mindless telephone chatter, and even computer e-mail. Spend time alone each day thinking, reading, exercising, or writing in a journal. Meditate on a regular basis. Create daily patterns of stability by choosing a morning ritual of renewal for beginning each day, and an evening ritual of closure for ending the day. Enjoy the world as it is meant to be enjoyed—simply, and free of false values, possessions, and endless striving.

❧   ❧   ❧

LIVING A SIMPLE LIFE KEEPS ME HEALTHY AND HAPPY.

MAY 11

"Not everyone's life is what they make it. Some people's life is what other people make it."

— writer Alice Walker

BUILDING A NEST OF PEACE

A bird builds its nest by first searching for the perfect twigs, pieces of string, weeds, scraps of paper, and other materials. Then it patiently interweaves these substances until its nest achieves the right shape, size, depth, and warmth. No two nests are alike, even within the same species; each has its own unique blending of materials that makes it distinguishable from other nests.

So, too, do you need to build your own special "nest" for yourself. While you may have already spent a good part of your life taking care of others or may now find yourself devoting a lot of time to the care of a spouse, child, or aging family member, you still need a safe nesting space for yourself in which you can be at peace with your own thoughts, feelings, and dreams. This nest could be an apartment, a retirement home you've always dreamed of, a quiet room, or even a cozy corner that has your favorite chair and a comforting afghan.

But your nest doesn't always have to be a place. Sometimes your nest can be derived from intangible things that bring you peace—a picture of a loved one, a soothing cup of tea, or a book you enjoy rereading—or from living things that comfort you—the sound of your cat's gentle purr or the feel of your dog's warm tongue on your face.

From now on, "build" your own special nest of peace, one that enables you to spend time away or apart from others so you can create and savor precious moments just for yourself.

I CREATE A NEST OF PEACE FOR MYSELF IN MY WORLD.

MAY 12

"When a man imagines, even after years of striving, that he has attained perfection, his decline begins."

— poet/essayist Sir Theodore Martin

PERCEPTIONS OF PERFECTION

Everyone and everything in the world has imperfections. Just as there's no such thing as a perfect person, neither is there a perfect living thing. There are certainly very attractive people, there are certainly highly creative people, and there are certainly quite charismatic people, but there are no perfect people. Also, in nature there are wonderfully fragrant roses; there are those with soft, velvety petals; and there are symmetrically shaped ones, but there are no perfect roses.

Life teaches you that every living thing is valuable and has its vital contribution to make, even when it's not perfect. As Ralph Waldo Emerson once commented, "What is a weed? A plant whose virtues have not yet been discovered." Every living thing has its own expression, its own capabilities, its own skills, its own way of being.

Nothing you can do, say, think, or imagine ought to convince you that you—above every other living thing—can be perfect, even when you've spent years aiming for such perfection. As an anonymous jokester once proclaimed, "When you aim for perfection, you'll discover it's a moving target." Being able to attain perfection is as impossible as being able to find the pot of gold at the end of the rainbow.

Why waste your lifetime trying to always hit the bull's-eye? The point of life is to do your best and enjoy yourself while doing so. Let go of unrealistic perfectionistic expectations, and you'll find that your best effort—not your perfect effort—is what really matters.

I ACCEPT LIFE ON ITS OWN IMPERFECT TERMS.

MAY 13

*"I postpone death by living, by suffering, by error, by risking,
by giving, by losing."*

— novelist/diarist Anaïs Nin

THE THREE PHASES OF LIFE

If life could be divided into three phases, each phase could be seen as a level of personal triumph you need to attain in order to progress successfully towards the end of your life. Move from phase to phase, experience your share of triumphs, and then you'll know when it's time to depart—when your soul has triumphed well.

The first phase involves learning as a way to seek the appropriate steps that will lead you towards mastery—like the process of crawling before you learn to walk or needing a hand to steady you as you strive to take your first bike ride. Often this phase involves an awful lot of awkward struggling prior to experiencing triumph.

The next phase is one of competition, where you test what you've learned, although this phase doesn't mean competition against others, but against yourself. For example, learning the fundamentals of swimming and then being able to dive into a lake and swim means you're competing against your own inability so you can triumph over it; even competing in a swim meet and beating your opponents still means that you're triumphing over yourself by achieving your personal best.

The third phase involves knowing when to retire from the need to triumph, for constant competition need not ever be a lasting way of life. Once you've reached the top, there's really no need for further triumph in that area; you can then start over, moving once again from phase to phase, or you can accept that there's no need to go any further. When you realize this concept, then that is true triumph.

I TRIUMPH OVER MYSELF IN ORDER TO
COMPLETE MY LIFE.

MAY 14

"The birds sing louder when you grow old."

— activist Rose Chernin

SPRING SONGS

All of nature is song. Sometimes the song is a joyous burst of sheer ecstasy, full of bright, rich melodies and thrilling chords that inspire movement. Sometimes the song is an answering call, an echoed response of reassurance and companionship. Sometimes the song is deep and mournful, with steady, repeated refrains filled with sorrow and longing. Sometimes the song is a soothing lullaby, providing comfort and closure as darkness falls.

Do you pay attention to the songs of life that the birds serenade you with each spring? Do you know what their songs mean? Do you know how to respond to such songs, to harmonize with them, to open your throat and sing accompaniment?

For so many years, you may have been too busy to listen to the melodies of the birds in the springtime, in the evening, at sunrise, at sunset, when winter comes, when it rains. Also, you may have been so caught up in chipping away at lists of obligations, responsibilities, and countless other pursuits in your day-to-day living that you may have neglected to give yourself time to listen to nature's spring symphony. You may have gone through life taking for granted that the birds sang every spring day without ever really hearing them, or you may have treated nature's solos as part of the normal background noise of life.

But the song of the birds is the song of life; to experience it, you need to listen closely to it, appreciate it, even harmonize with it. The song is an everlasting proclamation to life in all of its glories—you can't help but hear the song of the birds and feel how wonderful it is to be alive.

ᘒ   ᘒ   ᘒ

I LISTEN TO THE BIRDS SING THEIR SONGS OF LIFE.

MAY 15

*"Aging in itself worries us moderns more than it worried our
ancestors. They had other troubles to think about, especially the
threat of early, painful terrifying disease and death. They all had
reason to fear that they would die fairly soon. Why fear old age
when early death was much more probable?"*

— writer Wayne Booth

100 YEARS...AND COUNTING

Centuries ago, it was impossible to grow old. Living past the age
of 40 was akin to achieving a certain level of immortality; living
to 100 was downright freakish. Disease after disease kept people dying young. In the 14th century, the bubonic plague killed 20
million Europeans. In America, diseases such as whooping cough,
typhoid, and diphtheria regularly wiped out entire households. And
between the years 1917 and 1919, 20 million people died worldwide in an influenza epidemic.

Today, in most industrialized societies, one person in 10,000
passes the century mark, and the ratio is steadily rising. While the
eradication and control of many diseases plays a contributing role,
there are physical and psychological characteristics that contribute
to a healthy longevity, enabling many older women and men to get
around on their own without the assistance of crutches or walkers,
to continue to work, and to keep house and care for themselves.

Weight control is a contributing factor, along with good muscle tone. Also, a keen interest in current events, adaptability and
flexibility, optimism, a sense of humor, and sheer enjoyment of life
help. Finally, independence in the choice of occupations—that is,
being your own boss—and avoiding early retirement can help you
to be around for a long, long time.

I'M PRO-LONGEVITY!

MAY 16

*"PRESCRIPTIONS FOR LONGEVITY: Swim, dance a little,
go to Paris every August, and live within walking distance
of two hospitals."*

— Horatio Luro, at 80 years old

LAUGHING AT LIFE'S PUNCHLINES

There's a story about a poor farmer who was sentenced to death but miraculously obtained a reprieve by assuring the king that he would teach his majesty's horse to fly within the year. Even though the king's advisors protested the king's decision, exclaiming that the ruler was being duped by a mere farmer, the king stuck by his decision.

"And just how do you think you'll ever live up to your promise?" a fellow prisoner asked the farmer.

"Within the year," the farmer explained, "the king may die. Or the horse may die. After all, in a year, who knows what will happen? Maybe the horse *will* learn to fly!"

Being able to face life with such a lighthearted outlook can add years to your life and make your remaining years, as difficult as they may be, much more bearable. Comedienne Gilda Radner, who lost a long battle with cancer, kept her spirits up as her health failed by trying to take things lightly. A phrase she often used to help her deal with her difficult experience was, "If it's not one thing, it's another."

Actor George Burns smartly chose to make his longevity part of his appeal as a comedian. "It's nice to be here," he would typically announce at the beginning of his acts. "At my age, it's nice to be *anywhere*." And he would often quip, "I get a standing ovation just standing," and then would add, about his social life, "I *would* go out with women my age. But there *are* no women my age!"

I RESPOND TO LIFE WITH HUMOR.

MAY 17

"People do not live nowadays—
they get about ten percent out of life."
— dancer/educator Isadora Duncan

HIGH-INTEREST, LOW-BUDGET TRAVEL

Do you think that because you're getting older and living on a tighter budget, fun and exciting vacations are out of the question? There are lots of great deals at some of the most popular destinations, some of which are geared to older people.

For example, Grand Canyon National Park has inexpensive camping sites, great off-season rates at the park's lodge, and a one-time admission fee for life if you're over the age of 62. Or, you can buy an inexpensive visitor's pass for unlimited travel on the Metrorail, and then see nearly all of the sights in Washington, D.C.—from the Smithsonian to the White House to the Capitol building—for free. Self-guided downtown walks and other walking tours of major U.S. cities such as New York and San Francisco allow you to go at your own pace; maps and many of the guided tours are free.

If you're looking for excitement, Las Vegas offers decent rooms during the off-season and mid-week, and many out-of-casino activities are free, such as a hike in Red Rock Canyon. The Jazz and Heritage Festival and the French Quarter Festival in New Orleans promise good food and good music, all within walking distance of most affordable bed-and-breakfast accommodations.

Finally, Hawaii-on-a-budget isn't out of the question. By shopping around for package deals that include airfare, accommodations, a rental car, and, in some cases, meals, you'll be able to experience the romance of a moonlit stroll on the beach, a dramatic view from the top of Diamond Head, a tasty visit to a pineapple garden, or an exotic treat of a Japanese tea ceremony—all for free!

❀   ❀   ❀

I EXPLORE EXCITING VACATIONS THAT ARE
WITHIN MY BUDGET.

MAY 18

*"In my embarrassment I wandered off and pondered the
marvelous devices offered in this medical center for the use and
easement of old age—canes and braces and pans and wheelchairs, and toilet seats thickened like a clubfoot's shoe, and long
canelike pincers to retrieve what can no longer be bent over for:
a veritable armory as complex as a medieval knight's, our Grail
now simply the indefinite prolongation of life."*

— writer John Updike, while waiting for
his aging mother at a medical center

BOOSTING YOUR INDEPENDENCE

Is there a dignity in devices designed to assist you in old age to
help yourself or to enable others to take better care of you, or do
such aids and devices as canes, wheelchairs, walkers, hearing aids,
and bladder-control diapers only serve to highlight your infirmities?

While most people wish to get around in their older years as
independently as they did when they were younger, it's unrealistic
to think that you'll be able to totally escape hearing loss, eye problems, frailty, fractures, aches and pains, memory lapses, and other
signs of normal "wear and tear" that require you to be dependent
upon devices, equipment, drugs, and other common "accouter-
ments" of aging.

What's more realistic, however, is doing all that you can now
to stay active, alert, and lively in order to increase the length of time
that you can remain independent of such age-assistance devices.
Exercise a little every day. Even if you're not interested in sports or
workouts, you can be just as active doing chores such as weeding
the garden, mowing the lawn, or housecleaning. Also, you can
climb stairs instead of taking the elevator, walk to lunch instead of
taking a taxi, or cart a bag of groceries home on your bicycle. Any
exercise will improve your agility and may even postpone your
need for something to lean on for a while.

I APPRECIATE THE DEVICES THAT ASSIST MY INDEPENDENCE.

MAY 19

*"Paradoxical as it may seem, to believe in youth is to look
backward; to look forward we must believe in age."*
— mystery writer Dorothy L. Sayers

THE WISDOM OF THE YEARS

You were born into a tremendous bind. On the one hand, when you were young, you were frequently cautioned not to grow up too quickly. But you probably threw such caution to the wind and forged ahead as quickly as you could. You rarely thought about growing old or what that meant, even in the presence of grandparents and elderly neighbors, for that's not what the young think about.

Then, as you grew older, you were told to enjoy your maturity and the "golden years" that lay ahead of you. Yet today your mind may frequently wander back to your youth, to wondering if you did the right things, to questioning your value as a friend, a student, a lover, and a parent.

When you're young, you're not supposed to understand what it means to grow old; when you're old, you're not permitted to go back in time. When you're young and vibrant, you don't have the wisdom to put your energy to good use or the perspective to know how to value time; when you're old and finally have the wisdom and know the value of time, the passage of years may make you too weak to take action.

How ironic life can be! Yet the secret of aging well is knowing how to pass into the years gracefully, without regret, without longing, and without looking back over your shoulder and sighing, "If only I could be 21 again—yet with all the wisdom I've gained at 61." To age well...is to accept your age well.

I REVEL IN THE WISDOM OF MY YEARS.

MAY 20

MENTAL FITNESS

Aging is not necessarily a process of everything going downhill. In fact, some things improve with age—surprisingly, your mental skills and abilities. That's because aging brains hold larger vocabularies, are able to better understand written materials, have a greater ability to reason, display more wisdom, and process information better.

Also, older people often employ effective methods for memory recall that enable them to exhibit sharper mental abilities than most younger people. "Ask a group of 80-year-olds and 20-year-olds to phone a particular number on a particular day," explains Claudia H. Kawas, associate professor of geriatric neurology at Johns Hopkins, "and the 80-year-olds will perform far better...." Kawas recommends that "[as] long as you can adapt new strategies to accomplish tasks, you are a successful ager."

To keep your brain as fit and sharp as that of a much younger person, it helps to keep exercising your mind. Attend classes, read magazine articles and books on subjects that are new to you, or learn a new skill. Concentrate on those things you want to remember. Use a notepad to jot down reminders. Carry a calendar with you. And keep in mind that forgetfulness isn't necessarily a sign that something's wrong with your brain. Rather, it's a natural response to the incredible amount of memory overload of names, information, experiences, and so many other things that you have stored in your mind over the years.

I KEEP MY BRAIN FIT FOR LIFE.

MAY 21

*"Old age, to the unlearned, is winter; to the learned,
it is harvest time."*

—Yiddish proverb

LIVING WITH THE SEASONS

Seasons teach you about transitions. Just as winter slides into spring, spring into summer, summer into fall, and fall into winter, so too does infancy ease into childhood, childhood into adolescence, adolescence into youth, youth into midlife, and midlife into maturity. The natural seasons that occur outside you, as well as the seasons of change that occur within you, provide you with a valuable life lesson: while every new beginning brings you closer to an end, every ending has within it the hope of a future celebration.

Seasons, then, are valuable teachers that can convey to you the subtle lessons of how to live better. Respect the seasons, and you'll be more ready to accept the give-and-take that's a natural part of seasonal constancy and flux. The love that seems eternal now may soon be a memory; an illness that seems unbeatable now may soon give way to health; a pain or sadness that seems all-consuming now may open the doors to happiness. Perhaps this is why writer Pico Iyer observes that the seasons "...teach us that suffering is inevitable, and in that inevitability is a constancy that helps take the edge off suffering. We cherish flowers more than evergreens, precisely because they do not last."

Also, the seasons teach that there are no hard and fast divisions. Just when you think winter is over, an unseasonable blizzard reminds you that there are also overlaps in life. Thus, the winter of your life can be the spring—a time for joyful growth and bountiful harvest.

I EMBRACE THE SEASONS OF MY LIFE.

MAY 22

"Because we are obsessed with sex (we being all of us as well as American society in general), we think it unfortunate when someone is not 'doing it.' For myself it is a great relief not to be so motivated by lust. When I was making love a great deal, I did not ask myself about the significance of sex in my life, about how I used it, how I might go about it differently. If I felt desire, I did everything possible to satisfy that desire—without hesitation or reflection, and without regret."

— writer Sandy Boucher

NONORGASMIC PLEASURE

Do you define sex in terms of intercourse or stimulation that results in orgasm? Or, is sex any physical activity from which you derive pleasure? Cuddling, caressing, embracing, kissing, and other forms of physical contact can still be satisfying to you and your partner even if one or both of you doesn't achieve orgasm.

The great engine of lust that once propelled you, as a young person, toward exploring territories of undiscovered sexuality may have also kept you locked into a one-track mode of thinking: that the only truly satisfying and acceptable sexual activity culminates in mutual orgasm.

Yet, your age now allows you freedom to escape from such one-track, driven thinking. You can now explore the many ways in which to satisfy and to be satisfied, to express love and tenderness, to relax and enjoy the pleasures of the body as well as the soul, to pay attention to another and to be paid attention to. Today you can view sex as an experience, rather than an activity—something to be enjoyed and appreciated, no matter where it leads. As Greek philosopher Plato once remarked: "Old age has a great sense of calm and freedom. When the passions have relaxed their hold, you have escaped, not from one master, but from many."

❧   ❧   ❧

I MAKE LOVE FROM MY HEART AND SOUL.

MAY 23

*"There are no old people nowadays; they are either
'wonderful for their age' or dead."*
— writer Mary Pettibone Poole

SENIOR SUPERIORITY

You live in a society that features slick, appealing, youthful packaging. For example, advertisers consider the most desirable television audiences to be those in the 18- to 49-year-old age bracket, even though people over 55 comprise nearly 30 percent of the viewing audience. Yet, people over the age of 50 are often considered to be staid, crusty, out-of-it, old-fashioned, and behind the times. Such opinions are expressed by television advertisers; employers, politicians, and salespeople; countless others share in the ageist belief that a person's worth and abilities are determined solely by chronological age.

How can *you* deal with this attitude? When you're viewed as intellectually, physically, and psychologically inferior after you pass midlife, considered to be a senior citizen at the age of 60—and therefore obsolete—then it's going to be next to impossible to convince anyone your life isn't over or that you're not dead already. As one woman over 50 complained, "I'm a lot more interesting than I was at 25 or 35, but it's a lot harder to get anyone to pay attention."

The best way to personally handle ageism is to build supportive networks of peers for socializing as well as for influencing others. Join an organization such as the AARP, and push for opportunities on a local and national level to improve the status and image of older people. By banding together with other middle-aged and older men and women, you create a strong, allied force that can effectively advocate for social change.

I SUPPORT A CONSCIOUSNESS THAT REFLECTS HOW
"SUPER" SENIORS REALLY ARE.

MAY 24

"Wisdom doesn't automatically come with old age. Nothing does—except wrinkles. It's true, some wines improve with age. But only if the grapes were good in the first place."

— syndicated columnist Abigail Van Buren

LIVING LIFE DELIBERATELY

You may have figured out by now that to get the most out of life, you need to put effort into it; you don't get something for nothing. When you're willing to try, to do, to dare, and to risk, you're living life deliberately—and often reap rewards from doing so. But in order to get, you have to give. You need to expend energy.

However, if you look back to a time were you were younger, you may remember how much easier things seemed to have come to you. You may recall that very little effort was expended on your part for great rewards—a scholarship to a renowned university, awards and honors bestowed upon you, a coveted job offer, a terrific graduation gift, a wonderful first apartment.

What you may forget, though, is that most things come easier when you have no expectations, when everything is new, and when there really is no starting point. When you're young, you're a beginner; you're ready for anything, open to everything, and therefore rewarded by much. As you grow older, your options become more limited as your expectations increase; those things that may be handed to you often don't measure up to what you'd like or need.

That's why as you grow older, you sometimes need to live life with more effort and determination. As Henry David Thoreau once said, "I went to the woods because I wished to live deliberately, to confront only the essential facts of life, and see if I could not learn what it had to teach, and not, when I came to die, discover that I had not lived."

❀   ❀   ❀

I CREATE A LIFE FULL OF RICHNESS AND REWARDS.

"It is so hard for us little human beings to accept this deal that we get. It's really crazy, isn't it? We get to live, then we have to die. What we put into every moment is all we have....What spirit human beings have! It is a pretty cheesy deal—all the pleasures of life, and then death."

— comedienne Gilda Radner

THE PARTNERSHIP BETWEEN LIFE AND DEATH

Do you realize that at this time of your life, this season of marvelous growth—another spring of renewal, rebirth, and regeneration—everything you see has started toward the end of its life? American physician and writer Lewis Thomas once remarked, "If you stand in a meadow, at the edge of a hillside, and look around carefully, almost everything you can catch sight of is in the process of dying, and most things will be dead long before you are."

So many things in life present you with opposing points of view—good and bad, benefits and detriments, gains and losses. Yet, it may be hard to see both points of view when you're only focused on one. In those intense moments in which you confront death, it may be hard to see the seeds of new growth that are being planted.

Even though you know you're dying, remember that the person you are now will soon be transformed into someone new—a soul who has moved on to a different plane in the universe. Even though someone you love is dying, the person he or she is now will become someone new to you after they're gone—a beloved human being who has left you with endless memories and reasons to smile. Think of death as that gentle spring rain of hope Thoreau witnessed years ago; remember that new stirrings of growth are forever within you.

❈ ❈ ❈

I REMEMBER THAT WITHOUT DEATH,
LIFE WOULD NOT EXIST.

MAY 26

"People who cannot find time for recreation are obliged sooner or later to find time for illness."

— department-store founder John Wanamaker

ADDING ENJOYMENT TO YOUR DAY

Are there things in your life that you love to do? Albert Schweitzer loved to work in his clinic in Lambarene, Africa. Audrey Hepburn loved her work with needy children overseas. Eleanora "Billie" Holiday loved to sing. Amelia Earhart and Charles Lindbergh loved to fly. John F. Kennedy loved to sail and read.

When you love what you do and have the opportunity to do that very thing, you can be creative and passionate. You can be energetic and enthusiastic. You can be joyful and positive. And you can be so focused on what you do that external "rewards"—money, recognition, respect—pale in comparison to the physical, emotional, and spiritual rewards you elicit.

Retired and senior volunteer programs offer a wide range of opportunities to do the things you love to do. For example, a group of retired men in Newton, Massachusetts, formed the Small Appliance Repair Group because they loved to tinker with and repair failed appliances. Group members experience the joy of doing what they love to do—tinker on a toaster oven, antique pizzelle maker, snowblower, antique waffle maker, clock radio, or a lamp—and get the appliance to work again.

Also, they have the chance to enjoy one another's company. Two of the group's steadiest members, both in their seventies, met over broken appliances and have since become such good friends that they now lunch together once a week before digging into the repairs.

I DEVOTE TIME TODAY TO DOING SOMETHING I LOVE.

"To grow old is to pass from passion to compassion."

— philosopher/writer Albert Camus

CARING FOR CAREGIVERS

Caring, in the sense of loving concern, can be expressed not only by those who are giving care, but also by those who are receiving it. Can you be thoughtful and considerate to those who assist you when you need it, despite your pain or discomfort? Can you be grateful and kind to those who devote a good deal of time to you as they juggle countless other responsibilities in their lives? Can you express your appreciation—without judgment or criticism—to a son or daughter who shovels your walkway, replaces your storm windows, installs your air conditioner, takes care of your yard, prepares meals for you, drives you to the store, or helps you out financially?

It's not always easy to accept that you need others more than they need you, that you can't give equally in return to those who give to you, and that there may be things you used to do on your own that now can only be accomplished with the help of others. Sometimes such dependency can create resentment, guilt, shame, remorse, and fear, which overpowers your ability to remain calm, focused, and objective; you may lose your temper, say harsh words, or reject the advice and efforts of others.

While such responses are to be expected from time to time, behaving in such a way most or all of the time is downright selfish. If you truly can't accept the help those who love you are prepared to give, then seek alternative caregiving arrangements with trained professionals. But if you can temper your frustrations with compassion, you can continue to strengthen your relationship with those you love.

❀　❀　❀

I GIVE COMPASSION TO THOSE WHO GIVE TO ME.

"But perhaps what we call thinking about death is not really thinking at all. It seems more like a slow unclenching of the will, a readiness to wait for the angel at the door."

— writer/publisher Irving Howe

A WISE AND NOBLE LIFE

Once there was a king who ruled over a spacious and magnificent kingdom. The king so loved his land that he would often ride his horse across it, marveling at the natural beauty and bounty of the land.

One day, as he was out surveying his domain with his nobles, he stopped at a scenic spot and cried out, "To think that one day I must die and leave this behind! Wouldn't it be wonderful if we could live forever? Then we'd always be able to enjoy what we have for an eternity. We'd never have to give it up—none of it!"

All the nobles except one nodded in agreement. "Not me, sire," the one noble replied. "I wouldn't want life to be everlasting. And neither would you!"

The nobles gasped at the audacity of such a direct contradiction to the king's wish. The king turned to the dissenting noble and said, in an icy tone, "Do tell, noble, why you know this would be so."

"Well, sire," the noble began, "if life were everlasting, then the first king would still be among us—the one who was so horrible—as would all of his terrible nobles. And I would still be a farmer, and you, sire, would still be a clerk."

The king thought for a moment about the noble's words. Then he smiled. "I'm foolish to even think about living forever," he said. "You have shown me, wise noble, that to truly appreciate what I have while I'm alive, I need to be able to let it go."

I APPRECIATE MY LIFE...WHILE I'M ALIVE.

MAY 29

"Except for our higher order of minds we, are like the little moles under the earth carrying out blindly the work of digging, thinking our own dark passage-ways constitute all there is to the world."

— writer Bess Streeter Aldrich

A VISION OF HARMONY

Years ago, John Donne wrote that no man was an island, that each human being was "...a piece of the continent, a part of the main." This means that every person, place, and thing is a part of humanity—a part of a larger pattern of harmony that intrinsically links each together in a dynamic web of life.

To understand this principle of oneness, think about a loved one you may have lost from your life. Do you remember what your first holiday gathering after this loss was like? You may have felt a definite void, a sense that a vital piece of you and your family was missing, a feeling that the gathering was in some way imbalanced or "out of sync." Later on, there may have been a time when you had good news to share and, in your excitement, you reached automatically for the phone to dial the once-familiar number before you stopped short with the recollection that the special person was no longer there. Once again, you may have felt your world disrupted, a pattern to which you had grown accustomed taken away from you, leaving you with the feeling of being disconnected from the world around you.

Whenever you feel as if you've lost your vision of oneness in some way and begin to see yourself as an island, you lose your ability to live in harmony with the world around you. That's when you need to reach out to others so you can open your eyes and see the integral part you play in the much larger pattern. You may only be one link in the great chain that connects you to all of life, but you're a very vital link!

I RESTORE MY VISION OF ONENESS WITH THE WORLD.

MAY 30

"Every soul is a melody which needs renewing."

— poet Stèphane Mallarmé

THE VALUE OF REGULARITY AND ROUTINE

In the 1960s, Swedish physiologist Bengt Saltin, who doubted that recuperation in bed for seriously ill patients was sound advice, wanted to observe the effects complete bed rest had on the human body. So he asked five young men, who ranged in condition from extremely fit to sedentary, to remain lying in bed 24 hours a day for three weeks. At the end of that time, he made an astonishing discovery: regardless of each man's previous physical condition, all the men suffered a decrease in aerobic capacity that was equal to 20 years of aging!

What this means is that it's best to bring a balance of rest into your life, with moderation, so you avoid excesses and extremes. Renewal in all living things comes from maintaining a balance between the cycles of rest and activity. Animals do this instinctively, but human beings often override this cycle by either getting too much rest and too little activity, or too little rest and too much activity.

In every area of your life, the key is balance. To develop this balance, remember that exercise has to be tempered with rest; the muscle deterioration that naturally occurs during exercise needs to be restored, or else exercise will do you more harm than good. Be active, but be respectful of your body's need to recover. Use moderation to ensure that you're not going to extremes either in your rest or your activities, and strive for regularity to maintain a consistent, healthful routine.

※　　※　　※

I BALANCE REST AND EXERCISE CYCLES
TO RENEW MYSELF.

MAY 31

*"A good marriage is that in which each appoints the other
guardian of his solitude. Once the realization is accepted that
even between the closest human beings infinite distances continue
to exist, a wonderful living side by side can grow up if they succeed in loving the distance between them which makes it possible
for each to see the other whole and against a wide sky."*
— poet Rainer Maria Rilke

GROWING SEPARATELY, GROWING TOGETHER

Sunrise and sunset together represent the measure of a day. When
the sun rises, the moon sets; when the moon rises, the sun sets.
Without such a relationship between the sun and the moon, a day
would have no beginning and no end.

You and your partner together comprise a relationship, but the
success of your relationship depends upon whether there are times
you can be as separate as the sun and the moon. Although you may
share much in common, can you both think, act, and feel as two
individuals?

Too often when you've been in a close friendship or intimate
relationship for a long time, establishing and maintaining a sense of
individuality can be threatening. You may feel that taking separate
paths from one another, even for short periods of time, may force
you apart or in some way damage the peaceful resonance you've
formed in your relationship.

Yet time spent apart, with others or by yourself, is not only
essential to both people in any relationship, but also strengthening
for the union. Healthy relationships are made up of two individuals, not one, who can both seek out and enjoy a variety of friendships and outside interests. Separation from one another is necessary to help you to connect.

I ENCOURAGE AND SUPPORT SEPARATENESS
IN MY RELATIONSHIPS.

JUNE 1

"Miss Scheiber...could have lived lavishly over the years, but she chose not to. Instead she lived frugally in a small apartment. She watched her money, took care of herself and lived a long life. In the end, she knew that despite amassing great wealth, she couldn't take it with her. Rather than squandering her millions before she died, she used her wealth to help society."
— stockbroker William Fay

INVESTING IN YOUR FUTURE

When Anne Scheiber died in 1995 at the age of 101, her passing made front-page news—not because of her age, but due to her stunning generosity. She left her entire estate—valued at nearly $22 million—to a private religious school in New York.

But even more astonishing than her unexpected donation was the revelation that she had made her fortune in the stock market by starting with a mere $5,000 investment in the mid-1930s. Although she knew the risks involved in playing the market, her job as an IRS auditor taught her that much wealth could be accumulated by investing in common stocks.

Miss Scheiber wasn't interested in get-rich-quick schemes, nor did she listen to tips or rumors. Rather, her investments were the result of thorough research of companies and well thought-out strategies. Also, she bought stock in industry leaders whose products she believed would stand the test of time, with a portfolio that included Coca-Cola, PepsiCo, Loews, Bristol-Myers, Squibb, Monsanto, and many others.

You, too, can invest for the long-term. But keep in mind, as Miss Scheiber did, that you should never invest unless and until you can afford the risk.

❊   ❊   ❊

I INVEST WISELY FOR FUTURE FINANCIAL GROWTH.

"Words of comfort, skillfully administered, are the oldest therapy known to man."

— literary critic Louis Nizer

COMFORTING COMMUNICATION

When Dr. Bernie Siegel's son Keith was four years old, the child was scheduled to undergo a hernia repair in the hospital. The father reassured his son about the surgery by carefully communicating, in great detail, all of the medical details of the procedure. As his son was wheeled into the operating room, the doctor felt that his words had provided ample comfort.

But when Keith awoke after surgery and saw his father standing by his bedside, he mumbled, "Daddy, you forgot to tell me something."

"What's that?" his father asked.

"You forgot to tell me it was going to hurt."

Sometimes when a friend or relative is going through a hard time, you may be quick to provide them with words designed to help them solve their problems or ease them through their pain. But what those in need really want from you may not be answers, rational advice, or logical thinking. What they may yearn for is for someone to hear them and to respond to them with simple words of comfort—"I wish I could make this hard time better for you; I know it's not easy," "I'm sorry things are so rough for you right now," or "You know I can be there for you anytime." Also, they may need you to listen, to pay attention to their emotional outpouring, and to give them a space in which they can express their feelings without having to "get over them."

Rather than search for the right words that will magically make someone else's problems go away, speak the most comforting words that empathize with their pain.

I AM A PATIENT, CARING LISTENER AND ADVISOR.

JUNE 3

*"What lies behind us and what lies before us are small matters
compared to what lies within us."*

— Ralph Waldo Emerson

CREATIVE RISK-TAKING

All growth in life springs from the tension between limits and drive. You can believe that you can't do anything about a limitation and simply give up, or you can believe that there's got to be another way around the limitation—and then strive to find it.

In his parable of two frogs, related by creativity consultant Roger Von Oech, two frogs fall into a bucket of cream. The first frog, after frantically thrashing about in the cream for several seconds trying to seek footing, concludes that there's no way out of the bucket, accepts its fate, and drowns. But the second frog does whatever it can to stay afloat, thrashing about minute after agonizing minute until all his churning gradually turns the cream into butter. Though exhausted by his efforts, the frog then finds his footing and hops out of the bucket.

You may believe that there's no way around any of your age-limiting circumstances. Yet as Rollo May writes in his book *The Courage to Create,* "The creative act arises out of the struggle of human beings with and against that which limits them." You can be like the frog that believes it can't do anything about its situation and gives up, or you can be like the other frog, who refuses to accept defeat.

Dig deep within yourself to find the determination to struggle against your limitations. Be creative. Invent new ways of doing things. Change old attitudes. Revise former behaviors. Try out new paths. In short, don't be afraid to try to make some things in your life "butter"!

❧   ❧   ❧

I CREATE WAYS TO MOVE BEYOND MY LIMITATIONS.

JUNE 4

"I've always wanted to be somebody, but I see now I should have been more specific."

— comedienne/actress Lily Tomlin

BEING AN INDIVIDUAL

What do you think it takes for you to feel like your own person, for you to believe yourself to be an individual, for you to think that you're not only somebody, but somebody special?

Some people think that being an individual means differentiating themselves as much as possible from others in a variety of ways—in their style of dress, the mannerisms they employ, the beliefs they develop, and so on. Some people think this means just the opposite; that by distinguishing themselves in situations that require uniformity—such as in the military or in the corporate world, for instance—they're perceived to be individuals. And still others strive to be individuals by living by the philosophy proposed by Henry David Thoreau when he said, "If a man does not keep pace with his companions, perhaps it is because he hears a different drummer. Let him step to the music he hears, however measured or far away."

Yet, being more unique than others or marching to a different beat than others doesn't necessarily make you more of an individual. Individuality isn't about making a statement, changing people's perceptions of you, breaking out of a former way of being, or meeting the approval of others. No, individuality isn't about other people's opinions, it's about *your* opinion. To be an individual, you simply need to be yourself—the self with whom you're most comfortable—and then continue to be yourself, in spite of what others think or say.

I AM A UNIQUE, SPECIAL SOMEBODY.

JUNE 5

"The soul would have no rainbow had the eyes no tears."

— Minquass tribe proverb

SURVIVING THE STORMS OF LIFE

You know that all wounds need time to heal, whether the wounds be physical, emotional, or spiritual. But when you've been wounded—by an illness or injury, by the loss of a relationship or loved one, or by a sense of hopelessness and despair—you may believe that you'll never be able to heal. You may feel that from this moment on, you'll always be in pain or you'll always feel sad, empty, hopeless, depressed, lost, and lonely. Suffering will become your permanent state of living; your suffering will have no end.

Yet, no present hour ever endures; nothing in the universe stands still. Torrents of rain yield glorious sunshine and magnificent rainbows. The saying, "And this, too, shall pass away" provides an apt reminder that the world's a scene of perpetual change, constant in its inconstancy, fluctuating from sorrow to joy.

Rather than sit around and bemoan your suffering, use this difficult time to work with the natural cycles of change—the comings and goings of life. First, accept that, eventually, this moment of struggle will pass. Then, rather than focus on the agonizingly slow passage of each minute, strive to see the opportunity that can come out of your crisis—look for the rainbow after the storm. Philosopher Aeschylus once said, "By suffering comes wisdom." So think about what you can learn from your experience. Then be willing to look beyond your dilemma to what lies well past the horizon. Look outside yourself—to the sunshine, the lush greenery, and the sights, sounds, and smells of forthcoming summer life— and what's inside will soon be healed.

I LET MY TEARS CLEANSE MY SOUL.

JUNE 6

"Those we call the ancients were really new in everything."
— scientist/philosopher Blaise Pascal

REINVENTING THE FAMILY

Just as the shift from an agrarian to an industrial lifestyle in America transformed the isolated, home-based patriarchal family into a more socialized, neighborly nuclear family unit, in a society now blessed by the extended life of family members, new family structures are being forged. Today's family units are becoming more adult-centered, with relationships not only between adults and children, but adults and their adult children. Generations have become linked as peers under the same roof, placing the focus of home life not only on raising children, but also on maintaining a supportive network of adult relationships.

Yet, such an evolution of the family unit isn't new to history. The family, as a basic social unit, has always changed in size, shape, and focus, depending upon the economics and demographics at the time. And today's new family styles hearken back to the influence of ancient times, where grandparents and grandchildren would live together, where households were sometimes transgenerational—crossing, combining, or even skipping generations—and members were quite likely to be bound together as much by friendship and choice as by blood and obligation.

What this means to you today is that the family, in a general sense, and your family, in particular, are being reinvented. While the essential purposes of the family—to provide love, caregiving, friendship, discipline, support, and to share in celebrations—won't change, what will change is the unique style of your particular family. So welcome such changes, and honor your family.

I EMBRACE THE METAMORPHOSIS OF MY FAMILY.

JUNE 7

ENJOYING A SLOWER PACE

"In my later years," begins a journal entry written by a woman in her seventies, "my concept of time has changed and, because of this, my concept of myself has changed, too. For years I've always lived life at a grand pace. I've cooked and cleaned and washed and hung laundry and polished and waxed and shopped. When others would rest or sit down and read the newspaper, I'd be in the kitchen or the backyard or the basement or the attic, always doing something.

"For years, I showed no signs of slowing down. Go, go, go. That was me. I thought that slowing down was bad. That once I slowed down, it would mean I was getting old.

"Then my husband died. I couldn't take care of the house and the yard myself, so I sold it and moved to a smaller apartment. I didn't know what to do with myself. Because now I was slowing down.

"Then I met a woman my age who invited me with her on a week-long camping and hiking trip with the Appalachian Mountain Club. I didn't think I could keep up with everyone, but I did. I had a pack on my back and fashioned a strong stick for support, and I found myself going up modest elevations and enjoying myself thoroughly.

"It was then that I realized I didn't have to run through my life anymore. I could walk. I could take my time. In going slower, I've become more aware of who I am. I'm slowing down, but I'm slowly discovering who I am."

❀   ❀   ❀

I TAKE TIME TO GET TO KNOW MYSELF.

JUNE 8

"This grand show is eternal. It is always sunrise somewhere; the dew is never all dried at once; a shower is forever falling; vapor is ever rising. Eternal sunrise, eternal sunset, eternal dawn and gloaming, on sea and continents and islands, each in its turn, as the round earth rolls."

— naturalist/writer John Muir

BREAKING OUT OF ROUTINES

There may be many different words and phrases you use to describe your view of a stable life, such as *rigid, routine, inflexible, tedious,* and *monotonous.* Year after year of doing the same things in the same way may make you crave variation, long for a change of pace, and strive to be more spontaneous and flexible.

Yet, you live in a world which, in many ways, never breaks out of its routines. Day after day, the sun rises in the east; day after day, the sun sets in the west. "Monotony is the law of nature," spiritual leader Mahatma Gandhi once said. "Look at the monotonous manner in which the sun rises." Nature teaches you that you must have some sort of order to start from; somewhere in your life, there must be some level of stability. Yet within that framework, there can be differences and variations. Nature has such a need to break out of routines from time to time, with unpredictable winds and storms, lightning and thunder, droughts and floods.

So, at times, you may enjoy the sense of expectation, dependability, security, and familiarity that comes as a result of an undisrupted daily schedule, from the usual way of doing things, and from the "sure things" on which you can depend. Other times you may long to interrupt the usual progression of your time and do something out of the ordinary. How you balance the two in your life will determine whether you'll live a monotonous, unfulfilling life or a life that provides you with a safe, secure—and interesting—foundation.

❀   ❀   ❀

I CREATE FLEXIBLE STABILITY IN MY LIFE.

JUNE 9

"I like living. I have sometimes been wildly, despairingly, acutely miserable, racked with sorrow, but through it all I still know quite certainly that just to be alive is a grand thing."

— mystery writer Agatha Christie

AFFIRMING LIFE

When you're feeling physically, emotionally, and spiritually drained, you may welcome suicidal thoughts. But you may also feel like you don't really want to kill yourself. What you want may not be death, but a cessation to the pain and discomfort you're experiencing as a result of growing older.

If, at any time today, you feel hopeless, morose, powerless, fearful, anxious, confused, sad, achy, tired, or lonely, remind yourself that no matter how you feel, there's a Higher Power who's there for you and who understands what you're going through. Your Higher Power is always there to protect and care for you. And because there's always a loving and comforting spiritual presence around you, you're safe and secure at all times.

As you read these words about the presence and protection of a Higher Power, it may be hard for you to release your apprehension, doubts, and concerns. If that's how you feel, then you might find prayer beneficial. Prayer is the personal and private dialogue you have with your Higher Power. Through this conscious contact, you allow yourself to become more willing to receive reassurance and peace from a spiritual source. Prayer is your connection to your Higher Power's wisdom and love and, also, your connection to the wisdom and love you have inside you.

Rely upon a treasured or familiar prayer, or simply turn to your Higher Power and ask for peace and protection whenever you need to be reminded of the good that exists in your life.

❊   ❊   ❊

I PRAY TO REMEMBER TRUST, SERENITY, AND HAPPINESS.

JUNE 10

"Maybe it's best to treat happiness like a deer in the forest. Sometimes it will emerge from the woods and pay you a visit. But it dislikes undue attention. And if you chase it, it will run away."
— writer Phyllis Theroux

CONNECTING WITH OTHERS

One day a member of a tribe living in a remote area in central Brazil left his village and journeyed to São Paulo. After spending a few years experiencing life in this bustling modern city of millions of people, he went back to his small village of three hundred. When he got home, he told the members of the tribe why he had returned. "Here," he said, "we know each other and are with each other." He explained that even though he had looked for happiness in the city, he hadn't found it; rather, the close personal and social connections typical of his way of life in the tribe were what was lacking in the city and what truly made him happy.

Tribal societies don't abandon old people the way many in today's society do, shuttling grandparents and aging parents to the homes of siblings or nursing homes, sticking an obligatory birthday card in the mail once a year, or using holidays as the only times of gathering. In tribes, younger family members, as well as everyone in the village, share in all responsibilities together, and it's this ongoing connection that brings great happiness to both the younger and older members.

Writer Thomas Tryon once wrote, "I think the most important thing is caring about someone. It's being by themselves that does people in, makes them old and bitter....I think real happiness only comes when we are joined to another human being." Even though society can be an alienating place in which to live and grow old, you can find happiness by connecting with those who are near and dear to you.

❊   ❊   ❊

I LOOK FOR HAPPINESS IN MY "TRIBE."

"No wise man ever wished to be younger."
— writer Jonathan Swift

GROWING UP WELL

Should the focus of mature adulthood be a longing for youth? Although you may hope, in some measure, for youthful health and vitality to stay with you as you grow older, perhaps it's not wise to long to be forever trapped in the body and spirit of a young man or woman without ever being able to experience the benefits of wisdom, and the peace in serenity and fulfillment.

Then how about wishing you could live forever? Such a wish may also have its drawbacks. In J. R. R. Tolkien's trilogy, *The Lord of the Rings,* hobbit Smaegol discovers a magic ring that grants him two powers—invisibility and immortality. The problem is, the ring doesn't bring about greater quality to his life; it just gives him the ability to live on and on. As Smaegol lives longer and longer, his skin grows pale, his voice thins to a whisper, he loses his attachment to others, and he stumbles around without a purpose to his existence. He eventually retreats to an island in an underground lake, where he lives in darkness, muttering to himself, calling himself Gollum, and living in a never-ending eternal hell where he's hundreds of years old and can't die.

The point to living a long, full life is not to long to be younger, but to hope that you can grow older with a quality of living that disregards the years. In reality, the experiences you have when you're older can be even more unique, more rewarding, and more enjoyable than the experiences of your youth.

While your overall fitness may decline gradually in the coming years, your spirit, your senses, your mind, and your heart can always soar to great heights.

I LEAP AT NEW OPPORTUNITIES FOR PERSONAL GROWTH.

JUNE 12

"If you are smart and manage to stay healthy, you'll also stay smart, although it may take you longer to demonstrate that fact at sixty-five than it did at twenty-five...."

— psychologist Ward Edwards

MAKING A DIFFERENCE

Does it sometimes seem as if you've made it to this point in life without really feeling like you've accomplished something or without achieving at least one of your lifelong dreams? Do you sometimes feel that you've left many challenges unanswered, many broken fences in disrepair, or many needs unfulfilled? Do you wonder if what you feel is true—that your life really hasn't made a difference?

There's a story of an old man who was walking along the beach at dawn. His joints were stiff and sore, his heart heavy with the recent loss of his wife, his view of the future hopeless. He noticed a little boy ahead of him who was picking up starfish and flinging them into the sea. Catching up to the youth, the old man asked why he was doing this. The answer was that the stranded starfish would die if left until the morning sun came up.

"But the beach goes on for miles, and there are thousands of starfish," the old man grumbled. "How can your effort make any difference?"

The boy looked down at the starfish he held in his hand, then threw it to safety in the waves. "It makes a difference to this one."

So, too, had the interaction made a difference to the old man. As he bent down and joined the boy in his task, he realized that the only way to work through his sorrow, pain, and hopelessness was to instill joy, relief, and hope in others.

NO MATTER HOW I FEEL TODAY, I CAN MAKE A
DIFFERENCE TO SOMEONE ELSE.

JUNE 13

"The raindrops patter on the basho leaf, but these are not the tears of grief; this is only the anguish of him who is listening to them."

— Zen saying

WORKING THROUGH A HARD TIME

Everyone goes through ups and downs in life. Here are some simple ways to let nature help you work through a difficult or sad time, a dark mood, or grief:

• Notice the weather today, and discover at least one positive thing about it. Sunshine is a warming and encouraging sign for the beginning of summer; wind promotes the movement of air and precedes change and renewal; rain nourishes the seeds, bulbs, and roots and washes away grit and grime, and also provides assurance of a good, long drink for flowers that will sustain them throughout the upcoming dry months.

• Observe the wild animals as they go about their daily activities, scurrying to and fro or flitting about as if they had some great business deals to close or a meeting they needed to rush off to when, in reality, they are simply overjoyed by living on the earth another day.

• Go outdoors. Close your eyes and listen to the songs of the birds. Feel the rush of wind or the wetness of nature's shower on your face. Open your mouth and taste the air. Be aware of how your feet are planted on the earth and how the earth is supporting you.

• Get active. Take your dog for a walk. Play with your cat. Exercise. Spend time with your children or friends. Clean out a closet, and recycle what you no longer need. Feel your existence. Know your value.

❀   ❀   ❀

I USE NATURE TO TAKE POSITIVE ACTION
WHEN I'M FEELING BLUE.

JUNE 14

"The length of your education is less important than its breadth, and the length of your life is less important than its depth."
— columnist Marilyn vos Savant

MAKING SENSE OUT OF LIFE

Have you ever seen the ocean in a storm? The water is in constant, frightening motion, capable of sinking boats, eroding shorelines, and sweeping away entire homes. Yet, below the churning surface is a stillness that enables the tiniest fish to dart gently to and fro.

Deep within you is a similar "center"—a part of you that remains free of outside turmoil and tempests and stays calm, still, and focused on the more important, more meaningful matters of life. Getting in touch with this center—or being centered—is like being a tree in a storm: while wind, rain, and lightning may affect you on the outside, your roots hold you fast and firm in the ground. Such rootedness gives you a tremendous feeling of assurance in yourself and in your meaningful place in life.

There's certainly much more to life than what you see on the surface, what you've learned, or how long you've lived. Sometimes you're able to see this incredible vision of life in fragments—little pieces that you know fit together to make up one majestic whole— and sometimes things suddenly snap into focus for a clear, but momentary, vision before disappearing from view.

Yet, while the meaning of your life will probably never be fully revealed to you—it's much too big—you can certainly strive to make sense of the glimpses and inferences that are given to you. Like treasures that have been pulled up from a sunken ship, you can marvel over the fragments of the much bigger whole that lies hidden below the surface.

MY LIFE'S DESTINY IS A MARVELOUS MYSTERY.

JUNE 15

*"Every morning I wake up in pain. I wiggle my toes. Good. They
still obey. I open my eyes. Good. I can see. Everything hurts but I
get dressed. I walk down to the ocean. Good. It's still there. Now
my day can start. About tomorrow I never know.
After all, I'm 89. I can't live forever."*

— an anonymous 89-year-old woman

FINDING TRUE HAPPINESS

There's an old story about a man who approached Buddha to ask
the learned man for the secret of happiness. Buddha asked the
man, "Did you eat breakfast?"

"Yes," the man replied, confused at the question. "But what I'd
really like to know—"

"Did you wash your bowl?" Buddha pursued.

"Yes, yes," the man replied, a bit impatient. "Now can we get
back to—"

"Did you do a good job?" Buddha asked.

"What does that have to do with anything?" the man snapped.

Rather than answer him, Buddha turned and walked away.

So the man sat down and reviewed the conversation he had had
with Buddha.

And then, suddenly, he knew the answer Buddha had given
him. "If I simply wanted to be happy," he spoke out loud, "then the
answer would be simple. True happiness can be found by living in
the present moment, attending to what I need to do, and then enjoying it. But if I place my happiness outside myself—if I strive to be
happier than other people or if I look for my happiness to come
from something more, something bigger, or something better, then
I'll only feel distress. So I must always keep my focus in the
present."

ॐ   ॐ   ॐ

I LIVE IN THE PRESENT MOMENT.

JUNE 16

"[As Jung says], we spend the first half of our span of years...finding our place in the world, finding our sexual orientation, finding our appointed work, finding what things can serve us and what we must avoid or abjure. But by the age of 40 or so we take a change of direction, and henceforth seek knowledge of the world and of mankind, and above all knowledge of ourselves."

— writer Robertson Davies

LATE-IN-LIFE DREAMS

Tina Cassidy writes lovingly about her grandmother who, at the age of 45, with three grown children, decided to take up ice skating at a nearby rink. Even though Tina lived a couple of hours away from her grandmother, she insisted that she be able to take skating lessons with her. So her parents shuttled her every weekend so the two could skate together, sharing words of advice and encouragement.

At the age of 53, Tina's grandmother became the national champion in the mixed pairs ice-dancing competition at Lake Placid, New York, one year after the Olympics was held on the same ice. But a year later, while practicing for another national competition, her grandmother fell on the ice and broke her hip. The accident ended her skating career.

But it wasn't long before her grandmother was competing again. She entered the Ms. Senior Rhode Island pageant and won twice, partly because she had taken up the piano and organ—instruments she had always dreamed of playing—in order to compete in the talent portion of the contest.

What Tina learned from her grandmother is that no matter what your age, it's never too late to do what you've always dreamed of doing!

THERE'S A SPECIAL JOY IN REALIZING MY DREAMS.

JUNE 17

"All the world's a stage, and you are not the first to play the part of old person....The role you are expected to play is not flattering. The old persons who have walked the boards before you have been crotchety, stingy, boastful, boring, demanding, and arrogant. They have complained of their illnesses and many other things. You may be surprised at how easy it is to play the part that way...."

— psychologist B.F. Skinner

"GRAY DESIGN"

While the tendency in the past has been to view those who are aging as totally dependent on others, today the emphasis is on viewing even those older people who have physical limitations as capable of living as independent and normal a life as possible. The trend in "gray design" has helped integrate older people into society by making changes in physical environments so they can remain self-sufficient and comfortable. For example, showers and bathtubs have been redesigned with bars to facilitate entry and exit. Movie theaters provide equipment for those who are hearing impaired. Nonskid slippers and socks help prevent falls. Automatic light switches turn lights on and off in a room. Talking clocks announce the time when touched. Ramps are required at all public buildings. Velcro fasteners have replaced buttons, snaps, zippers, and shoelaces. Books are printed in large type. Frozen and microwaveable foods are available for special diets. And, pet partners not only provide companionship, but have been trained to perform life-saving services.

While you may still be able to find much to gripe about in the world around you, there's much you can be grateful for. Many things have been redesigned or repackaged to make it much easier to live on your own.

❧   ❧   ❧

I APPRECIATE THE WONDERFUL NEW ADVANCES
IN "GRAY DESIGN."

JUNE 18

"I enjoy talking with very old people. They have gone before us on a road by which we too may have to travel, and I think we do well to learn from them what it is like, easy or difficult, rough or smooth."

— Socrates

KNOWING WHAT'S THERE

There's a story told about a king who suddenly awakens in the middle of the night and summons the kingdom's wisest seer into his bedchambers. "Oh, Great Seer," the king says, "my sleep is troubled for I do not know the answer to this question: What is holding up the earth?"

"Your majesty," replies the seer, "the earth rests on the back of a giant elephant."

The king sighs in relief, and then goes back to sleep. But it isn't long before he awakens in a cold sweat and once again summons the seer to his bedchambers. "Tell me, Great Seer," the king says, "what is holding up the elephant?"

The seer replies, "The elephant stands on the back of a giant turtle."

The king sighs again, reaches for his bed candle to blow out the flame, and then stops. "But Seer..." the king begins.

The seer holds up his hand. "You can stop right there, your Majesty," he says. "It's turtles, all the way down."

The point of the story is that people live and learn through the support of others, particularly those who have lived and learned longer. As theologian Harry Emerson Fosdick wrote, "Life is like a library owned by an author. In it are a few books which he wrote himself, but most of them were written for him." Every person you meet contributes to your library of knowledge and experience. That means that you need to listen to the older people in your life and learn from them.

✿   ✿   ✿

I TRUST WHAT I LEARN FROM LIFE AND OTHERS.

JUNE 19

"Sometimes it seemed to him that his life was delicate as a dandelion. One little puff from any direction, and it was blown to bits."
— writer Katherine Paterson

SOARING IN STRENGTH

When a bird hops around on the ground, it becomes vulnerable and weak; at such a time, it would be easy for a cat to quickly snatch the bird in its mouth. Yet, when the bird is in flight, it becomes powerful and strong.

You, too, can be like that bird—weak and vulnerable as well as powerful and strong. Yet too often you may be more conscious of your weaknesses and vulnerabilities and let them dictate how you feel about yourself. One of the greatest mistakes any human being can make is to spend too much time and effort trying to correct or deal with one or more weaknesses, rather than focusing on developing one or more of their strengths.

So what if you're not as fleet of foot as you used to be? So what if you've forgotten that you've retold the same story to the same person? So what if you can't understand the lyrics to the music your children or grandchildren are listening to? So what if other drivers pass you on the road? So what if you can't open the pickle jar without asking for help? So what if you need to take the escalator or an elevator rather than the stairs? So what?

A proverb of unknown origin states, "Even when a bird is walking, we sense that it has wings." Today, you can soar with your strengths in mind, or you can let your weaknesses ground you. Focus on what you do right, rather than what you do wrong; focus on what you *can* do rather than what you *can't*, and focus on moments of success rather than times of failure.

I FOCUS ON MY STRENGTHS AND MY SUCCESSES.

JUNE 20

"The days potter by here much the same; sometimes the sad sound of their ticking feet gets into my ears as they disappear into history, carrying nothing in their delicate hands but a yawn."

— writer E. M. Forster

THE CURIOSITIES OF LIFE

During her 30-year career, talk show hostess Sally Jessy Raphaël has been fired 18 times. Every time this happened, however, she has focused on something she could do. When no mainland radio station would hire her—they thought women couldn't attract an audience—she moved to Puerto Rico, became fluent in Spanish, and proved them wrong. To sell her hit radio program, she pitched her idea time and time again to several network executives until it sold. Now she's the Emmy award-winning hostess of her own television show, reaching eight million viewers on a daily basis.

When you believe that nothing will change or ever get better, chances are pretty good that nothing will change or get better. If you do little to facilitate change, you'll have little change. So if you're stuck in a rut or plagued by the same problems, you need to recognize that much of it is your own doing—and much of it can be your own undoing.

Writer Robertson Davies recommends that the best way to add some zest and spice to your life is to become interested in your life. "Curiosity," he wrote, "is the great preservative and the supreme emollient. Not, of course, curiosity about theater or history alone or at all, but curiosity about *something*. Enthusiasm. Zest. That is what makes old age...a delight." Use what bores you as a springboard, and then dive on into your life!

I EXPLORE THE WORLD TODAY LIKE A CURIOUS CAT.

JUNE 21

*"To live fully, outwardly and inwardly, not to ignore external
reality for the sake of the inner life, or the reverse—
that's quite a task."*

— mystic/writer Etty Hillesum

BECOMING IMMORTAL

The ultimate boundary to human life is death. What your life is like depends on how you live within that boundary—on how well you live in the world within yourself, as well as within the confines dictated by death's limitations. If your world contains sickness, aging, and death, then these become inevitable parts of the "scenery" of your world. If, on the other hand, you see health, wisdom, love, pleasure, serenity, and other similarly positive elements, then these become scenic vistas in your world that you're able to experience and enjoy.

Ancient sages believed that the existence of a timeless reality is possible—a world in which there's an existence that either can't or won't see boundaries. Renowned physicist Albert Einstein espoused such liberation from boundaries when he said, "At such moments, one imagines that one stands on some spot of a small planet gazing in amazement at the cold and yet profoundly moving beauty of the eternal, the unfathomable. Life and death flow into one, and there is neither evolution nor eternity, only Being."

If you can view death not as a boundary or a restricting force in your life, but as just another transformation, death no longer represents an end point, an extinction, a limiting factor in how you live today. To live fully in the present, you must be true to life. Value the moment, act on it, live in it. See yourself as timeless, your life as limitless, and your being as immortal. Then you can truly live in what Dr. Deepak Chopra calls an "ageless body" and a "timeless mind."

I BREAK THE SPELL OF MORTALITY.

JUNE 22

"The older son was supposed to be 3,000 miles away, living in a high-rise dorm with a foggy view of San Francisco, calling sporadically and collect. His bedroom at home was supposed to be frozen in time—plaques, trophies, yearbook, winter clothes hanging unneeded in the closet....He's still here."

— writer John Powers

THE NOT-SO-EMPTY NEST

Do you feel as if you're in a state of limbo with your adult children, who you know ought to be off on their own, making their way in the world the way you had to when you were their age, but who are now living at home for one reason or another? Perhaps your son or daughter has lost a job or just graduated from college and can't find a job, and so is unable to pay for rent and living expenses. Maybe he or she is going through a separation or divorce and needs an interim place to stay. Perhaps one of your children is recovering from a life crisis—surgery, an addiction, bankruptcy, and so on—and needs to be in a supportive, caring environment. Or maybe your son or daughter has decided to go back to school to prepare for a future in a higher-paying career.

No matter what the reason, it can be difficult in your later years to still have your children living at home. It can be frustrating to put your own plans to spend more time with your partner on hold or to give up plans to convert your kid's room into a home office or hobby room. And it can be confusing, too, for what rules do you establish for adult children so they can take responsibility for themselves and respect the needs of their older "roommates"? That's why it's important to put into place and practice a rights-and-responsibilities list for your live-at-home adult children to safeguard your sanity and to ease them into their maturity.

MY ADULT CHILDREN WHO LIVE AT HOME TAKE
RESPONSIBILITY FOR THEMSELVES.

JUNE 23

SIXTY AND SINGLE

Finding a new love later in life is one of the sweetest pleasures reported by seniors who have lost a life partner either through death or divorce. "When I fell in love again at 60," said a 65-year-old Arkansas widow, "it was unexpected, but not a whole lot different than when I was a teenager. And I realized one very important thing. No matter what anyone's age, older people still have a lot to give and to receive."

After a time of grieving over the end of a relationship, most older men and women redefine themselves as single people who have continuing needs for love, affection, and sexual expression—and are therefore "available." And, because out of the total population of Americans age 60 and older nearly 43 percent are single, many options exist to promote such availability. Support groups for widows and widowers and divorcées bring them in touch with others who share a similar reason for being single. Retirement living communities are often built around hobbies, sports, and social activities enjoyed by the majority of its population. Travel packages and cruises specifically geared for seniors offer inexpensive trips to exotic locales. And singles dances and a variety of other social activities focus on the union of new, loving couples.

❀   ❀   ❀

I WELCOME A NEW LOVE LIFE AT ANY AGE.

JUNE 24

"Life is action and passion. It is expected of a man that he share in the action and passion of his time under penalty of being judged not to have lived."
— Judge Oliver Wendell Holmes, Jr.

MOTHER TERESA

Every morning, well before sunrise, she is on her knees on the floor, praying. Those who glimpse this devout woman see a tiny, frail-looking, elderly person. But the woman is Mother Teresa, and those who watch her work or know of her work recognize that the tiny woman is not only the center of a remarkable global spiritual movement, but an individual who is filled with nonstop action and intense passion.

Yet, the work for which Mother Teresa is most revered didn't become a reality until she reached midlife. Her early passion for missionary work and teaching led her to St. Mary's High School in Calcutta. At 36, she was principal, highly respected in her profession and her order. It seemed that she had found her calling in life.

But her journeys into Moti Jheel, one of the slums of Calcutta, awakened a new passion within her. One night, while riding the hot and crowded night train to Darjeeling at the age of 40, she "heard" her call to "leave the convent and help the poor while living among them."

And that is what Mother Teresa has done. She founded the Missionaries of Charity order and moved into the industrial slum in Calcutta where the lepers lived; she gave them food and medicine. At 58, she opened a house in Rome; at 60, with her order over three million strong, she moved to London and considered retiring. Instead, she relocated to New York and started the first North American mission in the ravaged and dangerous "Fort Apache" area of the South Bronx. The Nobel Prize brought her worldwide acclaim at the age of 69.

❦   ❦   ❦

I AIM TO LIVE AN ACTIVE, PASSIONATE LIFE STARTING NOW!

JUNE 25

*"I have a seventy-five-year-old friend whose fantasy, he says,
is to intervene in some cruel mugging and thus get himself
killed as a hero. Why? Why of course to avoid old age by
dying with his boots on."*

— writer Wayne Booth

CHOOSING YOUR WAY OUT

Do you dream of being able to leave this world in some glorious way? Do you long to leave this world doing what you love doing best rather than wasting away in a nursing home, being doped up on drugs to dull your pain, or being ignorant of who you are? Do you pray you can go before your loved ones so you can avoid the grief of losing them?

While you may wish to be able to have some control over your death—to have a "say" or even a vote in when you die as well as how you die—you know that can't happen. Death is a finger that arbitrarily points where it may; like the spin-the-bottle game that you may have played when you were a teenager, you're chosen only when the bottle points to you.

When baseball's National League home plate umpire John McSherry collapsed on the field seven pitches into the Reds-Expos opening day game in 1996 and died an hour later from a heart attack, one of his close friends and colleagues remarked, "He went out the way he wanted to go out. He was baseball. Baseball was him." But 51-year-old McSherry had scheduled a doctor's appointment for the next day for treatment for heart arrhythmia; clearly he wanted to live on and work many more opening days. So while you can't choose how or when you're going to die, what you can do is choose how you're going to live.

I FOCUS ON LIVING WELL IN THE MOMENT.

JUNE 26

"Age does not protect you from love. But love, to some extent, protects you from age."

— actress Jeanne Moreau

LIVING FOR LOVING

If you were just to pick and choose a few select people to love—people on whom you would bestow and from whom you'd receive compassion, passion, tenderness, acceptance, support, peace, harmony, honesty, trust, and openness—and then not love others, you would be eliminating people from your life who might be vital to the quality of your existence. For, the natural way of love is one that brings greater harmony not only to your present world, but also to your future world.

Taoist Chuang-Tzu taught that, "...through love, we experience the inherent connections between ourselves and others, seeing all creation as one." But you can only experience love in this way when you're able to look beyond your ego and beyond individual personalities and passions to perceive your part in a much larger pattern—one that exists beyond heart and head. Love can unite you with the good of all, but only if you're able to express love with no thought of return, transcend judgment and break the habit of analysis and comparison to others, release your anger, seek outlets for harmonious and peaceful interactions, live comfortably in the present to avoid regret over the past and expectations for the future, and circulate loving energy to protect yourself from the disappointments you may feel from growing older. Give and receive love, and you'll discover many treasures that can keep you young for years to come in very special, very loving ways.

I FILL A TREASURE CHEST OF LOVE IN MY LIFE.

JUNE 27

BODY TALK

As much as you'd like to stay young, you may notice that even if you're in good physical condition, that thickness around your middle takes a much longer time to disappear than it did when you were younger, when it would melt like a pat of butter in a hot frying pan. Your hair has turned a shade you once admired as "that cool salt-'n-pepper look" but which you now know signals you're a Master, although of what, you might not know. Or perhaps you no longer have hair in the spots you once warmed by a blow dryer and then laboriously styled with gobs of gel. And, you may hope that the wrinkles on your face give you a permanently relaxed look but, upon closer examination, you realize that you look like an angry prune.

You may have even finally admitted, after returning several runners' watches that you believed to be defective, that you're no longer going to break or even meet some of the terrific personal records you once set when you were in your twenties; it's no longer a question of time, but the lack of "fresh legs." And you know now that when you purchase a new pair of running shoes, you can't buy the "real" racing shoes that the fast guys use, but need the ones that offer back support, arch support, heel support, and enough room for your orthotics.

Admit it—you're getting older. But, as 47-year-old runner and writer J.D. Denton said, "Being an old guy who runs isn't so bad. Sure, we've been listening to our bodies for years, and we don't like what they've been telling us lately, but at least they're still talking."

I GRIN AT THE GROANS AND GRIPES OF MY BODY.

JUNE 28

"These years are still the years of my prime. It is important to recognize the years of one's prime, always remember that.... One's prime is elusive."
— from *The Prime of Miss Jean Brodie*, by Muriel Spark

GREAT DECADES

You must live your life from beginning to end, but do you ever think that you can live your life in-between, too? Middle age—and the decades beyond middle age—have much to offer if you can focus less on your actual age and more on the benefits that can be derived from each age.

Novelist Victor Hugo paid tribute to the age of 50—half a century—when he penned, "Forty is the old age of youth; fifty is the youth of old age." French writer Colette celebrated six decades when she wrote, "You must not pity me because my sixtieth year finds me still astonished. To be astonished is one of the surest ways of not growing old too quickly." Statesman Oliver Wendell Holmes similarly rejoiced in his seventh decade: "To be seventy years young is sometimes far more cheerful and hopeful than to be forty years old."

But writer Franck C. Laubach, who glorified eight decades, made aging sound like something to really look forward to. "Once you reach 80," he observed, "everyone wants to carry your baggage and help you up the steps. If you forget your name or anybody else's name, or an appointment, or your own telephone number, or promise to be three places at the same time, or can't remember how many grandchildren you have, you need only explain that you are 80....So please, folks, try to make it to 80. It's the best time of life. People forgive you for anything. If you ask me, life begins at 80."

Your age is your prime—no matter what age you are!

I LOOK FORWARD TO ENJOYING THE OTHER SIDE OF 50.

JUNE 29

"When you have seen one ant, one bird, one tree, you have not seen them all."

— entomologist Edward O. Wilson

LIFE'S SIGNIFICANCE

When nursing student Joann C. Jones was in her second year of nursing, her professor gave the class a pop quiz. Having kept up with her studies, Joann was pleased that the questions proved to be easy. However, the last question stumped her: "What is the name of the woman who cleans the school?" At first she thought the question was a joke. She shrugged her shoulders, left the question blank, and handed her paper in. She was not the only student who was thrown by the final question. As the future nurses filed out of class after the lecture, one asked the professor if the last question on the quiz would count towards the grade.

"Absolutely," the professor replied. "In your careers you will meet many people. All are significant. They deserve your attention and care, even if all you do is smile and say hello."

So, too, this is the case in your life. Every person with whom you've come in contact is significant—from your kindergarten teacher to your best friend to your first love to your last boss. Every event in your life is important—from the obvious meaningful events such as graduating from high school or getting married, to the not-so-obvious events such as taking a spontaneous side trip or signing up for an adult-education course. Also, every cause has an effect that can prove to be significant; you wouldn't be where you are today or who you are without all the steps you took along the way, all the people you met, everything you learned, and all that you did. Everything in your life—including the cleaning woman named Dorothy—is significant.

I TRUST THAT EVERYTHING IN MY LIFE HAS MEANING.

JUNE 30

*"People don't discuss their blood pressure or latest operation.
They talk about their recent trip to China or a lecture.
Everyone is with it."*

— 74-year-old Ruth Schwartz

COLLEGE "SENIORS"

When Ruth Schwartz and her husband, Arthur, who graduated from Cornell Medical School, chose where they wanted to live in retirement, they initially shuttled for years between homes in Miami, and Asheville, North Carolina. But although they loved their Key Biscayne home, they became disillusioned with the crime and overcrowding in South Florida. And while they liked Asheville, a leg injury made it hard for Ruth to climb the hills there.

Then the couple heard about a group of former Cornell faculty and alumni who wanted to develop a senior community near the Ithaca, New York, campus. Now Ruth and Arthur have become two more seniors who have shunned traditional retirement spots and opted for life in a college town. For this new class of "seniors," life is now filled with never-ending opportunities for learning, activity, community involvement, and culture. Many seniors attend class-room lectures, enjoy college concerts and plays, cheer at NCAA basketball and football games, haunt the rare books rooms at the extensive libraries, and assist the colleges and universities in orga-nizing their archives.

Living in a college town also helps seniors feel as if they're a real part of life rather than just a bystander. When 81-year old Carol Scott and her husband visited Florida to check it out as a possible retirement spot, she remarked, "I don't think we saw anything but gray heads." Now the Scotts, who live in Charlottesville, Virginia, keep themselves busy with activities at the University of Virginia.

I CONSIDER THE REWARDS OF LIVING IN A
COLLEGE TOWN WHEN I RETIRE.

JULY 1

"Life is always walking up to us and saying, 'Come on in, the living's fine,' and what do we do? Back off and take its picture."
— writer Russell Baker

FINDING YOUR ALIVENESS

Imagine that you have the opportunity to take a coast-to-coast trip across the United States. You can stop wherever you'd like, spend however long you want at any location, and have no set timetable. Are you going to focus solely on reaching your destination and simply drive there as quickly as you can? Or are you going to release the need to arrive at a specific time and simply enjoy the scenery, the people you meet along the way, and the interesting places you happen upon?

Every day you have the opportunity to go on a "cross-country trip"—a once-in-a-lifetime adventure never to be repeated. How do you wish to spend your time? If you focus on getting from one place to the next—from breakfast to lunch to dinner or from the morning newspaper to the afternoon mail delivery to the network news—then you'll certainly reach your appointed destination. But what if you allow yourself to get sidetracked from time to time— you water your plants and then eat breakfast and then weed the garden and have a snack as you read the morning paper, and then take a walk and eat a late lunch and maybe rent a movie for the evening? Wouldn't the lack of a set schedule help you enjoy every minute and sometimes stop to savor a unique opportunity?

"Aliveness," says writer Richard Moss, "is not necessarily about feeling better, curing ills, or solving problems; it is about feeling more, being in touch with a larger dimension of awareness." Today, see what happens when you get in touch with that larger dimension.

I OPEN UP TO A LARGER DIMENSION OF AWARENESS.

JULY 2

"The most common victim of age discrimination is becoming someone in his or her mid-50s who is replaced by someone in the mid-40s. Now those people will have their day in court."

— Sally Dunaway of the
American Association of Retired Persons

AGE-BIAS DISCRIMINATION

In 1989, James O'Connor was doing so well in his position as a salesman for Consolidated Coin Caterers, a North Carolina vending machine company, that he won a bonus of $37,000, the highest award his employer gave out that year. But the next year, when O'Connor turned 56, his supervisor told O'Connor he was "too damn old for this kind of work." O'Connor was fired and replaced by a 40-year-old. In response, O'Connor sued.

After repeated losses at the lower court level, O'Connor won a significant victory in the U.S. Supreme Court, which ruled that workers can sue employers for age discrimination even when they've been replaced by employees who are 40 years old—or even older. This ruling will certainly help the over 30,000 age-bias cases that are filed with the Equal Employment Opportunity Commission annually, as well as those that are filed in decisions based on firings, not being hired, or getting demoted or transferred because of age.

Up until this time, some prior rulings determined that lawsuits could only be brought if the replacement worker was under 40, outside the category of workers who are protected by the federal Age Discrimination in Employment Act. But now the courts have widened the field for suits on age bias. So, although it may be hard for you to prove an age-bias case against your employer, if you feel that you're being discriminated against in any way on your job, you have the right to expose such bias.

❈   ❈   ❈

I USE MY EXPERIENCE TO PROMOTE AND
PROTECT MY EXPERIENCE.

JULY 3

*"The heart is the toughest part of the body.
Tenderness is in the hands."*

— writer Carolyn Forché

HAND CARE

Do you ever look at your hands and think, These are the hands of my grandfather or My mother's hands used to look like this? You may be shocked, frightened, or even disgusted by the appearance of your hands; seeing them look like the hands of a family member from an older generation signals that you're truly growing old.

Skin diseases, scaly dryness, swelling of the joints, redness, skin chapping, and brown spots are normal signs of skin aging. Skin cells grow more slowly with age, and the outer layer of skin isn't shed and replaced at the same rate as in younger years. With age, cells lose some of their ability to retain water, causing dryness. Also, changes in a protein called collagen make the skin stiffer and less pliable. Sometimes applying cream or oil immediately after a shower or bath can keep the skin moist, as can using a mild or creamy soap on trouble areas.

But what's most important is to keep in mind that although your hands may look rough and toughened, they can still convey tenderness, comfort, and warmth. One 64-year-old woman remarked, "I am trying to recognize that my hands are indeed a part of me, and a part of me that I love. Because I do a great deal with my hands, of course, they are very capable despite the fact that they have these configurations [arthritic swelling]. And I realize that I have indeed been taken in by what a woman's hands should look like, and mostly they're supposed to look pretty useless. My hands don't look useless at all. In fact, they look as though they've been used a great deal."

I ADMIRE MY HANDS AS EVIDENCE OF MY LIFE EXPERIENCES.

JULY 4

"The best remedy for those who are afraid, lonely, or unhappy is to go outside, somewhere where they can be quite alone with the heavens, nature, and God. Because only then does one feel that all is as it should be and that God wishes to see people happy, amidst the simple beauty of nature. As long as this exists, and it certainly always will, I know that then there will always be comfort for every sorrow, whatever the circumstances may be."

— diarist Anne Frank

FINDING "OPEN DOORS"

When you're not at peace with yourself, you're not a free person. When you're not at peace with yourself, you're restricted from living life to the fullest. When you're not at peace with yourself, you're held down, powerless, limited, dominated, and weakened, subservient to your fears, loneliness, and unhappiness.

To find such peace, you need to stop struggling to free yourself. For the moment you stop struggling, you're free. To illustrate this, one day a robin mistakenly flew into an apartment through sliding glass doors. Confused and frightened by its confining new environment, the distressed bird frantically fluttered about the living room, banging into walls and hitting the ceiling. In a panic, it repeatedly hurled itself against the windows and screens in its efforts to get out.

Finally, exhausted and dazed, it perched on the back of a chair. As the small creature panted through its wide-open beak, it suddenly cocked its head to the side. It listened to the sounds of other birds coming from outside the open glass doors. It hopped down from the chair, fluttered across the floor to the doors, then quickly flew outside to a nearby tree branch, where it soon began to sing.

You, too, need to find the "open doors" that will release you from feelings of confinement. Perhaps you can find this in nature or in your spiritual beliefs.

❧   ❧   ❧

I LIBERATE MYSELF AND, IN SO DOING, FIND INNER PEACE.

JULY 5

"It is not by muscle, speed, or physical dexterity that great things are achieved, but by reflection, force of character, and judgement; in these qualities old age is usually not only not poorer, but is even richer."

— Roman orator Cicero

USING YOUR BEST JUDGMENT

It has been said, "To make a peach you need a winter, a summer, an autumn and a bee, so many nights and days and sun and rain, petals rosy with pollen—all that your mouth may know a few minutes of pleasure." So it is in your life, too, for anything worthwhile to be accomplished, you need to let gentleness, rather than strength, prevail.

There's the story of a man who, for years, had owned a peach orchard. One year he harvested a crop of much smaller peaches than usual. He apologized to all of his customers, explaining that his orchards needed constant attention. He said that it took him an entire day just to prune one tree properly, and with over 500 trees to tend, he couldn't keep up with the difficulty of the project.

"This makes me very upset," he confided to one of his regular customers. "I'm getting on, you know, so I guess I'm slowing down. I can't prune all of my trees with the same speed and skill I once had. I tried rushing the job, but ended up severely damaging some of the trees in my haste. So I decided to let the trees grow as they wanted to. And this is what happened," he sighed as he indicated the smaller peaches with a wave of his hand.

The customer took a bite of a smaller peach. "This is the most delicious peach I've ever tasted," she said. "Even though the peaches are smaller, they're even more tasty. Maybe you used good judgment in letting the trees grow as they wanted to."

∞ ∞ ∞

I REFLECT RATHER THAN REACT FOR
THE BEST OUTCOME.

JULY 6

"Cancer is a reminder of how short a leash you're on. As I read somewhere, 'You want to make God laugh? Tell him your plans.'"
— news anchorman John Chancellor

A LITTLE HELP FROM YOUR FRIENDS

When the late John Chancellor ended his broadcasting career, he was looking forward to a comfortable retirement. But then he was stricken with an aggressive form of stomach cancer. It was then that he started to make a personal moral inventory, analyzing and reflecting upon how he had lived his life up to that point in time. Had I smoked or drunk too much? he wondered. Not exercised or prayed enough? Cancer didn't run in my family. Why me?

You, too, may have gone through or are now going through similar ponderings about a disease, illness, or injury that's impacted your life. The onset of any disabling condition can bring about feelings of guilt, remorse, depression, dejection, anger, shame, and the need for rationalization. Also, you may also be tempted to "bargain" with a Higher Power—to make your recovery conditional. For example, you might say, "If I get better, I'll break my bad habits. I'll go to church more often. I'll spend less time on my work. I'll help out more around the house." The list of promises you make may go on and on.

But rather than strive to find easy ways out of a disabling condition or look ahead to a future which, in reality, may be shorter than you'd like, you simply need to get through your difficult time as best you can by living in the present moment and reaching out for help. Before his death, Chancellor remarked that he was able to get through the dreaded side effects of chemotherapy with the help of his best friend—his wife, Barbara. You, too, need to reach out for your own help.

🕸️ 🕸️ 🕸️

I CAN GET THROUGH ANYTHING WITH A LITTLE
HELP FROM MY FRIENDS.

JULY 7

"On the seventh day of the seventh month pick seven ounces of lotus flowers; on the eighth day of the eighth month gather eight ounces of lotus root; on the ninth day of the ninth month collect nine ounces of lotus seeds. Dry in the shade and eat the mixture and you will never grow old."

— Yin Shan Cheng Yao

THE SEARCH FOR ETERNAL YOUTH

Not a day goes by when you don't hear of a new "weapon" in the eternal "battle" against aging. You've seen dramatic announcements of a new product or procedure that claims to keep skin looking younger, erases wrinkles, grows hair where none exists, or helps lose unwanted hair, promotes muscular vitality, or increases stamina. There are even products rumored to have age-reversing effects; rather than help you shed unwanted pounds, such products claim to be able to help you shed unwanted years.

Yet this search for immortal youth is nothing new; for centuries, humankind has longed for such an elixir to assure them of everlasting, youthful vitality and vigor. Explorers braved raging seas and traipsed through rugged wilderness to be forever young. Others concocted salves and brews from herbs, roots, barks, and berries. Fiction writers teased readers with stories of youthful transformations, and, when reality finally set in—that there really was no fountain or elixir of youth—movie producers coyly linked the young and old in romance, suggesting that such a sexual encounter might serve to "average out" the ages so the youth grew in maturity while the older person became young at heart.

While you may be tempted from time to time to try something new to make you feel or look new, remember that such things are hoaxes.

HOW YOUNG I FEEL IS MORE IMPORTANT THAN
HOW YOUNG I LOOK.

JULY 8

"If this is a valid study, we doctors ought to be writing on our order sheets, 'Pray three times a day.' If it works, it works."
— Dr. William Nolen

HEALING PRAYER

When Dr. Larry Dossey was in his residency training at Parkland Memorial Hospital in Dallas, Texas, he had his first patient with terminal cancer in both lungs. He advised the patient of available treatments but offered him no hope; the man opted for no treatment. But until his patient was discharged, the doctor noticed that the man was always surrounded by visitors from his church who were singing to him and praying for him.

A year later, while working at another hospital, a colleague at Parkland called the doctor and asked if he wanted to see an old patient, who turned out to be the same terminally ill man, whose chest x-rays now showed his lungs to be completely free of cancer. Dr. Dossey wondered, Does prayer really heal? But he found no scientific research that could help him answer his question.

Then, in 1988, cardiologist Dr. Randolph Byrd assigned the coronary care patients at San Francisco General Hospital either to a group that was prayed for by prayer groups or to a group that was not remembered in prayer. No one knew which group they were in; those who were praying were simply given the name of the patient, a small bit of medical history, and the advice to pray for the patient each day until the patient was discharged. When the study was completed, those patients who were prayed for were five times less likely to need antibiotics, two-and-a-half times less likely to suffer congestive heart failure, and overall, less likely to go into cardiac arrest. Those who were prayed for lived longer.

I WELCOME BEING INCLUDED IN THE PRAYERS
OF MY LOVED ONES.

JULY 9

"Zorba came upon an old man planting an apricot seedling and asked why he, an old man, was planting a new tree. 'I live as though I would never die,' was his reply.
" 'And me, I live as though I might die tomorrow,' said Zorba.
'Which one of us is right?'"

— writer Nikos Kazantzakis

DEVELOPING A GREEN THUMB

You're being reborn every minute of the day; every cell in your body is constantly changing. In fact, you're not even the same person you were just a few short minutes ago. This means that, if you want, you can transform the cycles in your life in ways that can help you to feel hopeful, full of zest, carefree, free-spirited, and in love with life. As Henry David Thoreau once recommended, "We must learn to reawaken and keep ourselves awake...."

Remember that you get what you cultivate in your life. Think of yourself and your life as a garden, and then keep in mind what will happen if you don't plant new seeds each year, tend to them, and cultivate their growth. So if you focus solely on how you're getting older and how there never seems to be much new that's happening in your life, then you're going to feel dull and lifeless; your garden will become choked with weeds, and nothing will reach fruition.

But, if, instead, you begin to focus on living wholeheartedly from this moment on—to let your roots go deep into everything you do so you become immersed in the people, places, and things in your life—then you can transcend what you believe to be a descent into the twilight of your life. You can give birth to a whole new garden that's filled with soft, green shoots of exciting new growth.

I CULTIVATE THE GARDEN OF MY EXISTENCE.

JULY 10

"His weekend was routine: tennis, dining out, a movie. But days before his 80th birthday, Herb Caen was, as always, working. He is in constant search of journalistic morsels to entice readers into his daily column, which has entertained, informed and occasionally irked generations of Californians."

— writer Martin F. Nolan

HERB CAEN, COLUMNIST

Since 1938, with some time out to serve during World War II, well-known *San Francisco Chronicle* columnist Herb Caen has published more than 14.5 million words. His five-times-a-week newspaper column is a legend in American journalism; his column has lovingly refined and distilled the city of San Francisco (never, according to Caen, to be called "Frisco") for over half a century.

In those decades spent on the San Francisco beat, Caen has witnessed some incredible changes—the building of the Golden Gate and Bay bridges, for example, along with the full-time operation and then the abandonment of the prison at Alcatraz. He has met such notables as Frank Sinatra, Benny Goodman, and Jack Kerouac. He rode Ken Kesey's bus through Haight-Ashbury in the 1960s; when campus turmoil erupted across the bay, Caen christened the location "Berserkeley." And, in one of his most notable achievements, he helped save the city's most unique attraction—its cable cars. Caen now shares the status of being considered one of the city's living landmarks. Asked how he feels about his age, he replies "It's [80] just a large round number. Longevity isn't that big a deal."

You, too, can become a chronicler of your own locale—a sort of Herb Caen of your community. Research and write a column for a local newspaper, get involved with a garden club, and take an active interest in your community's political affairs.

✺   ✺   ✺

I STRIVE TO BECOME A "LIVING LANDMARK"
IN MY COMMUNITY.

July 11

"You cannot stay on the summit forever; you have to come down again. So why bother in the first place? Just this: what is above knows what is below, but what is below does not know what is above. One climbs, one sees. One descends, one sees no longer, but one has seen. There is an art of conducting oneself in the lower regions when one can no longer see, one can at least still know."

— naturalist/writer Rene Dumal

GROWING OLDER, OR GROWING BETTER?

Here are ways that you can grow older and keep growing older:

- See life as meaningless and having little value.
- Be resentful, crotchety, and hypercritical of everything and everybody.
- Avoid trying anything new; take no risks.
- Be mistrustful and fearful.
- Do the same things day after day after day.
- Revel in being stubborn and immovable.
- Go outside as little as possible.
- Give up.

Here are ways you can grow older and grow better:

- Get in motion; go outside, no matter what the weather.
- Take chances; take risks.
- Try something new—something totally out of your character.
- Do things that bring you joy and fulfillment.
- Make a positive contribution to your community.
- Develop a sense of humor; exercise it often.
- Love yourself and everyone else.

I DECIDE WHETHER TO JUST GROW OLDER,
OR TO GROW OLDER AND BETTER.

JULY 12

"Time is that which man is always trying to kill, but which ends in killing him."

— philosopher Herbert Spencer

MAKING TIME COUNT

How much time do you set aside as "free time"? Studies have shown that people who reach midlife spend fewer than three hours a week reading a book, newspaper, or magazine, and less than an hour a week relaxing and thinking!

Can you start to live today by saying, "Counting time is not so important as making time count"? Or will you continue to pack any free time you have with activities centered around household responsibilities, family obligations, errand running, or the latest self-improvement kick?

Free time is certainly not very "free" when it's relegated to activities that often require as much discipline, energy, and sustained effort as work—a rigorous rehearsal schedule for a community theater production, for example, taking an intensive workshop or course, or engaging in a strenuous step-aerobics class. In fact, you may feel now—if you're retired or your children have grown up and left home—that you need to quickly fill the idle time you have on your hands. As Will Rogers once joked, "Half our life is spent trying to find something to do with the time we have rushed through life trying to save."

From this moment on, strive to use your free time as that time in which you're neither too busy nor too idle. Read a bestseller. Meditate. Paint. Go for a walk or a run. Call up a friend or family member. Pick a movie to see tonight. Set a goal to enjoy at least one hour of free time every day. Then take advantage of the free time: put up your feet, relax, and enjoy every minute!

I REMEMBER THAT THERE'S NO ACTIVITY IN FREE TIME.

JULY 13

"So here we are, in what many are calling a 'belated' time....Much of the time, it is true, we still talk about how we can make sure that we will grow older and older. More often we talk about how bad it feels to grow old. And sometimes—not often enough in my view—we talk about what we can do to make aging not just endurable but a form of life worthy of celebration."

— writer Wayne Booth

CELEBRATING THE JOY OF LIFE

When was the last time you felt truly joyful? Joy is most often a wonderful surprise—totally unexpected, and yet never undesired. You may spend most of your life struggling to achieve some level of happiness and think that when you're happy, you're also joyful. However, happiness and joy are two different emotions. Happiness is an outcome, a by-product, from effort that you've exerted to achieve a goal, to realize a dream, to fulfill a desire. Happiness springs from things—a job promotion, a vacation, a kiss, walking with your dog, getting out of financial debt, eating a delicious meal, spending time with a friend.

But joy is a gift that's given to you even when it's not your birthday, a holiday, or an anniversary. Joy happens simply because joy *is*. Joy is spontaneous. Joy is playful. Joy is lighthearted. Joy is lively. Joy is one with the moment, one with life.

Life teaches you to welcome joy when it comes to you, but not to desire joy as a goal or as an expected outcome for things that are sought after, worked hard for, or struggled over. You can't just say, "Today I'll be more joyful," and expect that joy will suddenly appear. But what you can do from now on is to celebrate and embrace the good in life as much as you can, in the hopes of discovering the joy of life.

JOY OF LIFE COMES FROM ENJOYING MY LIFE.

JULY 14

"The middle-aged, who have lived through their strongest emotions, but are yet in the time when memory is still half passionate and not merely contemplative, should surely be a sort of natural priesthood, whom life has disciplined and consecrated to be the refuge and rescue of early stumblers and victims of self-despair.

— writer George Eliot

SUPPORTING YOUTH

During the Great Depression of the 1930s, everyone was in the same boat and knew that their fellow human beings were suffering equally. Due to this common bond, people as a whole were able to pull together in ways that aided themselves as well as their country. Families who may have been living apart moved in together under the same roof. Grandmothers and mothers baked goods for sale and stitched clothing, grandfathers and fathers labored at odd jobs, and young children sold newspapers and apples on street corners. Because the members of all generations worked together, households survived.

Today, times can be pretty tough for those in the younger generation. The present-day disparity between the "haves" and the "have-nots," the pressures and stresses brought about by competitiveness, the disconnections at home due to the need for both parents to work, and many other factors, may make youngsters, teenagers, and young adults feel lost, insecure, and fearful of their futures.

In many ways, you've certainly "been there." While you may not always be able to identify with the circumstances being experienced by young people, you can usually identify with their feelings. Be willing to reach out to someone younger so you can offer your guidance and experience to help them through a tough or confusing time.

I SEEK TO BECOME A "BIG SISTER" OR "BIG BROTHER"
TO A YOUNGER PERSON.

JULY 15

*"I asked myself the question, 'What do you want of your life?' and
I realized with a start of recognition and terror, 'Exactly what I
have—but to be commensurate, to handle it all better.'"*

— poet/diarist May Sarton

HANDLING LIFE BETTER

Author, publisher, and metaphysical lecturer and teacher Louise
Hay recommends that you imagine that your thoughts are like
drops of water. As you repeat thoughts over and over to yourself on
a daily basis, you may first notice a small stain on the carpet on
which you're standing. Later on, you may notice a much larger
stain. A short time later, you may that find you're in the middle of
a small puddle, then a pond, and—as your "thought-drops" continue—that you're in a lake and then in an ocean. The question she
asks you is: "What kind of ocean are you creating with your
thoughts? Is it one that is polluted and toxic, or one that invites you
to enjoy its refreshing waters?"

For so many years, you may have handled your experiences in
life in ways that may not have always benefited you. For example,
you may have responded to even the gentlest and most helpful
advice and criticism with defensiveness, sensitivity, overreaction,
or anger. You may have shied away from people who wanted to
develop closer friendships with you, responding to their friendly
invitations and proffered support with rebuffs and excuses. You
may have worshiped your work rather than a God and sought out
wealth rather than wisdom.

Today you have your first opportunity to start to handle all of
your experiences in a different, more positive way—to enjoy your
life, appreciate the good things, and to reconnect with yourself.

I CHOOSE TO RESPOND POSITIVELY TO LIFE.

JULY 16

"I don't want to get around it. I want to live it. I don't want to 'treat' it or 'cure' it, though I do want to honor it with curiosity and with therapy...attention of the kind one devotes to sacred mysteries. I want menopause to be a soul event, which means letting it be transformative."

— writer Christine Downing

A WONDERFUL, TRANSFORMING EXPERIENCE

The common folk expression "change of life" has been used for years to describe the transitional time in a woman's life when she passes from her reproductive into her postreproductive years. Often the butt of jokes as well as the bane of a woman's existence, menopause has, for the most part, been portrayed in negative ways. So, rather than look forward to this period of life, most women dread the onset of menopause and its signs—hot flashes, irritability, vaginal dryness, hormonal imbalances, and so on.

Yet menopause can also be a wonderful experience—one that can be welcomed rather than dreaded. Women can become more self-confident and assertive at this time. They can experience the freedom from the monthly onslaught of premenstrual syndrome, bleeding, and juggling schedules or limiting activities to accommodate cramping or heavy flows. They can show less interest in pleasing others and more in pleasing and taking care of themselves. And they can go through a profound emotional and spiritual transformation.

One 42-year-old woman had this to say about her experience with menopause: "[The menopause] is a rebirth of sorts, an incredible opportunity to rediscover who I am as a human being. The truth is that I have a very long life ahead, and now I can choose how I am going to experience it and what I am going to do."

❧   ❧   ❧

I WELCOME MY CHANGE OF LIFE.

JULY 17

"One of the many things nobody ever tells you about middle age is that it's such a nice change from being young."
— writer Dorothy Canfield Fisher

NEW PERSPECTIVES

In her book *The Tao of Inner Peace,* Diane Dreher tells the story of a Midwestern farm boy who was the only one in his family to go to college. Al felt privileged to be accepted to a state university, even though most of his friends went off to colleges and universities in other states. After years of hard work, Al then earned a graduate fellowship, this time to a fancy Eastern school. There, Al often felt embarrassed when his classmates asked if he had read this or that lofty-sounding book; he often felt way out of his league going to school in a big city and trying to converse with classmates who sounded so intellectual and knowledgeable. So, he would remain quiet as his classmates discussed theories and authors he didn't know. But then, one day, he decided to tell the truth. "No, I haven't read that book," he responded when asked. "Could you tell me more about it?"

Thinking back on your youth, do you remember times when you felt embarrassment, shame, or guilt about something you didn't know that others did know, about something you didn't own that others had, about an interest that was different from that of your peers, about a religious belief that you held that was in the minority, or about any number of other things?

Writer W. Somerset Maugham once penned, "It wasn't until late in life that I discovered how easy it is to say, 'I don't know.'" You, too, may notice how freeing it is to recognize that the areas of ignorance, differences, and contrasts that once caused you difficulty are now valued components of your individuality.

I MUCH PREFER THE FREEDOM AND HONESTY
INHERENT IN MATURITY.

JULY 18

"You can only perceive real beauty in a person as they get older."
— actress Anouk Aimée

VALUABLE BEAUTY

If you've used beauty in the past to get you something—a job or a partner, for instance—or have considered beauty to be that which can be seen rather than that which can be felt, then you're always going to be indebted to beauty. You're always going to be chasing it, you're always going to be worrying whether or not you have it, you're always going to be demanding it, and you're always going to be looking in the mirror to see if it's still there.

But what is beauty, really? Is it the exquisite rose that grows in fertile, watered soil—the rose that always wins the prize? Or is it the wildflower that pushes its way through a crack in the concrete and rises above a sidewalk littered with glass and cigarette butts, to be plucked by a child and placed in a paper cup with water to greet a hard-working parent?

Maturity teaches you that while beauty on the outside can be eye-catching and attractive, what really matters is the beauty on the inside. Not many people take the time to notice how beautiful a person's mind is or how beautiful the words and actions of another can be. There's beauty in tenderness and thoughtfulness. There's beauty in love. There's beauty in being able to hold an intelligent and lively conversation.

Society tells people as they get older, "Because you're no longer gorgeous—because you have wrinkles and your hair is gray and your muscles sag—you're no longer valuable." But you know you're valuable because you know you're beautiful. You're a whole person, and a beautiful person.

I LOOK OLDER, AND THAT MAKES ME BEAUTIFUL.

JULY 19

"Softride of Bellingham, Wash., unveiled its PowerWing MTB mountain bike frame this month. It uses the company's unique carbon-fiber, shock-absorbing leveraged seat beam that turns bumps into butter.

"Softride's target: over-50 riders with back problems."

— writer Sal Ruibal

THE BOOMER'S LATEST CYCLE

The number of mountain bikers is soaring, especially among baby boomers. Growth in the 1990s has risen to nearly two million riders between the ages of 35 and 55. For many mountain bikers, age is irrelevant; rather, what's more important is that mountain biking is a nonimpact sport that can provide any kind of stress relief you'd like—from a fast-paced, hill-climbing, downhill soaring slalom ride to a quiet, solitary ride on a gently winding bike trail or on a logging road cut through a thick, lush forest.

Mountain biking got its start in 1971, when a gang of 20-something California speed seekers began racing thick-framed clunker bikes down Marin County's Mount Tamalpais. Cross-country mountain bike racing was a medal sport at the 1996 summer Olympic games; in just 25 years, mountain biking has become the fastest rising sport in modern Olympics history.

Today's mountain bikes are built with lightweight materials, but offer the full suspension of shock absorbers on the front and rear wheels to smooth out bumps and give more traction going up hills, making the sport easier for older riders. The fact that car manufacturers that cater to an older market—Volvo and Volkswagen, for instance—are offering car packages that include a high-quality mountain bike and rack shows the impact that boomers have made upon mountain biking.

❀　　❀　　❀

I AM AN ENTHUSIASTIC BIKER OR A
RECREATIONAL RIDER.

JULY 20

"We turn not older with years, but newer every day."
— poet Emily Dickinson

WHAT'S NEW?

Nature is always able to transform itself; it does so by constantly renewing itself with vigor and fresh life. In the spring, this is most evident, with robins returning from their winter homes and chirping from sunup to sundown; with the popping and cracking sound of ice melting on rivers and the gurgling of cold streams rushing down mountainsides; with the green blades of flowers and grasses heaving clumps of earth out of their way. Summer yields a steady and energetic growth, and autumn reveals a freshness in crisp brilliance that belies the oncoming stillness of winter.

Yet even in winter there's new growth; prolonged periods of cold temperatures and dormancy are necessary for trees to blossom and bear fruit, for roots to push deep into the ground to support lush new green life, and for animals to conserve their energy in order to mate and give birth. The endless cycles of nature develop thousands of living things year after year, gradually bring them into decline, and then bring about new life.

So, too, it can be with you. Each minute you age represents a passage of time as well as a fresh advance of the clock. There's something new in store for you, something waiting right around the corner. It's knowing that there's such newness, and being ready to explore it that keeps you young in your heart as well as your mind. As writer Elizabeth Janeway once noted, "I have a problem about being nearly 60: I keep waking up in the morning and thinking I'm 31."

❄️ ❄️ ❄️

THERE'S GOING TO BE SOMETHING NEW TO
LOOK FORWARD TO TODAY.

JULY 21

"The book of nature is like a page written over or printed upon with different-sized characters and in many different languages, interlined and crosslined, and with a great variety of notes and references. There is coarse print and fine print; there are obscure signs and hieroglyphics....It is a book which he reads best who goes most slowly or even tarries long by the way."
— writer/naturalist John Burroughs

ABOUT JOHN BURROUGHS

The richness of nature was well understood by John Burroughs, preeminent naturalist of the mid-Hudson River and Catskill regions of New York, who lived from 1837 to 1921. A teacher for a short time, as well as a government employee, he spent most of his life working—in his own words—as a "nature essayist." The 27 volumes of Burrough's work that provide a lasting legacy today were the product of a writing career that spanned half a century.

Although Burroughs camped in Yosemite with Scottish-born American naturalist John Muir and in Yellowstone with Theodore Roosevelt, and also traveled with Muir to the Grand Canyon and Alaska, Burroughs was less interested in the intensities of such wild, rough locales. Instead, he felt more in tune and in touch with intimate, calm, and more personal natural places. It was in those places, he felt, that nature was more easily understood and far more accessible. "One has only to sit in the woods or fields," Burroughs wrote, "or by the shore of a river or lake, and nearly everything of interest will come round to him, the birds, the animals, the insects."

Today, sit in nature for a short time—in the woods, in the fields, or even on a city park bench. Then wait and watch the nature that comes around to you.

I FIND NATURE IN AN INTIMATE, PERSONAL LOCALE.

JULY 22

"There on the flat stone, on which we so often have sat to weep and pray, we look down, and see it covered with the fossil footprints of great birds and the beautiful skeleton of a fish. We have so often tried to picture in our mind what the fossilized remains of creatures must be like, and all the while we sat on them. We have been so blinded by thinking and feeling that we have never seen the world."

— writer/feminist Olive Schreiner

OPENING YOUR SENSES

Imagine that you travel to a remote jungle village. The locals gather around you, peering at you and touching you, for they've never seen anything like you. They're curious, too, about what's in your backpack. One native pulls out your radio. You turn the radio on. Music suddenly blasts from the speaker, startling the natives, who turn the radio in every direction to find the musicians. In sign language, you explain to them that the music comes from the air, through radio waves.

Later that day, the natives guide you through the jungle to their village. Along the way, they sign for you to look at a snake. You stop and look, but can't see it. Then a native grabs you from behind and pushes you off the path, saving you from falling into a concealed trap. Before you reach the village, the natives cup their hands around their ears and nod to one another, but you hear nothing.

Everyone has limited detection abilities, limited awareness, limited sensitivities. Sometimes such limitations are good, as when you can block out the jarring sounds of a jackhammer. But other times such limitations deprive you of unique experiences, interesting sightings, curious sounds, or sometimes even the most obvious things around you. Today, strive to open all of your senses so you can truly see the world in which you live.

I EXPERIENCE THE WORLD IN A WAY I NEVER HAVE BEFORE.

"It seems to me nowadays that the most important task for some-one who is aging is to spread love and warmth wherever possible."
— sculptor Käthe Kollwitz

A LITTLE TENDERNESS GOES A LONG WAY

To be kind and loving to others every day as you go through the ups and downs of aging can sometimes be difficult. When you're tired or your body is twisted in pain, when you've just learned that you have a medical problem that will require lengthy treatment, when you've been forced into an early retirement and now must struggle to find new work, when you see your health or the health of your partner deteriorating, when you're unhappy, or when a cherished relationship has been broken, the last thing in the world you may want to do is be nice to someone close to you. In your anger, frustration, pain, or misery, you may knowingly or unknowingly lash out at this loved one.

"Is there any stab as deep as wondering where and how much you failed those you love?" asks writer Florida Scott Maxwell. Treating your loved ones as you would hope to be treated by them—no matter what the circumstances—is your best assurance against failing them. When you can look beyond your infirmities, fears, anxieties, and stresses to the love you truly feel inside, then you can exhibit the right behavior, provide thoughtful and calm responses, and assume a respectful and tender posture.

Scottish author and preacher George Matteson, who was blind, often expressed this prayer: "I have thanked Thee a thousand times for my roses [and]...for my 'thorn'....Show me that my tears have made my rainbow." Be mindful that you're sharing your experiences in this life with others you care about.

I TREAT THOSE I LOVE LOVINGLY.

JULY 24

"Statistically, the probability of any one of us being here is so small that you'd think the mere fact of existing would keep us all in a contented dazzlement of surprise."

— biologist/writer Lewis Thomas

THE WORLD OF WONDER

When Orson Welles relayed his famous broadcast, *The War of the Worlds*, he could never have imagined that his listeners would have believed that an invasion by Martians was imminent. But the planet that is over 40 million miles from Earth had already been brought into bedrooms and living rooms with the creation of the telescope. Even though the American space program was decades away, the possibility of space flight and Hollywood's conception of spaceships had already been instilled in the imaginations of many. So all Orson Welles did was what H.G. Wells had done when he first wrote his story, *The War of the Worlds*. He used his imagination to create surprise and wonder.

Imagination is the unending ability to wonder—to be continually astonished by the world around you. For many, this sense of wonder may have ended in childhood at about the same time learning focused on the memorization of facts such as the year Christopher Columbus set sail, the capital of North Dakota, and the number of acres in a square mile. But this sense of wonder—this ability to appreciate the world around you, to treat it with awe and curiosity, to approach new things willingly and with a sense of innocence—can be restored at any age.

Begin today to look at your life, your environment, and the universe as if for the first time, without preconceptions, without searching for quick answers, and with a willingness to discover as much as you can from what you see. Exercise your imagination in this way every day, and you'll be endlessly dazzled by your world.

THE WORLD IN WHICH I LIVE NEVER CEASES TO AMAZE ME.

JULY 25

"The life...that she had complained against, had murmured at, had raged at and defied—none the less she had loved it so, joyed in it so, both in good days and evil, that not one day had there been when 'twould not have seemed hard to give it back to God, nor one grief that she could have forgone without regret."

— writer Sigrid Undset

DIVINE GUIDANCE

Have you ever marveled at how fate has drawn you to different people and certain situations? Maybe you met the person of your dreams by a chance encounter or an interesting turn of events. Perhaps you stopped at a store you've never been in before and discovered a childhood friend working there. Maybe you just happened to meet up with someone who had valuable information to share that you had been looking for. Or perhaps a great retirement opportunity came your way while golfing with strangers.

There's a lesson to be learned from each person you meet and each chance encounter you have. Your contact, however brief, happens for a reason. As writer Ruth P. Freedman has commented, "There is a divine plan of good at work in my life. I will let go and let it unfold." Although not all the lessons you'll learn will be easy or all the contacts you make feel wonderful—some people may treat you badly, and some enticing opportunities may not work out—all will have given you a valuable lesson.

Trust that your life is being guided not only by the decisions you make, but also from the input of a divine source. Rather than marvel at chance meetings and amazing connections with people, accept them as fulfilling a useful purpose. Every lesson you learn is meaningful.

I TRUST THAT THERE'S A DIVINE PLAN IN MY LIFE.

July 26

*"We come into this world crying while all around us are smiling.
May we so live that we go out of this world while everyone
around us is weeping."*

— Persian proverb

THE BITTER WITH THE SWEET

At the end of Dostoevsky's *The Brothers Karamozov*, a young man dies. After the funeral, his friend Alyosha reminds those who are gathered to mourn the loss through the custom of eating pancakes. The purpose is to mix the sweetness of life with the bitterness of death.

When you can only see death as a terrible loss or a devastating upset, it will continually cause you pain. When death only leaves you with sorrow—with no memory of the joys, the laughter, and the pleasures—you'll never be able to experience a little sweetness with the bitterness. In either case, it will be hard for you to accept how much death is part of life.

The process of living includes many dimensions. Some are joyful. Some are not. Yet if you can allow yourself to experience some lighter moments in ceremonies such as funerals or remembrances of anniversaries of losses, such events can become a celebration of a life lived rather than just a mourning of a life lost.

Death can be a homecoming for anyone you've known in your life—a homecoming that's mixed with considerable joy as well as deep sadness. But rather than let death forever sadden you, remember to sweeten it from time to time with memories of the special times you shared with someone. Death, when it approaches, ought not to take you by surprise, but should be part of your full experience of life.

I WELCOME DEATH WITH A TEAR AS WELL AS A SMILE.

JULY 27

*"If you'd known when you were younger what you know now,
you would have made different mistakes."*

— writer/runner Joe Henderson

PROVERBS TO LIVE BY

Inspirational words can sometimes find their way into your life at just the moment you need them, providing you with the right focus you need to solve a problem, the right words you need to ease your discomfort or pain, the right wisdom to make you think, or the right lightheartedness to make you smile.

Here are some proverbs that may have a place in your life today:

- When an old man dies, a library burns down. (African proverb)
- It is easier to snatch a pearl from the jaws of a crocodile, or to twist an angry serpent 'round one's head, like a garland of flowers, without incurring danger, than to make an ignorant and obstinate person change his ideas. (Hindu proverb)
- Old age is not as honorable as death, but most people want it. (Crow proverb)
- Guard your tongue in youth, and in age you may mature a thought that will be of service to your people. (Sioux proverb)
- If you continually give, you will continually have. (Chinese proverb)
- Love makes time pass away, and time makes love pass away. (French proverb)
- The old days will never be again, even as a man will never again be a child. (Dakota proverb)
- Cherish youth, but trust old age. (Pueblo proverb)
- If a family has an old person in it, it possesses a jewel. (Chinese proverb)

I HONOR THE PROVERBS OF MANY GENERATIONS.

JULY 28

"When you consider something like death, after which (there being no news flash to the contrary) we may well go out like a candle flame, then it probably doesn't matter if we try too hard, are awkward sometimes, care for one another too deeply, are excessively curious about nature, are too open to experience, enjoy a nonstop expense of the senses in an effort to know life intimately and lovingly."

— poet/writer Diane Ackerman

SENSING LIFE'S SENSUALITY

Even though Helen Keller was blind, deaf, and mute, she knew what a mountain lion looked like. She could describe its color, the texture of its fur, the feel of its twitching tail, the ferocity that burned in its eyes, the sharpness of its teeth, the sound of its snarl and purr, the firmness of the pads of its feet, the sharp prick and tear its claws could inflict upon its prey. She knew all this from a mountain lion she had examined at the hands-on museum at the Perkins School for the Blind in Watertown, Massachusetts, when she was a student there.

The subtlety of nature is sometimes greater than the subtlety of the senses; Helen Keller learned this by holding out her hands to stroke the mountain lion, to turn her hands palms up to feel a sunbeam, or to cup them together to catch water gushing out from a pump. But to be able to distinguish nature's even more mysterious subtleties—the delicacies of color hidden away in the chalice of a flower; the orchestral-like movement of a sea of grass as it shifts and bends in response to the wind, its invisible conductor; the lively sound of waves rolling pebbles, grains of sand, and shells on the shore as they drone on in incessant "wavespeak" to anyone who will listen—requires you to make the transition from sensory awareness to pure sensual abandonment to the world around you.

LIFE IS A TRULY SENSUAL EXPERIENCE.

JULY 29

"Nothing so dates a man as to decry the younger generation."
— politician Adlai Stevenson

GENERATION X

Eighty million young men and women, ranging in age from 11 to 31, today make up the largest generation in American history—bigger even than the baby boomer generation. It's the most ethically, culturally, and economically diverse American generation to date. It's the only generation born since the Civil War that will unlikely match parental economic fortunes. And it's the only generation born in the 19th century to grow up being blamed for the decline of American society's greatness. Is it any wonder, then, that reporter Nancy Smith wrote in *The Washington Post,* "It's like, we don't even have a name. Yours—'Baby Boomers'—is so big we fall in its shadow."

Yet today's teenagers and young adults may appear to be in need of being overshadowed. With their garish hairstyles, screaming music with offensive lyrics, slovenly style of dress, and a defiant, in-your-face attitude—epitomized by cartoon character Bart Simpson's typical response, "I didn't do it, nobody saw me do it, you can't prove anything"—you may feel that the Puritan proverb, "Children should be seen and not heard" should be revised to "Today's children should never be seen or heard."

Yet how bad is today's generation? Are they really any different from the rebellious youth of the 1950s, with their slicked-back hair, revved-up cars, and delinquent diversions; or the young adults of the 1960s, with their drugged-out, dropped-out, spaced-out attitudes? Isn't it time you got to know more about the younger generation instead of condemning who you think they are?

I TAKE A MORE DISCERNING LOOK AT
TODAY'S YOUNGER GENERATION.

"In the past few years, I have made a thrilling discovery...that until one is over sixty, one can never really learn the secret of living. One can then begin to live, not simply with the intense part of oneself, but with one's entire being."
— writer Ellen Glasgow

A PERSONAL WELLNESS PROGRAM

Growing old well—maintaining or even improving your physical, emotional, and spiritual health—is something you have more control over in midlife and beyond than you've ever had before. That's because today you have more health choices to choose from.

While there are no magic wands or potions for good health, no fountains of youth, no products that can cure all your ills, and no vitamins or holistic remedies that can prevent all ailments, what does exist is your freedom to choose; you have the ability to change your health habits for the better and, in so doing, to improve the quality of your life.

When you strive for wellness, you end up feeling good. And when you're feeling good, you're more likely to exercise, more likely to prepare healthy foods and eat regular, well-balanced meals, more likely to shed unwanted pounds, more likely to decrease unhealthy consumption of alcohol and kick the smoking habit, and, in general, you're more likely to take better care of yourself. Such things improve your sense of well-being so that you have more energy to participate in life, to try new things, to make greater efforts, and to be more persistent. As one man explained, "At 60, I used to say to myself, 'Whatever you were supposed to do in this world, you've already done. There's nothing more.' But at 68 I discovered how to take care of myself, and a new world opened up to me."

I ESTABLISH A WELLNESS PROGRAM THAT
ENHANCES MY LIFE.

JULY 31

"We are all happier in many ways when we are old than when we were young. The young sow wild oats. The old grow sage."

— Sir Winston Churchill

HOLDING ON TO HAPPINESS

In 1987, journalist Nancy Mairs wrote an article about happiness, which she highlighted with a brief, but personally moving description of her midlife experiences. She wrote: "If anyone had told me then that by the time I was 43 I would be crippled and George would have cancer and my beloved family would have begun to die, I would have cried out, 'Oh, no! I could never stand the pain!' But if anyone had told me that, in the presence of these realities, I would find myself, without warning, pierced by joy, I would have been stunned speechless, certain that my information was either perverse or outright mad."

Do you think that you can be happy, joyful, and confident no matter what life places in your path—the traumas as well as the triumphs? While there's much tragedy in life that happens when you're young, such things appear to be quite unbearable. And yet the same things can occur to you later on in life and you, in mature adulthood, know that you can not only handle them, but handle them well.

Age has taught you a very valuable lesson: knowing the extent to which you can be content has little to do with what happens to you. Rather, happiness depends more upon your ability to find pleasure in life—in spite of what happens to you—and to hold on to that happiness.

I ADJUST TO ALL CIRCUMSTANCES IN MY LIFE IN WAYS
THAT CONTRIBUTE TO MY HAPPINESS.

AUGUST 1

EXERCISING NATURAL CONTROL

Just one generation ago, most people bought food in bulk at local stores. You probably remember being in your mother's or grandmother's kitchen and seeing, on the countertop, canisters filled with sugar, tea, rice, flour, coffee, and other dry goods that were purchased in reusable cotton bags. But today you live in a "paper-or-plastic?" world; you live in a wasteful society that thinks nothing of destroying thousands of trees to read a single edition of a Sunday newspaper.

Can you learn to exercise natural control in your life—to learn how not to waste things in your home or business? Can you start to have an impact on controlling the amount of new construction that's being done in your neighborhood or the city or town in which you live by showing your opposition to the continued destruction of natural areas? Can you visit museums, local zoos, and nearby aquariums and observe the treatment of animals that are being held in captivity to ensure that there's no abuse? Can you purchase less plastic and fewer packaged materials and buy in larger quantities or in bulk? Can you exert more control in your life by becoming aware of how much you crave and by starting to limit such excesses? Can you do all these things—and more? Your fate, and that of future generations, depends upon it.

I PRESERVE MY WORLD AND THE WORLD OF OTHERS.

AUGUST 2

"The great thing about getting older is that you don't lose all the other ages you've been."

— writer Madeleine L'Engle

MEMORY TRIGGERS

Did you experience something today that returned you to a time in your life that you haven't thought about for a while? The scent of a particular perfume may have reminded you of your mother. A song that played on the radio may have transported you back in time to a summer your family spent at the beach, when you fell in love for the first time. A stranger you passed on the street may have looked like your best friend from childhood—the one you learned to ride a bike with, the one you played ball with, and the one who got to sleep over your house on weekends. A picture in a photo album may have helped you to recall that special honeymoon trip you took.

One of the most wonderful benefits of getting old is realizing how certain moments of your present life—which, at the time, may seem almost insignificant—magically breathe life back into memories of past joys, laughter, friendships, loves, adventures, great times, and special occasions. Such memory triggers are pleasant reminders of all the wonderful people, places, and things you've been blessed to experience in your life. Each is like a panel on a comforting quilt that warms your heart; also, each is like a note which, when joined with many other notes, creates a moving symphony of a rich and fulfilling life. For even though those special times are over, those special people may be gone, and those special feelings can never be reexperienced, the fact that they existed and you can remember them makes them forever young, forever alive, and forever lasting in your mind.

I TREASURE THE WAY LIFE IS NOW—AND THEN.

AUGUST 3

*"It is one of the deadliest and heaviest feelings of my life to feel
that I was no longer a boy. From that moment I began to grow old
in my own esteem—and in my esteem age is not estimable."*

— poet Lord Byron

EXPLORING TIMELESSNESS

Being able to live a life that's not bounded by time can be extremely vital to your overall well-being when you age. For, when you're not held captive by time, you don't have a sense of what you can and can't do; with time boundaries, there's no escape from the physical and emotional decay that time inevitably brings.

To prove this, choose a time of day when you can feel unpressured and relaxed. Sit quietly in a comfortable chair. Take off your watch, but place it or a clock nearby so you can easily look at the timepiece without having to move your head very much. Now close your eyes and take slow, deep breaths. Concentrate only on your breathing, on the steady stream of air flowing gently in and out of your body. Do this for a few minutes, until you feel your muscles relax.

When your mind and body feel stilled, slowly open your eyes and concentrate on the second hand on your watch or clock. Depending on how relaxed you are, it may seem at first as if the hand isn't moving. Or the hand may seem to hesitate in its movement or even appear to be moving much slower than it would if you were to glance at it during the normal course of events in the day.

What does this mean? It means that when your mind is filled with restless thoughts, time seems to be fleeting—positively fleeing—into some distant, future space. But when your mind is relaxed and you're "one with the moment," time, in reality, moves quite slowly. This experience can ease your fears about moving away from your youth and instead teach you that life can be full and rich at any age.

ฟ๎   ฟ๎   ฟ๎

I MAKE LIVING IN EACH MOMENT MY PRIMARY FOCUS.

AUGUST 4

"Our notion of success is being able to purchase what you need and not be obligated to anyone. Yet in other cultures, people have always accepted leaning on each other as part of life."
— psychiatrists/writers Jacqueline Olds and Richard Schwartz; journalist Harriet Webster

LIVE-LONGER FRIENDSHIPS

In their book *Overcoming Loneliness in Everyday Life,* authors Olds, Schwartz, and Webster describe loneliness not just as a painful experience, but as a major public health problem. Also, it's a problem that is more commonly felt today by older people rather than younger individuals because the former are more likely to live alone. In fact, the percent of one-person households has dramatically increased since the 1950s, when only 10 percent of households consisted of just one person; by the mid-1990s, the number had soared to 24 percent.

What this means is that while the ability to spend time alone happily is one of the great joys of life and a hallmark of a mature personality, having meaningful social ties can increase your health and longevity. Studies have shown that people who are isolated but healthy are twice as likely to die over a period of a decade or so as healthy people who are not isolated. People who live alone and have heart disease have a poorer chance of survival and more risks following a heart attack than those who have lots of friends. And women with advanced breast cancer who join a support group live twice as long as those who don't.

So, for your health and well-being, remain socially active throughout your life. If you find yourself widowed, divorced, or similarly alone, strive to establish contact with others. Reestablish ties with old friends or seek out new friendships.

❊   ❊   ❊

I SEEK FRIENDS FOR COMPANIONSHIP AND
HEALTH REASONS.

AUGUST 5

"For is it not possible that middle age can be looked upon as a period of second flowering, second growth, even a kind of second adolescence? It is true that society in general does not help one accept this interpretation of the second half of life."

— writer Anne Morrow Lindbergh

EXERCISING YOUR LIFE CYCLES

Until recently, the charting of how life was supposed to be lived was structured and predictable. In a world where most people didn't often expect to live longer than six decades, it was essential that key personal and social tasks be accomplished by specific ages. Traditionally, schooling and job preparation, courtship and marriage, childrearing and home ownership, and retirement were assigned to particular periods of life and were supposed to occur only once in a lifetime. So if you were a 30-year-old unmarried woman, for instance, you were thought to be a spinster because your window of opportunity for parenthood had long since passed; if you were a 20-year-old man who didn't know what he wanted to do for the rest of your life, you were considered a ne'er-do-well.

Yet today you can be a grandparent without even being a parent. You can be a freshman in college when you're over 60. You can stay in such good physical shape that you can wear a skimpy bathing suit to the beach when you're 50. You can be retired before your hair is gray and have enough money saved to last the rest of your life.

Today you're living a cyclical life plan rather than a linear one. Life experiences have no age restrictions; age no longer dictates periods of emotional, physical, or even fiscal growth. Education, work, parenthood, sex, recreation, and a variety of other life activities can blend into and influence one another at any age.

I ENJOY THE FREEDOM OF A CYCLICAL LIFE PLAN.

August 6

"These are the worst years, I tell you. It's gonna happen to you. I-I'm afraid to look inna mirror. I'm afraid I'm going to see an old lady with white hair, just like the old ladies inna park—little bundles in a black shawl waiting for the coffin....Am I an old dog to lay near the fire till my eyes close? These are terrible years...!"

— from the film *Marty*

ENJOYING INDIVIDUALITY

Do you feel, at your age, vital to life itself? Traditional cultures often hold their elders in high regard, seeing them as store-houses of wisdom to be transmitted to the next generation. The Pueblo Indians, in fact, believed that their elders' rituals helped the sun to rise each morning.

Western civilization, however, isn't as kind and respectful of its older citizens. American society teaches its children to look at an older person and say, "I hope I'm never like you," rather than, "I want to be just like you." Such a degrading attitude is one that's founded on fear—fear of the passage of time. This fear can be so blinding that it doesn't show a person, but rather an age, doesn't acknowledge a personality, but reveals peculiarities, hides pride due to prejudice.

Yet, you're an individual—one who has different gifts to offer that are enhanced by your own unique experiences and heritage. You fill a place that no other person can fill. Imagine how dull life would be if there was only one variety of tree, if everything had one drab color, or the landscape was totally flat. Forests are filled with young saplings as well as towering trees that have lived for cen-turies, and each benefits the other. It's your personal responsibility to develop and maintain your own self-respect, to grow in your own part of the forest, and to add your own particular color to life—no matter what others think or how they treat you.

I PRAISE THE GOD THAT HAS MADE ME AND
HAS MADE US ALL.

AUGUST 7

"One of the misfortunes of advancing age is that you get out of touch with the sunrise. You take it for granted, and it is over and done with before you settle yourself for the daily routine. That is one reason, I think, why, when we grow older, the days seem shorter. We miss the high mountains of their beginning."

— statesman/writer John Buchan

FOCUSING ON THE WORLD AROUND YOU

There's a Chinese parable in which a wise man talks about moving a mountain in his village, and he explains that it will be accomplished over generations. Rather than cry out, "We've got to get this project finished!" those workers who chose to participate in moving the mountain did so with a smile on their faces. They chose to live in the present moment and focused on the task of moving the mountain, bit by bit. In performing the task, time meant nothing to them, nor did completing the actual goal of moving the mountain. Rather, it was the task itself, and the ability to focus on that task, that became most important to them.

This lesson of focus is echoed by writer Robert Pirsig, who writes about the challenge of mountain climbing: "Mountains should be climbed with as little effort as possible, and without desire. The reality of your own nature should determine the speed. If you become restless, speed up. If you become winded, slow down."

The mad rush of living—the crush of places to go, people to see, and things to do—and the beepers and alarms and billboards that determine the direction your life takes can put you out of touch with the things that really matter—a hug from a loved one, the wet warmth of your dog's tongue upon your face, a walk through the woods on a summer's evening, the scent of wild herbs, the flight of a hummingbird, or the simple beauty of a sunrise.

I TAKE TIME TO FOCUS TODAY ON THE SIMPLE PLEASURES.

AUGUST 8

"I do not intend to pause, or rest, or rust. I will survive."
— marathoner/writer Dr. George Sheehan

AGE OF OPPORTUNITY

Sometimes it's tough to be a master's runner—you're one of those men or women who rarely, if ever, gets to break the tape at the finish line of a race and who always feels as if you're slogging through a vat of molasses while being passed by those who seem to be gliding on ice.

In fact, you may find it tough at your age to be active in any event or athletic endeavor. Even though you may be out there training and exercising every day just like the younger runners and athletes, you may need more recovery days, may feel less flexible than you did were when you were younger, and may be carrying around a bit more weight—even an annoying few pounds that seem to be impossible to take off—than you once did.

Yet there is one area where an "old-time" runner or athlete has an edge over those who are younger. During extended layoffs, masters' athletes rather than younger athletes maintain their fitness for much longer. Recent studies have revealed that a young athlete who stops training can start slipping in fitness in from as little as one to three weeks, while someone over 50 may not see a difference in fitness until as long as 12 weeks. Additionally, older athletes continued to feel fine during their layoffs and slept just as well as when they were active; such benefits weren't experienced by the younger athletes.

"Nobody's saying lungs of 50 work the same as lungs of 25," says Dr. John Bland, a competitive cross-country skier in the 75 to 79 age group. "What we are saying is that your fitness seems to grow less fragile as you get older."

I KEEP FINE-TUNING MY BODY.

AUGUST 9

*"The really frightening thing about middle age is the knowledge
that you'll grow out of it."*
— actress/humanitarian Doris Day

THE DIFFERENCES OF OLDER BODIES

Try as you might to ignore it, there's no getting around the fact that you're going to experience natural declines in your physical functioning as you get older. Here are just a few of things you can expect:

- A decline of about two percent per decade in the speed at which nerve impulses are transmitted. This means that you'll gradually have slower reaction time to various stimuli and find that your performance of certain tasks that require a combination of functions involving transmission of nerve impulses—driving a car, for example, or using a computer—will be slower.

- Your kinesthetic sense—or your awareness of your body's position and location in space—will decline with age. This means that you may experience some unsteadiness and become increasingly susceptible to slips and falls.

- It will become harder for you to discriminate among the four basic taste sensations—sweet, bitter, sour, and salty—because your taste buds will decrease. Food simply won't taste the way it used to.

- You'll have diminished circulation, making it more difficult to keep warm; sweaters and extra blankets will become a must.

- You'll have increasing stiffness and loss of dexterity in your fingers.

While the physical changes of aging that you'll experience can be annoying, accepting them is the first step in becoming willing to redesign your environment and lifestyle in order to cope with them.

I ACCEPT THE CHANGES IN MY OLDER BODY.

AUGUST 10

*"You don't get to choose how you're going to die. Or when.
You can only decide how you're going to live. Now."*

— singer Joan Baez

DEATH AS PART OF LIFE

Do you think you're "ready" for death? You might be in the sense that you've made all the necessary arrangements to help those who'll handle your affairs when you're gone. But one of the most important developmental tasks in the second half of your life is coming to a personal understanding—even an acceptance—of your death. Rather than feeling ambivalent about death or frightened to even acknowledge it, you can prepare yourself for death in a variety of ways. Here are some ways older people have come to terms with their own deaths:

- "I feel a greater awareness of mystery and beauty in life since I have accepted death as a personal eventuality for me." (78 years old)
- "I believe that I am not just a body that is perishable, but I am a spirit which is eternal. I believe that death is only an exit from this temporary life of unreality into a glorious new life of reality." (92 years old)
- "I do not look to the future with dread. It has to be shorter than my past, but it does not have to be less rich. I'm more relaxed. I don't try to do everything." (78 years old)
- "Death, I am learning through my own experience, need not be frightening. After all, we are all born terminal cases, because we will all die, at one time or another....I have lived life fully and enjoyed it greatly, which makes it easier to consider bowing out than if you feel that you have missed out on a lot." (78 years old)

I APPRECIATE HOW LIFE IS BALANCED WITH DEATH.

AUGUST 11

"When I was young I was amazed at Plutarch's statement that the elder Cato began at the age of eighty to learn Greek. I am amazed no longer. Old age is ready to undertake tasks that youth shirked because they would take too long."

— writer W. Somerset Maugham

MAGGIE KUHN, GRAY PANTHER

When she was 65 years old, the national office of the United Presbyterian Church forcibly retired Maggie Kuhn. But rather than accept that, by society's standards, she had become a "senior citizen" who was at the end of her career, Kuhn and five of her friends who had also been booted out of the work force formed a radical group designed to challenge society's ageist ways.

Initially, the group—Consultation of Older and Younger Adults—issued a call to action to both young and old to join forces to work for a better world for all, regardless of age. But a New York television news reporter who admired the group's radical pride, which he likened to the Black Panthers, dubbed them the "Gray Panthers."

Maggie Kuhn, with her white hair and arthritic fingers, provided a voice for justice for the "elders of the tribe," her name for older people. Her social and political involvement contributed greatly to a better future for herself as well as for others. As she once so eloquently remarked: "In this age of self-determination and liberation, many groups are struggling for freedom. All these struggles are linked in the worldwide struggle for a new humanity....Old people have a large stake in this new community—in helping to create it and extend it. The winds of change are impellling and empowering. They can free us or destroy us."

I BRING A LIFETIME'S WORTH OF EXPERIENCE
INTO MY FUTURE.

AUGUST 12

"Every time I think that I'm getting old, and gradually going to the grave, something else happens."
— civil rights worker/peace activist Lillian Carter

TRAVELING NEW ROADS

Think for a moment about a nearby city. Now, picture the many roads that lead to that city. One may be a winding, tree-lined country road. Another may be an efficient eight-lane highway. And still another may be rutted and filled with potholes.

No matter which road is taken, it will lead to the same destination as the others. But what will be different is the experience of the journey, depending on which road you take and on what day you make the journey. Some days you'll make a choice that will result in a pleasant, hassle-free ride; other days you'll find yourself stuck in traffic or meandering behind a slow school bus, wondering if you'll ever reach your destination.

Now, consider that this city is your life. Every day you wake up and need to choose a road that will take you into the city. But which one will you choose? Even though the highway may seem to be the best choice, traffic tie-ups and accidents can make your journey on this road a nightmare. While the bumpy, pothole-ridden road may seem to be the least enjoyable road to take, it may end up not only being the speediest, but the one that gives you the greatest challenge.

From one day to the next, you never know what life has in store for you. There's always a new road to travel, if you're willing to try it out. For, as writer Marion Zimmer Bradley has pointed out, "It has never been, and never will be, easy work! But the road that is built in hope is more pleasant to the traveler than the road built in despair, even though they both lead to the same destination."

I TRAVEL ON A NEW ROAD OF DISCOVERY EACH DAY.

AUGUST 13

"When you are younger you get blamed for crimes you never committed and when you're older you begin to get credit for virtues you never possessed. It evens itself out."

— writer I.F. Stone

THE HABIT OF BLAME

The habit of blaming others is something you may have learned years ago, the first time one of your parents accused you of doing something you didn't do—for example, it may not have been you but another sibling who left the sprinkler on—or when an adult such as a grandparent or teacher blamed you for something that was way beyond your capabilities—that is, contributing to the decline of society. "You kids today..." may have been the opening to all blame-based statements adults hurled in your direction; you may have just shrugged your shoulders and assumed you were guilty as charged.

Today, as an adult, you're well aware of how the habit of blaming others is a sure sign of weakness; it shows an inability to take responsibility for self. The list of scapegoats people use for their life miseries is endless—parents, communities, teachers, the government—even demons and gods. But, now that you're an adult, "kids today" may be—as it was for your parents—an easy group to blame for the issues and problems in society.

Each person lives on this planet with the desire to simply develop a pure sense of self—a special self inside—so they can look at shortcomings and strive to take steps to eliminate them. Each person desires to rise above blame and build upon self-esteem rather than feel as if they have to defend or protect who they are. No one generation is worse than another; each can be praised in some way.

I BREAK THE HABIT OF BLAMING OTHERS.

AUGUST 14

"Women over fifty already form one of the largest groups in the population structure of the western world. As long as they like themselves, they will not be an oppressed minority. In order to like themselves they must reject trivialization by others of who and what they are. A grown woman should not have to masquerade as a girl in order to remain in the land of the living."

— feminist writer Germaine Greer

GROWING BEAUTIFUL WITH AGE

The fashion industry lives in a world of pretend. The industry pretends that there are no women in the country who are over the age of 35, there are no women who require sizes larger than 10 unless they're pregnant, there are no women with gray hair, and there are no women with wrinkles.

In reality, however, the midlife woman is the major clothes buyer today; it's estimated that a 40-year-old woman spends four times the amount of money on clothing, shoes, and other accessories that a 25-year-old woman does. Also, women's magazines that reach a midlife and older women's audience have finally pushed for advertisements that include models whom their readers can relate to. Kaylan Pickford was 44 years old when she broke into modeling; she didn't dye her gray hair or try to hide her age because, as she said, "I didn't want to look young, just beautiful." Now in her 60s, Pickford is still modeling and shares the fashion limelight in leading women's magazines with a number of top 50-plus models who not only display fashion, but who are also used in major ad campaigns for such clients as Smirnoff vodka and De Beers diamonds.

You don't have to look younger. You don't have to cover up your gray hair. You don't have to dress like you're a teenager. You can just be yourself—your older, more beautiful self!

❈　　❈　　❈

AS I GROW OLDER, I BECOME MORE ATTRACTIVE.

AUGUST 15

"...If one advances confidently in the direction of his dreams, and endeavors to live the life which he has imagined, he will meet with a success unexpected in common hours....If you have built castles in the air, your work need not be lost; that is where they should be. Now put the foundation under them."
— naturalist/writer Henry David Thoreau

THE POSSIBILITIES OF A DREAM

"Never in my wildest imagination did I ever think..." might be how you'd begin a story about a job promotion you had just received, a degree you had just earned, a dream house you had just purchased, a new love interest you had just met. There may be many other achievements in your life as well that you had once thought might never come true.

But did you ever really imagine that they'd *never* come true? More likely than not, such things had been part of your active imagination for a long time; you had probably visualized that they would happen and then not only hoped they would, but expended time and energy to ensure they could. So your wildest dreams did eventually come true, with help from your determination, your capabilities, a bit of good luck, and your imagination.

Yet as you grow older and realize that many of the dreams you wanted to accomplish by now haven't been attained, you may think you're living in a world of impossibilities rather than possibilities, a world not of "What if..." but "It won't work...." Yet dreaming is not only for the young. You have the ability at any age to refuse to place limits on your dreams. Now is the time to reclaim your ability to dream as a child would dream, to journey in your mind to a world where all things are possible. Recover a lost dream, and begin to make it happen.

❀   ❀   ❀

I BELIEVE THAT DREAMS CAN COME TRUE.

AUGUST 16

*"I would rather be ashes than dust! I would rather my sparks
should burn out in a blaze than it should be stifled by dry-rot. I
would rather be a superb meteor, every atom of me in magnificent
glow, than asleep and permanent as a planet. The proper function
of man is to live, not to exist. I shall not waste my days trying to
prolong them. I shall use my time."*

— writer Jack London

MAKING EVERY ACT COUNT

What do you wish to be doing when it becomes difficult for
you to move around without the assistance of a cane, crutch,
or wheelchair? What do you wish to be doing when you're told that
an illness or disease is going to beat you down? What do you wish
to be doing when death is breathing down your neck?

If you can think of anything better to do when you're so overtaken, then get to work on that right now. Do every act as if it were
your last. There's a story told about an old man who was thin and
frail, ravaged by an unmanageable disease. The doctor told those
who had gathered around the man's bedside, "It's pretty hopeless. It
doesn't look like he'll last through the night." So they left the man
alone for a few hours to prepare dinner, make some telephone calls,
and take a break until they would once again begin their death vigil.

But when they entered the room, they found the man sitting in
his favorite chair next to his bed, which he had made so well that
there wasn't even a wrinkle on the bedspread. The man sat hunched
over in the chair, his breathing labored and his weak arms and legs
shaking. But then he coughed and raised his head to look at his
astonished friends and family members.

"I wanted to leave this world feeling like I had accomplished
something right up until the very end," the man gasped. "And I did.
Now I can go."

I PUT MY HEART AND SOUL INTO EVEN THE SMALLEST ACTS.

AUGUST 17

RISKING IT ALL

Imagine that you've been given the chance to return to any previous time in your life and change a decision you made at that time. The only drawback is this: you must lose everything that has happened to you since that time. In effect, what you're faced with is an opportunity to risk it all—to risk losing everything you've earned and all the people you've been blessed to know in the hopes that you'll end up in a much happier, more successful life for yourself.

What would you do? If you decide to return to a pivotal point in your life and explore the road you opted not to take, then you might think that you're an incredible risk-taker—one of those "Las Vegas high rollers"—someone who is unafraid to lose it all in the hopes of winning it all. But if you don't decide to change the decision you once made, does that make you any less of a risk-taker?

Taking risks is not about loss, although often, when taking a risk, loss does occur. But the greatest risks are not those that have the greatest potential of loss; rather, sometimes the greatest risks are those in which you remain true to your beliefs and ideas, protect your security, continue to trust in yourself and your capabilities, and live without regret over the past.

Oftentimes the greatest risk is considering all the chances you could take and then having enough confidence in yourself to be able to decide whether something new and different is really what you want. The greatest risks are those that are made from freedom—freedom to choose, and to live without regret over your choice.

❀   ❀   ❀

I AM FREE TO LIVE MY LIFE IN THE WAY I
CHOOSE FOR MYSELF.

August 18

"It is often said that one has but one life to live, but that is nonsense. For one who reads, there is no limit to the number of lives that may be lived, for fiction, biography and history offer an inexhaustible number of lives in many parts of the world, in all periods of time."

— writer Louis L'Amour

THE FACE THAT YOU WEAR

Someone who is blind is unable to see a person's face when he or she is speaking. So the blind person needs to judge who the speaker is—that is, the character of that person—by the voice that's heard. When the speaker offers congratulations on some success, the blind person needs to consider whether it's a heartfelt response of shared happiness or one that's tinged with envy. When the speaker offers condolences over some failure, the blind person needs to consider whether it's a meaningful sadness or if it's colored by pleasure. When the speaker expresses happiness, the blind person needs to consider whether the voice is completely happy. When the speaker expresses sorrow, the blind person needs to consider whether sadness is all that's being heard.

Like a person's voice is to a blind person, you have many faces that you show others—faces that express a variety of emotions, faces that reflect a wealth of experiences, faces that display your traditions and heritage, faces that result from your childhood, faces that you put on to face the world. Each face is somewhat different; each is made up of different parts of your world—a world of self-discovery and history.

Sometimes you "put on" a particular face as if it were a mask, which you may use to disguise your feelings or hide your history. But to show the world the most honest face you can is an act of daring and courage.

❧   ❧   ❧

I PUT MY BEST FACE FORWARD AS I FACE THE WORLD TODAY.

AUGUST 19

"Body and mind, like man and wife, do not always agree to die together."
— writer/clergyman Charles C. Colton

REDEFINING FOREVER

Currently, older women make up the fastest growing group of single people in America. There are now five times as many widows as widowers, nearly half of the women over the age of 65 are widows, and there are well over 10 million single women over the age of 60 as opposed to about 3 million men who are in that age group. What this means is that not only are married women outlasting their husbands, but with the average life expectancy reaching well beyond the age of 65, women are faced with a variety of decisions: Will they spend their remaining years alone? Will they date one or more people? Will they settle down with one partner in a monogamous relationship? Will they remarry?

Also, "Until death do us part" is a phrase that many married couples believed would guide them into their twilight years. Yet statistics show that while there are many long-term marriages, there are also many divorces. Older couples are often more willing to honor traditional marriage values, but "younger couples"—those in midlife—are more accustomed to major life changes of all kinds, from changing majors in college; to shifting from job to job; to moving across town, across state, or even across the nation. However unsettling divorce may be, it can be viewed as a more normal, acceptable alternative to staying in an unsatisfying relationship, particularly when children have grown up and are no longer living at home.

As disturbing as death and divorce can be, they can also be liberating. Being single late in life can lead to new companions, new experiences, and new joys.

I ACCEPT THE NEW FREEDOM THAT COMES FROM BEING AN OLDER SINGLE PERSON.

AUGUST 20

"When we are young, we are slavishly employed in procuring something whereby we may live comfortably when we grow old; and when we are old, we perceive it is too late to live as we proposed."

— poet Alexander Pope

CALLING A TIME-OUT

In the heat of an intense sports competition, one of the best strategies a coach can use is to call a time-out. When the players have a chance to step away from the action and take a breather, they're given the opportunity to replenish their depleted energy, review their strategy, and renew their efforts to win.

After the "heat" of decades spent in a lifelong career, striving to advance to the top or to be the best you could be, you may need to take a time-out. That doesn't mean that you have to stop what you're doing now forever. It just means that perhaps if you give yourself a chance to take a breather, you'll be better able to assess how well you're balancing your work-related activities with your leisure-time interests. Also, you'll have a chance to decide whether you need to readjust or redirect your energy so you won't discover—too late—that you won't be able to do all those things you've always wanted to.

Perhaps you're at an age when retirement is a possibility, but you just aren't sure you'll like it. Maybe you'd like to continue to work, but would like a change from what you're doing or you just don't want to have to commute every day or put in a set number of hours each week. Or maybe you'd like to take a sabbatical so you have some time to make a decision about it all.

Midlife career changes, exits and re-entries into the job force, retraining, and early and late retirements are just some of the options you can pursue. You just need to decide what's right for *you.*

I CREATE A WORK SCHEDULE THAT ENRICHES MY LIFE.

AUGUST 21

"The great affair, the love affair with life, is to live as variously as possible, to groom one's curiosity like a high-spirited thoroughbred, climb aboard, and gallop over the thick, sun-struck hills every day. Where there is no risk, the emotional terrain is flat and unyielding, and, despite all its dimensions, valleys, pinnacles, and detours, life will seem to have none of its magnificent geography...."

— poet Diane Ackerman

THE WATERS OF LIFE

Go for a walk on a rainy day, and you'll know how brooks, creeks, and rivers are formed. The tiny rivulets you see at your feet run quickly by on their way to a newly formed stream; it takes hundreds of them to make a brook, hundreds more to create a creek, hundreds times hundreds more to flow as a river. Even the tiniest drops of rain have the power to stream down city streets, rapidly fill depressions on a road or sidewalk, surge into storm sewers, and urge leaves, sticks, and other debris along with them—all on a merry romp.

You, too, should flow as water does, running through life in a pattern of changes. But are there times when you resist such a journey? Do you live in dread over where the waters of life will take you? There's an old Chinese adage that says, "Flowing water does not decay." So when you go with the flow, you move; when you don't, you stagnate.

Get into motion! Move your mind, body, and spirit. Live! Do something new, different, exciting, and challenging. Be like Huckleberry Finn. Build your raft, and journey to wherever the river of life takes you. Don't be like the majestic ship that stays forever docked in the harbor of life—steam out into the open seas. Breathe in the salty air, watch the shore recede from view, and roll with the waves!

✿ ✿ ✿

I BUOYANTLY SAIL THROUGH LIFE.

AUGUST 22

"Knowledge and timber shouldn't be much used till they
are seasoned."
— Judge Oliver Wendell Holmes, Jr.

DEVELOPING WISDOM

Here is the path to wisdom:

First, you believe everything you're told, without being given any reasons.

Next, you believe in most things, but express some doubt about some things that you once accepted without question.

Then, you believe in nothing whatsoever.

After that, you believe in most things, but express some doubt about a few other things.

Then, you believe in everything again. Except now you know the reasons why you believe them.

Jazz musician Chick Corea offered this version of a similar path he followed to wisdom: "I searched through rebellion, drugs, diet, mysticism, religions, intellectualism, and much more, only to begin to find...that truth is basically simple—and feels good, clean, and right."

Sometimes it may seem to you that the more knowledge you acquire, the longer you live, and the more experiences you have, the less you know or the more confused you are. But that may be because you're trying to *know* all the pieces of life rather than simply trying to put them all together to create a total experience.

A tree that grows neither questions its existence nor the existence of all the trees around it; it simply grows and, in so doing, matures. So, too, should you. Recognize that knowledge isn't wisdom, but wisdom is what you know.

I STRIVE TO BECOME LIKE SEASONED WOOD.

AUGUST 23

"He is lucky who, in the full tide of life, has experienced a measure of the active environment that he most desires. In these days of upheaval and violent change, when the basic values of today are the vain and shattered dreams of tomorrow, there is much to be said for a philosophy which aims at living a full life while the opportunity offers."

— mountaineer Eric Earle Shipton

THE DANCE OF LIFE

Life is meant to be lived in motion, for all living things are in motion. Deep below the ocean's surface, for example, aquatic plant life undulates with the currents. Corals feed by waving their stinging tentacles from tubes to snare baby fish and other tiny sea animals. The constant motion also extends outward from the reef, for several kinds of fish live in or near it. Small fish flit quickly back and forth, feeding on microscopic animal and plant life. Larger fish propel themselves around, oftentimes feeding on the smaller fish. Along the coastline, in rock pools and shallows, lobsters and crabs crawl about while waves splash against the shore. Overhead gulls, terns, gannets, and other sea birds scan the shallow waters for something to eat while shore birds scamper back and forth along the sandy stretches of beach.

All this represents only a small segment of nature's bountiful, bounding activities. Yet the influence upon humanity can be profound. As American dancer Isadora Duncan once said, "I was born by the sea, and I have noticed that all the great events in my life have taken place by the sea. My first idea of movement, of the dance, certainly came from the rhythms of the waves."

Life, like nature, ought never to be still. Is there a natural motion that can so influence you, too?

I GLADLY PARTICIPATE IN THE DANCE OF LIFE.

"The middle years, caught between children and parents, free of neither: the past stretches back too densely, it is too thickly populated, the future has not yet thinned out."

— writer/critic Margaret Drabble

RESTRUCTURING CAREGIVING

Sometimes you may ask yourself, "When does the caregiving stop? When will I finally be able to just take care of myself?" It may seem that your life is a constant struggle to juggle caring for your children, who may be old enough to take a great deal of responsibility but not full responsibility for themselves; caring for your parents, who are getting on in years and becoming more and more dependent on you to help them with the things they used to be able to do; and caring for yourself, for you've reached that age in life—your midlife—where you'd like things to get easier rather than harder, decisions to become more self-focused rather than sacrificial, and plans for the future to exclude your children and your parents.

Sometimes you may feel that this kind of questioning and thinking is selfish. "After all," you may say, "I've still got my health. I've got lots more years to be productive on the job force. There will be time for me. So maybe I shouldn't be so upset about still having to devote so much time to my children and parents."

Yet it's when you are feeling good and you do have your whole life ahead of you that you'd like to be able to enjoy it more—to live it as much as you can for yourself as well as for others. The way to do this is to ask others to share in some of the caregiving or to even redistribute it within your family. For example, ask your children to help take care of their grandparents, and ask your grandparents to help take care of their grandchildren from time to time. You don't have to do everything; others are there to help you.

❄️ ❄️ ❄️

I ASK FOR HELP FROM MY CARE-RECEIVERS.

AUGUST 25

*"The big problem is that with somewhat declining vigor...
somewhat increasing deafness, and sleepiness in the afternoon,
and a less sharp eye for other people's conduct—I still have to
create or put together a body of work while there is still time."*
— writer Malcolm Cowley

ROBERT PARISH, "THE CHIEF"

You'd think, after getting banged and bruised night after night, year after year, that it would be delightful to see some sort of end in sight—a light at the end of tunnel that signals an escape from the effort of having to sweat and struggle up and down a basketball court in order to race against sets of legs that are half your age.

But the 40-plus towering giant of basketball—Robert Parish—doesn't want to see a light at the end of the tunnel that leads to the locker room. Instead, he looks forward at the end of each season to another one. His only worry, as he advances in age, is not that he can no longer do his best, but that teams won't be interested in him.

At the age of 42, the man who long ago earned the nickname "the Chief"—who is also a grandfather—played his 20th season with the NBA Charlotte Hornets. During that season, he leaped into the record books when he logged his 1,561st game, eclipsing Hall of Famer Kareem Abdul-Jabbar as the all-time leader in games played. Also, he averaged close to 8 points a game, 8 rebounds, and 27 minutes as a starter.

Parish collected three championship rings with the Boston Celtics in the 1980s; he began his career with the Golden State Warriors in 1976, when another aging player, Magic Johnson, was just a high school senior. Today Parish starts games and plays with and against rookies; he's never grown tired of the game.

I REVEL IN THE TIME I HAVE TO PURSUE
MY LIFE'S PASSION.

"Life is better than death, I believe, if only because it is less boring, and because it has fresh peaches in it."

— writer Alice Walker

VICTORY!

Author Joseph Conrad wrote a lengthy and intense novel, struggling repeatedly with the language. Because his native tongue was Polish, the task of working out precise English words and phrases in his story was very difficult for him. When he finally completed the book, he didn't write "The End." Instead, he scrawled a single word across the last page. It wasn't *finished* or *complete*. Conrad wrote the word *victory*. And that eventually became the title of his novel: *Victory!*

A Chinese proverb states, "The man who moves a mountain begins by carrying away small stones." Imagine that the mountain is life; each moment you live involves carrying away small stones so you can feel a certain level of success, or victory, each day. Some of your victories will be major achievements—you earn a degree or you move to a retirement community—while some will seem small and insignificant—you venture out of the house to the grocery store to buy fresh peaches for dessert. But no matter what their size or how much closer they bring you to moving your own mountain, each small stone is a victory. Without victory, there's no movement, there's no growth, and there's no progress.

Each victory in your life is like a birth. The aim of life is to be fully born, so you need to live every minute of your life seeking victory. Stop looking for victory, and the novel of your life will never be complete; the mountain of your life will stand steadfast. Stop looking for victory, and you'll die before you've even been born.

I LOOK FOR VICTORY IN EVERYTHING I DO.

"You're involved in the action and vaguely aware of it, but your focus is not on the commotion but on the opportunity ahead. I'd liken it to a sense of reverie—not a dreamlike state but the somehow insulated state that a great musician achieves in a great performance. He's aware of where he is and what he's doing, but his mind is on the playing of his instrument with an internal sense of rightness—it is not merely mechanical, it is not only spiritual; it is something of both, on a different plane and a more remote one."

— golf great Arnold Palmer

TAI CHI, THE MIND AND BODY STRENGTHENER

You can learn from an ordinary bamboo leaf that strength of the spirit is greater than physical strength—that softness can triumph over hardness and feebleness over power. In a snowstorm, the leaf will bend lower and lower under the weight of falling snow until it seems as if the leaf will snap. But suddenly the snow will slip to the ground without the leaf having stirred, and the leaf returns to its original position, with no damage done. What this proves is that being more flexible is always superior to being immovable; to control things, sometimes it's best to bend along with them.

So, too, it should be with the fitness program you design for yourself. The best activities are not necessarily those that strain your muscles and make you sweat; rather, some of the best and most beneficial activities are those that help you to attain total body flexibility as well as spiritual growth. Tai Chi is an example of such an exercise. Developed in ancient China, the exercise is becoming quite popular in America, particularly because of the positive effects it has on physical, emotional, and spiritual fitness. Through Tai Chi, you can develop not only flexibility and strength, but also inner awareness and concentration.

꙰   ꙰   ꙰

MY MIND AND SPIRIT ARE EVEN STRONGER
THAN MY BODY.

AUGUST 28

PARTY ON!

Aren't the best parties you've ever attended those that you're most reluctant to leave? Later on, as you drive home or get ready for bed, you may reflect on the reasons why the party was so great and you had such a good time. Was it the delicious food? The fascinating conversation? The superb wine? The festive decorations? The unexpected business contacts you made? The particular holiday or reason for the celebration? The familiar faces? The lively games you played? The new people you met? After much consideration, you may be uncertain as to why the party was so great; you just know you had a good time.

So, too, should life be that kind of excellent party—one that you never want to leave, one that makes you want to linger. Life ought to be a joyous celebration, filled with laughter and interesting conversation. Life ought to be a gathering of people that you find fascinating and whose company you enjoy. Life ought to be a festival of good things to eat and drink, with enticing pleasures of the palate that you can appreciate as well as savor. Life ought to be fun and lighthearted, to bring out childish joy and play. Life ought to be an event that leaves you with marvelous memories.

The festival of life is one that brings you closer to others in a community; it's a festival that kindles the fires of friendship, values your individuality, and affirms your sense of belonging to a group. Life's "perfect" party is one in which you gladly participate, always appreciate and enjoy, and never want to leave.

I EAT, DRINK, AND AM MERRY AT THE PARTY OF LIFE.

AUGUST 29

"My voice had a long, nonstop career. It deserves to be put to bed with quiet and dignity, not yanked out every once in a while to see if it can still do what it used to do. It can't."

— opera singer Beverly Sills

AVOIDING BURNOUT

You may be quite skilled at keeping yourself "in the fire" for just a little bit longer—in the work fire, in the child-rearing fire, in the errand-running fire, in the caretaking fire, in the moving-up-the-corporate-ladder fire. But at some point you're going to get burned up—and burned out.

What happens when the "fire alarms" in your life go off time and again and you're never allowed to take a break? Like a marshmallow that's been left too long to brown over a campfire flame, you can end up getting burned out pretty quickly. Your ability to respond quickly and effectively, putting in your best effort each time, will gradually diminish over time. Your energy will soon be depleted unless you take a break. But, most important, you're going to lose interest in what once used to bring you joy and fulfillment unless you step away for a time—either permanently or temporarily.

Think of how different you'd feel if you were able to set limits in your life that kept you from getting temporarily burned out or from feeling as if you're in a state of perpetual burnout. Imagine how you might handle things in your life if you were able to set limits rather than constantly force yourself to go beyond your limits. Imagine how restful and refreshing taking a break could be. Imagine how different you'd feel from this moment on—physically, emotionally, and spiritually—if you were able to say, "Enough!"

❧   ❧   ❧

I SET ASIDE TIME TODAY TO "COOL DOWN."

"In middle age we are apt to reach the horrifying conclusion that all sorrow, all pain, all passionate regret and loss and bitter disillusionment are self-made."
— poet/essayist Kathleen Norris

THE EEYORE ATTITUDE

Do you have the Eeyore Attitude? The Eeyore Attitude enables you to find something bad, something tragic, something hurtful, something impossible, something overwhelming, something unfair, and something wrong with every person and every thing. The Eeyore Attitude is like a garden that's sown with disgust, cultivated by complaint, enriched by pessimism, and harvested by hopelessness. The Eeyore Attitude gets in the way of things like wisdom and happiness, and pretty much prevents any sort of real accomplishment in life. The Eeyore Attitude is, by its very nature, humorless and not much fun to experience.

When the day starts for the old grey donkey Eeyore and he's greeted by a cheery good morning from his friends Pooh and Piglet, his gloomy response is always, "Good morning—if it *is* a good morning. Which I doubt." Yet Pooh and Piglet never see the world in this way. When Pooh starts his day, the first thing he wonders is what's for breakfast. When Piglet starts his day, he wonders what exciting thing is going to happen. Both Pooh and Piglet have noticeably different attitudes from Eeyore—an attitude of happy serenity. This attitude enables them to enjoy the simple things in life and to spontaneously find joy and humor in everyone and everything.

Today, think about the attitude you wish to cultivate from now on. You can be a grumpy Eeyore, or you can be a peaceful Pooh or Piglet. Which do you choose?

❧   ❧   ❧

I CONSIDER LIFE—AND EVERYTHING AND
EVERYONE IN IT—TO BE VERY GOOD!

AUGUST 31

"Get your grammar right! Live in the active voice rather than in the passive, thinking more about what you do than about what happens to you. Live in the indicative mood rather than in the subjunctive, concerned with things as they are, rather than as they might be. Live in the present tense, facing the duty at hand without regret for the past or worry about the future."
— educator William DeWitt Hyde

LIVING "ALL-OUT"

Kansas City Royals star George Brett, one of the most dedicated players in professional baseball, was once asked by a reporter what he wanted to do at his last at-bat. He replied, "I want to hit a routine grounder to second and run all-out to first base, then get thrown out by half a step. I want to leave an example to the young guys that that's how you play the game: all-out."

Staying active for as long as you can involves living "all-out." This means that you're willing to strive for the highest level of achievement possible, to strive for greatness in each moment. How do you do this? A team of researchers at the University of Chicago analyzed the careers of concert pianists, sculptors, research mathematicians, neurologists, Olympic swimmers, and tennis champions to determine what led them to go "all-out." What the researchers discovered is that talent alone didn't make them great at what they did; rather, their ultimate excellence was a product of total commitment and hard work over the long term. So your effectiveness is not only related to your ability and the effort you've put in up to this point in time, but your willingness to put such things into action. You can't worry about the past or the future or anything other than how you respond at the present moment.

❦   ❦   ❦

I LIVE "ALL-OUT" IN EVERYTHING I DO.

September 1

EVERYDAY LEARNING

Do you remember when you would return home in the afternoon after school, and one of the first questions your mother or father would ask was, "What did you learn today?" Because you were young and there was so much you didn't know, every day offered something new to you—a new word to spell, a new math problem to solve, a new bit of history to learn, a new grammar rule, a new piece of scientific information, a new physical challenge, a new drawing to create.

Now that you're much older, do you feel that each day you have the opportunity to learn something new? Sometimes you can discover something new by reading the paper every morning. Sometimes tuning in to a cable news show or a public broadcasting station can reveal something you didn't know. Sometimes listening to the chatter of the morning diners who are gathered at your favorite breakfast spot can bring to light a topic you've never really explored in great detail.

If you want to learn more about the world you live in, you don't have to go back to school. There are lots of ways you can learn something new. Take a book out of the library about a person you may have heard of, but know little about. Purchase a magazine on a subject you never really paid much attention to. Go out for coffee with someone who followed a different career or life path than you did. Visit a computer store and play with a computer. Channel surf and settle in on a program you wouldn't normally watch. Take the time and make the effort to expand your knowledge base, and you'll learn something new every day.

I LEARN MUCH IN THE SCHOOL OF LIFE TODAY.

SEPTEMBER 2

"The crucial task of old age is balance: keeping just well enough, just brave enough, just gay and interested and starkly honest enough to remain a sentient human being."
— writer Florida Scott-Maxwell

HABITS OF THE PAST

As you grow older, some habits that may have served you well when you were younger may now make you unwell. For example, the habitual morning rush and routine that once helped you and your family leave for school and work on time may now no longer be necessary. So, continuing to wake up and move out at such a frantic pace and high stress level may be detrimental to your serenity. Now you may find that you're happier and calmer waking up gradually to soft music, gentle yoga movements, and a hot cup of herbal tea.

If you think back to how you used to live when you were younger, you'll probably recall lots of late nights, endless cups of caffeinated coffee, and take-out meals. How likely were you to set aside—or even be allowed—enough time to get a good night's sleep; to prepare nutritious, well-balanced meals; to exercise regularly; and to just have time for yourself?

The lifestyle habits you formed when you were younger can become a backbone to you—a firm structure upon which you still rely. But how strong is that backbone? For how long will it help you to stand straight and tall? You need to start now to strengthen your own backbone and to slowly let go of some of your bad habits. You can do this by choosing one or two bad habits and altering them, or you can make a list of your bad habits and seek to eliminate them from your life "cold turkey." Remember, however, to always have a good habit to replace a bad one.

I RENEW MY HEALTH AND VITALITY WITH GOOD HABITS.

SEPTEMBER 3

*"Of all the self-fulfilling prophecies in our culture, the assumption
that aging means decline and poor health
is probably the deadliest."*

— writer/philosopher Marilyn Ferguson

GERONTOPHOBIA

Do you remember the game of opposites? One person says a word, and the other person responds with a word that has an opposite meaning. So if one person says, "hot," the other person can say, "cold." If one person says, "hungry," the other person can say, "full."

Society often plays a similar game of opposites when it comes to the perceptions, images, and attitudes it generally has toward aging. Because the image of youth is one that conveys vigor, power, and sexual appeal, the image of older people is perceived to be the opposite. Older people are thought to be "wheezers" and "geezers" who are slow, stubborn, sick, weak, disinterested in sex, incompetent—even stupid. In the game of opposites, the young earn all the positive words, while those who are older are labeled with the negatives. If young is good, old must be bad. If the young are beautiful, then the old are unattractive. If it's great to be young, then it's awful to be old. If the young represent hope and the future, then the old symbolize hopelessness and clinging on to the past.

Gerontophobia—fear of old age and aging—is ingrained in everyone, young and old. Out of this fear can come unfair contrasts to youth, as well as a myriad of negative and misleading myths about what it means to grow older.

But you can start to play a new game, one that compares rather than contrasts. In this game, the young are vigorous—and so are the old; the young are sexy—and so are the old; the young are your future—and so are you.

❀   ❀   ❀

I PLAY GAMES WHERE BOTH THE YOUNG AND THE OLD WIN.

SEPTEMBER 4

"I don't know what your destiny will be, but one thing I know: the only ones among you who will be really happy are those who will have sought and found how to serve."

— Albert Schweitzer

ALBERT SCHWEITZER

The selfless and renowned humanitarian Albert Schweitzer was, when a young man, as restless and dissatisfied with his life as many of today's youth. His first career was that of a musician; he was an organist and interpreter of Bach. Then he switched careers and became a theologian, philosopher, and writer. But at the age of 30, he returned to school and chose another career path—medicine.

Yet, after years of medical training, Schweitzer made still another career move. He set off to help those who were less fortunate by becoming a jungle doctor. At the age of 38, he established a hospital on the Ogowe River in Gabon, French West Africa. But then he was interned as an enemy alien by the French during World War I. Upon his release, he discovered his hospital in ruins—its buildings had collapsed from neglect in his absence—and he was fast approaching the age of 50. Should he or shouldn't he return to a more comfortable life, back in "civilization"?

Schweitzer returned to the jungle and rebuilt the hospital, which he ran until his death at the age of 90. In each of his many careers, he always achieved a level of renown that could have earned him plenty of money so he could have lived a comfortable life surrounded by luxuries and recognition. Instead, he chose to apply his talents in an African jungle and to use his gifted mind and giving soul to tend to the sick so that each of his patients could feel the recognition of their importance to him as a human being.

I FIND A WAY TO USE MY SKILLS TO SERVE OTHERS.

September 5

THE MARATHON OF LIFE

Imagine what it would be like to run a marathon—all 26.2 miles—backwards. You'd start out on wobbly legs, wearing sweaty clothes that stick to you and that have already chafed tender spots on your skin, your feet would be hot and swollen, your socks and shoes would be coated with grit and grime from the road, sweat would be streaming down your face, your blood-sugar level would be dangerously low, and you'd be almost crazy with thirst.

And you'd know that you'd still have 26.2 miles left to run!

But you might not feel so intimidated if you knew that each mile you ran, you'd feel better and better until you finally crossed the starting line with fresh legs, dry clothing, cool feet, clean socks and shoes, a high level of glucose, and the feeling that you're raring to go.

When you think about it, life is like a marathon you may wish you could run backwards. Each successive year you live would be like each reverse mile you'd run. You'd feel better and better until you finally reached the finish line—the end of life—and you'd be feeling great.

But life, like the marathon, has to be run mile after progressive mile. Life, like the marathon, has to be lived by looking ahead. And life, like the marathon, needs to be depleting. For what good is it to reach the end of your life with fresh legs and a high energy level? Wouldn't you rather reach the end of your life feeling that you've completed a distance that says more about your strong spirit than your weakened flesh?

I MOVE FORWARD, NOT BACKWARD, IN MY LIFE.

September 6

"Success—to laugh often and much; to win the respect of intelligent people and the affection of children; to earn the appreciation of honest critics and endure the betrayal of false friends; to appreciate beauty; to find the best in others; to leave the world a bit better, whether by a healthy child, a garden patch or a redeemed social condition; to know even one life has breathed easier because you lived. This is to have succeeded."
— clergyman Harry Emerson Fosdick

THE KEYS TO YOUR SUCCESS

Success means different things to different people. To some, it's a corner office and gold-embossed business cards. To others, it's an extensive client list and the feeling of being in demand. Still others believe success is measured in financial terms. And there are those who believe that success is helping others rather than helping themselves.

Africa-based English writer and aviator Beryl Markham once said, "I have had responsibilities and work, dangers and pleasures, good friends, and a world without walls to live in....I sit there in the firelight and see them all." Imagine sitting before the warm glow of a crackling fire. As you peer into the flames, recall moments of your life that have brought you the feeling of success. What do you see? A personal victory? Great friends? A wonderful relationship with your parents? A risk you took? A passionate romance? A trip to a country you'd always dreamed of visiting?

Take a moment to reflect upon the things in your life that have instilled you with the feeling that you've been or are successful. They can be measurable—such as owning the home you've always wanted—or found within you—such as being able to enjoy a beautiful sunset. Such things are the keys to your success.

I RECOGNIZE THE SUCCESSES IN MY LIFE.

SEPTEMBER 7

"Only a life lived for others is a life worth while."

— Albert Einstein

HELPING OUT

Every day hungry and homeless men, women, and children wander America's streets searching garbage cans for scraps, lining up outside crowded shelters and soup kitchens, or panhandling. Every night these same hungry and homeless fight in the cold for the privilege of attaining the "luxury" of being able to catch a few hours of precious sleep on a park bench, over a subway grating, or wrapped in a blanket while huddled inside a cardboard box.

Do you ever take the time to share some of your abundance with the hungry and homeless? You can donate a bag of groceries to a local food pantry, prepare or serve food at a soup kitchen or shelter, offer to clean up after meals are served, and donate an old sweater, winter coat, or blanket to a shelter or charity. Also, you can change your attitude toward those less fortunate than you by not turning away in disgust from a hungry and homeless person who approaches you, and instead extend a smile, a kind word, or spare change to purchase a hot cup of coffee.

Writer Leo Buscaglia points out the need for such charitable acts: "The majority of this world lead quiet, unheralded lives as we pass through this world. There will most likely be no ticker-tape parades for us, no monuments created in our honor. But that does not lessen our possible impact, for there are scores of people waiting for someone just like us to come along...."

There's much good that you can do for your brothers and sisters who share this planet with you. Giving just a little bit of your time or material possessions can make just one person in this world more comfortable.

❖   ❖   ❖

WHEN I HELP TO TURN A LIFE AROUND,
I TURN MY OWN LIFE AROUND.

SEPTEMBER 8

"When grace is joined with wrinkles, it is adorable. There is an unspeakable dawn in happy old age."

— writer Victor Hugo

LIFE TATTOOS

If you decided to go to a tattoo artist for a tattoo, you'd probably be given a great deal of options of possible images and words you could have engraved upon your body. Or you may have made your own sketch of something you'd like, and the artist would work with you in creating what you want.

But many of the marks upon your body are not evidence of such a creative exchange; rather, they're reminders of the passage of time. In many ways, life is like a tattoo artist. As a passage from the *Tao* roughly translates:

> *"Lines on the face, tattoos of aging.*
> *Life is proved upon the body*
> *Like needle-jabs from a blind machine."*

Every time you look in the mirror, you are faced with the aging mask you now wear. You may be surprised, shocked, or even dismayed when you look at photographs of your once-youthful and "unmarked" face. But is it really a bad-looking mask you now wear? You'll think it is if you allow yourself to be tattooed by life, if you let it take its own creative liberties with you. But what if you take more of an interest in the pattern and picture of yourself that emerges over time? It's really you who ought to be selecting what you'll look like by the actions you perform. Every experience you have, everything you do, and all the thoughts you think are registered upon your face as surely as the embroidery of a tattoo artist. Whether you emerge beautiful or ugly is really up to you.

I SELECT THE "PICTURE" THE TATTOO ARTIST WILL USE.

SEPTEMBER 9

"You cannot step twice into the same stream. For as you are stepping in, other and yet other waters flow on."

— Greek philosopher Heraclitus

ENDING STAGNATION

Here are some differences between living a life that embraces change and living a life that leads to stagnation:

- A life of change measures yourself against yourself; a life of stagnation measures yourself against others.

- A life of change refuses to give up to moderate inconvenience or mild discomfort; a life of stagnation opts to drop out for no other reason than a weak will.

- A life of change realizes that victory is attained by simply making an effort and trying; a life of stagnation is not trying anything unless success is assured.

- A life of change finishes every goal that is set, even the smallest ones; a life of stagnation refuses to set goals.

- A life of change revitalizes, refreshes, and renews; a life of stagnation is listless and lifeless.

- A life of change seeks to do something in a way that's never been done before; a life of stagnation accepts that something has never been done before in a certain way and therefore doesn't do it.

- A life of change walks forward; a life of stagnation walks away.

- A life of change refuses to stop after one try; a life of stagnation gives up after the first sign of failure.

- A life of change leads to the promise of greater change; a life of stagnation leads nowhere.

I LIVE A LIFE OF CHANGE TODAY.

SEPTEMBER 10

"It's wonderful to be married to an archaeologist—the older you get the more interested he is in you."

— writer Agatha Christie

LOVING ANOTHER

How do you convey your love to your partner? In an expensive gift? In a touching card? In a surprise night out on the town? By kisses and caresses? By saying, "I love you"?

Imagine that you've been given the assignment to convey "I love you" to your partner. You need to do this in 25 words or less, but there's just one catch. You can't use the words "I love you" in your essay, in any language.

Love isn't always an easy emotion to feel and can be even harder to express. It may be easier to write or say those three little words than it is to try to put into words and actions why you feel them.

Sometimes love can best be conveyed to a partner when you're able to remember that the person you've chosen to spend a lifetime with is, most of the time, also your best friend—someone who you can trust with all your secrets and with whom you can share anything and feel safe. When you look at those relationships around you that appear to be good—solid, secure, and loving—more likely than not what you see are two people who are good friends and who treat each other with respect, two people who have shared values and trust for one another, and two people who are willing to be vulnerable and intimate with each other.

Accept the "I love you" challenge today. Compose an essay to your partner that expresses the depth and breadth of the love you have. Let this serve as a reminder to both you and your partner of the wonderful relationship you have.

I WRITE A LOVING COMPOSITION TO MY PARTNER.

SEPTEMBER 11

"The body is not a permanent dwelling, but a sort of inn (with a brief sojourn at that) which is to be left behind when one perceives that one is a burden to the host."

— Roman philosopher/statesman Seneca

A COMFORTABLE INN

How you feel physically will not only change over time, but also vary widely from time to time. Depending on how well you treat your body, your mind, and your spirit at different times of your life, you may actually feel physically better at an older age than at a younger one. It depends on how in touch you can be with your body.

If you can learn to listen to your body's wisdom, you'll hear it express itself quite clearly to you through signals of comfort and discomfort. Should you decide to try a new activity such as yoga or walking, for example, you can complete a brief beginning session and ask your body, "How did you feel about that?" Your body will send you a signal of distress if it's not ready for what you're doing or incapable of doing what you want it to; it's not a good idea, then, to continue to subject your body to such undue stress. But if, on the other hand, your body conveys a signal of comfort and eagerness to continue, proceed with what you're doing and enjoy it!

Remember, too, that if you treat your body as if it were a special dwelling—a mansion, a cathedral, or a comfortable inn— you'll enjoy inhabiting this special place, will want to take good care of it, and will feel as if you "belong" in your body's abode. Keep in mind, however, the words of writer Herman Melville, who said, "Our souls belong to our bodies, not our bodies to our souls." Not always will you be able to inhabit this space in the same way from day to day, month to month, or year to year. Enjoy the space while you can, for as long as you can.

I TREAT MY BODY AS IF IT WERE A TEMPLE.

*"The compensation of growing old...was simply this:
that the passions remain as strong as ever, but one had gained—
at last!—the power which adds the supreme flavour to existence—
the power of taking hold of experience, of turning it round,
slowly, in the light."*

— writer Virginia Woolf

FINDING JOYFUL MEMORIES

It has been said that "much unhappiness results from an inability to remember the nice things that happen to us." You may find that when you have days of feeling like you're "down in the dumps" or find it hard to shake a particularly blue mood, it helps when you can recall a joyful memory. Reliving the memory in your mind can help you to wipe off a frown and put a smile on your face and walk with a bounce in your step instead of a dejected shuffle.

Are you able to review the past in ways that bring joy back into your life in the present? You can do so by taking emotional "time-outs" periodically, and by mentally revisiting special places you've been to, celebrations and rituals you've shared with family members, wonderful friends you've grown to know and love over the years, and significant achievements you've made in your life. Take out a photo album, call or visit a friend or family member, or go through your scrapbook or boxes filled with newspaper clippings, letters, high school and college yearbooks, military uniforms and decorations, college books and papers, and so on. Turn back the clock for a few moments on your own or in a conversation with another so you can re-experience feelings of joy and happiness.

Such time-outs can help you to reflect on the good that has been a part of your life and can continue to be part of your life in the present.

I TAKE TIME TO REMEMBER THE JOYFUL
MEMORIES OF MY LIFE.

*"Its mourners are few, perhaps, but the passing of the barn sign—
there on the side of the road, a friend to man—is another symbol
of the passing of an American era that was more rural,
more tied to the land...."*

— writer David M. Shribman

THE PASSING OF AN ERA

Are you young enough to remember the Mail Pouch barns, the ones painted for tobacco industry profit and which, today, serve as a historical tribute to a time in America when tobacco was one of the country's earliest cultivated crops? Today most of America views smoking as an annoying addiction rather than an enjoyable activity, and devotes time and energy to kicking the habit rather than paying tribute to it.

But the disappearance of Mail Pouch barns—and all barn advertising, for that matter—signals that the country is, in many ways, no longer *country*. Cable television today can reach into even the most remote and rugged rural areas; there's really no need for such advertising. The barn ads are fading out of existence, like the era they symbolized.

The man who was once known as "the Michelangelo of American barn painting," Harley Warrick, single-handedly painted more than 10,000 barns in 45 years. He worked without a stencil and, when Swisher International, the company that owns Mail Pouch, decided to cease barn advertising, he retired in his late sixties.

The passing of American eras can also point out the passage of time in your life. But you can still take a ride on a winding country road, look at the old barns and their advertisements, and, for a moment, recapture that time gone by.

❀   ❀   ❀

I APPRECIATE THE COUNTRYSIDE AND WHAT IT
STILL STANDS FOR.

SEPTEMBER 14

"Lacey always told me what she needed. A bark from the kitchen meant it was time for her supper. A paw slapping at the door said she was ready to come in—now. Toward the end of her life, a whimper meant she needed the water bowl brought over."

— writer Vicki Croke

SAYING GOODBYE TO A PET

Saying goodbye to a beloved pet can oftentimes be even more difficult than saying goodbye to a partner, dear friend, or family member. It's hard to lose what your pet gives you—unconditional love as well as a nearly perfect relationship that's free from conflict, issues, and emotional baggage. But what can make losing your animal companion even more difficult is that you oftentimes need to make the decision for the animal to terminate its life due to injury, disease, or painful debilitation from aging.

To further complicate matters, your friends and family members may not be able to understand the depth of your loss. "Hey, it's just a dog," you might be told, or "You can always get another kitten. There's plenty around." You may think that such callousness emanates from non-animal lovers, but oftentimes other pet owners don't share in a meaningful relationship with their own animals.

If you're faced with making the traumatic decision to terminate your pet's life or have lost your pet and find no validation for your grief, there are options for support. Contact your local chapter of the Society for the Prevention of Cruelty to Animals; group counseling sessions are often available. Also, many veterinarians are now willing to come to your house, so your pet can relax and you can say goodbye in privacy. You can also make it a point to talk to friends and family before your pet is sick so they understand your important relationship.

I PROVIDE LOVE AND COMFORT TO MY FRIEND
AND COMPANION.

SEPTEMBER 15

"Never lose sight of the fact that old age needs so little but needs that little so much."

— writer Margaret Willour

BE A CANDLELIGHTER

If you've ever seen a candlelight ceremony, you know how powerful just one candle can be. Countless tapers can be lit from that one small flame until a room, large meeting hall—even a darkened avenue—is brilliant with light.

Sometimes others may need your small flame from which they can light their own candles of hope, health, and happiness. Maybe your aging parent needs your daily telephone call to feel connected with you, as well as to help ward off feelings of loneliness and isolation. Perhaps your partner needs your reassurance that you'll be there for each other in retirement, sickness, and old age. Maybe your adult child needs your encouragement to help deal with a sometimes difficult world. Or perhaps a friend needs your support in helping to get through a period of grief.

Each day, you can give the gift of your light in small but meaningful ways to others. Offer encouragement to those who can use it, give support to those who are in need, provide strength to those who are weak, relate hope to those who are losing faith, and share your experience and knowledge with those who will listen.

Today, don't leave anyone you love and care for in the dark. Be a candlelighter to others; let them light their candles from you. This gift of light will illuminate your world as well as theirs. By sharing the warm glow of loving feelings, nurturing acceptance, and laughter and lightness with others, they, too, can learn how to glow with the strength of an eternal flame.

I LIGHT THE CANDLES OF OTHERS AND KEEP THEM LIT.

SEPTEMBER 16

"I am a restlessness inside a stillness inside a restlessness."
— writer/playwright Dodie Smith

GAZING MEDITATION

More and more people are using relaxation techniques—also referred to as meditation— to make themselves feel better, to gain a sense of control in their lives, to give them a feeling of safety, to enhance the ability to sleep, to restore clear thinking, to refresh their mind, to diminish tension, and to increase the ability to deal with symptoms of depression caused by age-related issues.

There are many different ways to meditate, but any way you choose leads to the same result. One meditation you can do while taking a hot bath or sitting quietly in your favorite chair is called gazing. Set the object of your choice that you'd like to look at on a surface that's at eye level and about a foot or two away from you. Choose something simple such as a flower, a burning candle or stick of incense, a crystal, a poster or postcard of a natural scene, or a favorite stuffed animal. Take three deep abdominal breaths, then gaze at the object while keeping your eyes and body relaxed. Notice everything about the object—its texture, shape, color, size, and how it smells. Trace the edge of the object with your eyes as you take in all the minute details that you might not ordinarily notice. If you become distracted, simply return your gaze to the object. You might like to listen to music or a guided meditation tape or one with recorded nature sounds.

Practice the gazing meditation twice a day for two weeks. Each day, compare how you felt before trying the meditation and then after. At the end of two weeks, consider whether this meditation has helped you to still your restlessness and to respond to life in a more relaxed way.

I MEDITATE FOR STILLNESS AND INNER PEACE.

SEPTEMBER 17

"If the world were merely seductive, that would be easy.
If it were merely challenging, that would be no problem. But I
arise in the morning torn between a desire to improve (or save)
the world and a desire to enjoy (or savor) the world. This makes
it hard to plan the day."

— writer E.B. White

FOSTERING A SPIRIT OF COOPERATION

Cooperation within nature happens in a multitude of ways: a gentle summer rain provides water for green, living things; a receding tide exposes food for gulls; dead leaves drop around a tree, slowly decay, and provide the tree with a rich source of nourishment. What you learn from such cooperation is that each element in nature becomes an integral, organic part of the overall "organization" of nature; each influences the other collectively and helps to shape it in some way through this influence.

In businesses, fellowships, organizations, families, group living situations, and other collectives, you know that the best way to function as a group is to work together in the spirit of cooperation. Even if there is a "leader," the leader needs to know when to act, when to be passive, and how to present himself or herself as an equal so the group will work together as one cohesive unit.

The power of leadership can be seductive; so, too, can the challenge presented by a problem to which you wish to devote your time and energy. You may feel that in order to enjoy life you need to decide between whether to lead or to follow when you're involved in a particular area of interest. But sometimes you don't need to choose; sometimes you just need to engage yourself through the spirit of cooperation in any project, task, or organization in which you're involved.

❧   ❧   ❧

I COOPERATE WITH OTHERS FOR A COMMON PURPOSE.

SEPTEMBER 18

"It is customary to call youth the happy, and age the sad part of life. This would be true if it were the passions that made a man happy. Youth is swayed to and fro by them, and they give a great deal of pain and little pleasure. In age the passions cool and leave a man at rest...the intellect is set free and attains the upper hand."
— philosopher Arthur Schopenhauer

PLEASURE OR PAIN?

Do you experience the world only as a source of pleasure or pain? Perhaps now you don't, but you can probably recall times when you were younger when life seemed to be one roller coaster ride after another. Sometimes you'd be riding high, experiencing thrills, adventures, risks, and emotional surges of delight; other times you'd be riding the depths of despair, filled with worry, anxiety, fear, boredom, and loneliness. For every positive emotion, you discovered a negative side to it—love could result in pain, for example; success could turn into a great loss; expectations could be dashed; hopes could be shattered; doubt could infiltrate even the most upbeat moods.

Now, at an older age, you probably can see that between the two extremes of pleasure and pain are levels of different emotions—gentle, rolling rides with less emotionally traumatic twists and turns. This is because you're now capable of looking outside yourself, of recognizing that there's much more to this world than your own little space with your own little issues.

When you're young, you're much more focused on yourself; when you're older, you can be much more focused on others. This is the time of your life to devote to causes, civic duties, worthwhile organizations, volunteering, and activism. Doing so will bring you great pleasure.

I DEVOTE MY TALENTS TO WORTHY CAUSES,
AND IT GIVES ME PLEASURE.

SEPTEMBER 19

"Notwithstanding the poverty of my outside experience, I have always had a significance for myself, and every chance to stumble along my straight and narrow little path, and to worship at the feet of my Deity, and what more can a human soul ask for?"

— diarist Alice James

TRUSTING YOURSELF

Do you remember the story of the man who thought God had deserted him during a most troubling time in his life because he only saw one set of footprints along the difficult path he had just walked? When he asked God why He wasn't with him when he needed Him the most, God told him that he had only seen one set of footprints because He had been carrying him.

Even though you may face difficulties in your life, you can trust that you're always in good hands—God's hands. God carries you whenever you need to be carried and provides you with a guiding voice of experience that reminds you that all things change, all wounds heal, and all is eased through the passage of time.

When you can trust in the existence of such a presence, then you can trust in yourself. Trusting in yourself means that you're open to learning all you can about yourself as well as about the people, places, and things that happen to cross your path. Also, it means that sometimes you must put yourself in situations where you *have* to learn—where you need to feel as if you're walking alone on a difficult path.

At such times you must not run away. Instead, you need to trust that you can take the next step, and the next, and the next. Then, you can slowly begin to feel sure of yourself, slowly start to feel your intent become stronger, and then gradually let go of the need to always wonder whether you're being carried.

❀   ❀   ❀

I TRUST IN GOD, AND I TRUST IN MYSELF.

SEPTEMBER 20

"When he was in his mid-80s, the great cellist Pablo Casals kept practicing his instrument for four or five hours each day. Someone once asked him why, at his age, he still worked so hard. 'Because,' he said, 'I have a notion that I am making some progress.'"

— writer Leonard Lyons

PROGRESS, NOT PERFECTION

The great poet John Milton once despaired how little he had accomplished at the age of 23. But at the age of 59, he wrote *Paradise Lost,* which some consider to be the greatest epic in the English language. Henri Matisse, who had achieved recognition at an early age as a post-Impressionist painter, decided to rest on his laurels and went into a period of semiretirement. But at the age of 66, he began creating again and then, at age 71 and bedridden most of the time, he invented ingenious ways to continue to create art. Between the ages of 75 and 80, he produced 6 major illustrated books. When he died at the age of 85, critics ranked the works of his last decade of life as some of his greatest achievements.

You may feel, as Milton did, that you've accomplished little in your life to date. Or you may feel, as Matisse did, that even though you've accomplished much, there's still much left you can achieve. You may be progressing more slowly than you'd like, but you are making progress. Remember that your time will come. *Have patience.* Your projects, goals, dreams, and desires will come to you when you're ready to receive them. Accept where you are right now. Each step you take leads you closer to your goal. But you'll reach that goal when the time is right for you.

🌸　🌸　🌸

I PATIENTLY MAKE PROGRESS IN MY LIFE.

September 21

"But how meager one's life becomes when it is reduced to its basic facts....And the last, most complete, reduction is on one's tombstone: a name, two dates."

— writer Helen MacInnes

THE PRACTICAL MATTERS OF DYING

Part of dealing with death means also dealing with practical matters—personal preferences and desires about the type of service and burial that you wish. But what happens when you can't communicate such preferences yourself? Rather than simply assuming that everything will be taken care of in the way you'd like or letting your life be reduced to a name and two dates on a tombstone, you can take the time now to plan ahead so your passing will not only respect your wishes, but respect those who will carry them out.

Before you die, for example, you may want to arrange to donate vitally needed organs, such as kidneys and corneas, for transplant. You can update the will for your estate in order to stay current with living relatives and friends and worthwhile charitable organizations for donations. This is also a good time to make a living will that can provide guidance for caregivers and family members when you can no longer communicate your wishes.

Now is also the time when you can plan the kind of funeral or memorial service you want. From preparing your body for burial, the burial or cremation itself, the last rites, and the music to be played or poetry to be read, all rituals can be designed now so your survivors can be comforted, and not confused; grateful for your assistance, and not plagued by guilt that they're not following your wishes; and free to devote their attention to saying goodbye to you and grieving their loss.

I MAKE MY PREFERENCES KNOWN FOR MY PASSING.

SEPTEMBER 22

*"From the letters which were written [when I was young],
I can easily see what advantages and disadvantages come with
every time of life, to balance those of earlier and later periods. In
my fortieth year, I was as clear and decided on some subjects as
at present, and, in many respects, superior to my present self; yet,
now, in my eightieth, I possess advantages which I would
not exchange for these."*
— poet/dramatist Johann Wolfgang von Goethe

DONATING AND GIVING

When 100-year-old Rhea Stambaugh made up her mind that the old house full of books could no longer suffice as a library for the 2,000 residents of Plymouth, Ohio, she took charge of the project. She scouted around for available land, purchased the land herself, hired an architect, and turned down the younger man's first four designs. She approved the final design, observed each phase of the construction, and delivered a speech at the dedication of the building. When asked how she felt, she commented, "Next to my marriage, it's the best thing I ever did."

Many people in midlife and older feel the need to involve themselves more in a chosen cause, in an activity that allows them to give to others, in ways that allow them to share some of their wealth—financial, professional, or experiential—and receive, from such actions, the personal satisfaction of knowing they may have made a difference in someone's life—or, as in Stambaugh's case—in the lives of many others.

Sometimes it's only when you're older that you can be so giving of yourself. Although you may have had similar desires when you were younger, now you're probably in a better position to donate money and property, to provide skills and resources, and to devote time and energy.

❊   ❊   ❊

I DONATE MY KNOWLEDGE, ENERGY, AND RESOURCES
TO SOMETHING I BELIEVE IN.

SEPTEMBER 23

"We have, inadvertently, trained our young doctors to consider it a virtue to prolong life for the sole purpose of prolonging it."
— physician James Howard Means

THE BATTLEFIELD OF LIFE

If life is viewed as a battlefield, then death is the enemy that's striving to defeat the army of living. How you go into battle becomes significant; your leaders need to be fearless and determined, and the weapons you use have to overpower the enemy's.

When you're young, your leaders are your parents, who seek to protect you from injury, illness, and danger; the weapons they use are discipline, guidance, and love. As you grow older, your leaders become teachers, coaches, and mentors; the weapons they provide you with are wisdom and experience. When you reach midlife, your leaders are often your peers; together you use strength and stamina to battle onward.

But then, without warning, your line of protection eventually breaks down. Enemy spies infiltrate and do damage; illness, injury, disabilities, and battle-fatigue set in. Those who then lead you out onto the battlefield are nurses and doctors, physical therapists and specialists; the weapons they give you are wheelchairs and crutches, medication and salves, shots and IVs, outpatient and inpatient surgeries.

At some point, the reasons for returning to the battlefield become muddied; you may feel as if you're no longer fighting to defeat the enemy but striving instead to throw down your weapons and give up the battle. Nothing can make people age faster than feeling as if they can't fight their own battles. To avoid such self-defeat, determine now just how long you'd like to prolong that battle. Determine the conditions and terms of your own surrender.

◦◦◦   ◦◦◦   ◦◦◦

I FIGHT MY OWN BATTLES AND DETERMINE THE
OUTCOMES MYSELF.

SEPTEMBER 24

*"Mother Nature has let us flounder all night in the fog. We fight
our way: she is telling us with her fog that life is not always a
direct sighting; you don't always know where you are or where
you are going; you can only keep fighting with a smile until it
breaks and the new light is seen, then you are on your way again.
It may be a new direction, but it is a life. Thanks for the fog."*
— writer Chapin Wright

THE NEW IN THE OLD

How well do you know the world around you? Although you
may study it endlessly, spend a great deal of time in it, and feel
that you're truly "in touch" with it, in reality you, as a human being,
are quite out of touch with even your most familiar environs.

To prove this, take a walk on a familiar path through the woods
when it's nearly dark. Without the aid of a light, you may stumble
over tree roots, have your hair snagged by low-lying branches, and
miss the turn you need to make. Or go for a drive on a road you
often travel—but on a foggy night. You'll find yourself leaning
over the steering wheel and struggling to figure out where you are
without familiar landmarks to guide you. Also, you could even
enter a darkened room in your home and stub your toe on a couch
that's been in the same location for decades.

What this means is that just because you reside at a location
you've lived in almost all of your life, you socialize with family
and friends you've known for years, you've worked at the same job
for decades, and you've enjoyed the same hobbies since childhood,
there are still new things to notice, new things to learn about, and
new ways of interacting with people, places, and things. No one
and no thing will ever grow old in your life unless you treat it as if
it was the same old thing.

I TAKE NOTHING AND NO ONE FOR GRANTED
IN MY LIFE.

"While jogging past a local high school last winter, I came to the realization that although I was probably faster and stronger than most 17-year-olds, my 37-year-old body and mind were in danger of falling apart. After years of diligently cross-training, gobbling vitamins and even forsaking artery-clogging ice cream, the sad truth was that I was becoming a wreck."

— writer Jill Yesko

POWER YOGA

Power yoga has changed the life of many midlife athletes who, because of overtraining and obsessive focus on one particular sport, have developed chronic aches and pains that they ignore for fear they'll have to give up their "first-love" activity. The harder you train, the tighter your body can become; ironically, while all the hours of training result in a fit, trim body, they also create muscular and spinal imbalances that can lead to injury and chronic pain.

Power yoga helps to balance the body while, at the same time, developing mindfulness—a valuable mental attunement that sharpens awareness of staying focused so you can avoid injury and overuse of particular muscles. Each session begins with *ujjayis*—Sanskrit for "expanded victory"—or deep inhalations that serve to relax the body, oxygenate the muscles so they become pliable, and stoke the energy stores needed for physical coordination and mental concentration.

Power yoga sessions include body-balancing postures and even handspring-like movements, equivalent to about 200 push-ups, that give your overworked and underused muscles the ultimate stretch, as well as a superior oxygenated cleansing. After each session, you'll feel stronger, more focused, and ready to return to your activity of choice with fewer side effects.

❀   ❀   ❀

I EMPOWER MYSELF WITH POWER YOGA.

"A human being should be able to change a diaper, plan an invasion, butcher a hog, conn a ship, design a building, write a sonnet, balance accounts, build a wall, set a bone, comfort the dying, take orders, give orders, cooperate, act alone, pitch manure, solve equations, analyze a new problem, program a computer, cook a tasty meal, fight efficiently, die gallantly. Specialization is for insects."

— writer Robert A. Heinlein

PREVENTION SOLUTIONS

Imagine today that you could do something you've never done before. Forget about the planning or training you'd need to do this, what it might cost, how it would fit into your current schedule, caretaking arrangements you'd need to make, and numerous other considerations which, in the past, may have prevented you from pursuing this particular activity. Know that at this particular moment you could do whatever you'd like to do. So what would you choose?

Now think about what it would be like to finally realize this dream or goal of yours. Picture yourself doing the activity. Then imagine how you'd feel after you had completed what you set out to do.

Return to the present moment. Ask yourself, "What's preventing me from pursuing this dream or achieving this goal?" Divide a piece of paper in half and label it "Preventions"; on this side, jot down all the reasons you feel you're prevented from doing this particular activity. Then, on the opposite side of the paper, write "Solutions." Opposite each prevention statement, write the following words, "But I can work this out by _____ ." Fill in the blank with one or more actions that will solve each problem or difficulty. Then, with all your preventions "fixed," you can make plans to pursue your dream!

❀   ❀   ❀

I SET A GOAL TO ACHIEVE A GOAL.

SEPTEMBER 27

"Nothing is more seductive, and at the same time more deceitful than wealth. It is extremely troublesome to acquire, to keep, to spend and to lose."

— Hindu saying

"BABY BOOMER" RETIREMENT

Are you one of the 76 million American "baby boomers"—born between the years 1946 and 1964? Are you a baby boomer looking ahead to your future retirement and wondering what you will do? It's not too early to plan today in ways that will safeguard your living standards and lifestyles of tomorrow.

Despite your current income, investments, and possessions, you—as well as few baby boomers—will have the funds that will enable you to enjoy a "country club" life in retirement. In fact, the baby boomers who can expect to be the wealthiest will either have been able to amass sizable retirement nest eggs on their own, from savings and/or retirement plans, or will get big windfalls from the estate of their parents.

That's why it's important to start now to contribute to a savings and/or retirement plan; you can't count on the retirement safety net your parents had, because Medicare and Social Security benefits are already being threatened. Also, the era of traditional company-paid pension benefits is also on the wane.

Even if you're 50 years old, there's still enough time to start to set money aside in a savings plan because you'll be able to work for at least 15 more years. What's important to keep in mind is that you need to save enough money to live a very long time. You can expect to live at least ten years longer than your parents—well into your eighties, at least.

I SAFEGUARD MY FINANCIAL FUTURE TODAY.

SEPTEMBER 28

"Though it sounds absurd, it is true to say I felt younger at sixty than I had felt at twenty."

— writer Ellen Glasgow

"GRAY PARKS"

When was the last time you really enjoyed an amusement park—when you took in all the rides, enjoyed all the exhibits and shows, indulged your cravings with a variety of tasty treats—maybe even won a kewpie doll or a stuffed animal?

"Gray parks"—theme and amusement parks specifically designed to attract those from their mid-thirties to mid-sixties—are already in existence today. Epcot Center, twinned with Disney World, is one of the most popular; it attracts a crowd whose median age is 35 years older than the average age at Disney World. At Epcot, the rides reflect the taste of older visitors, exhibits are geared towards such mature interests as hydroponic gardening and fish farming, holographic cinemas provide interesting breaks from walking, and a variety of international dishes can be sampled. Also, places such as the Smithsonian, world's fairs, planetariums, museums of fine arts, and intellectual amusement parks that offer hands-on exhibits and interactive experiments attract an older, more educated and mature audience.

However, good old-fashioned county fairs still abound—and can be lots of fun to attend at any age. Fairs with 4-H competitions and exhibits; carnivals that set up booths with games such as ring-toss; parks that offer cotton candy and fried dough along with roller coaster rides, water flumes, and twisting, turning, rides through dark, scary tunnels can make you feel like a kid all over again—screaming with delight and enjoying every minute of a stomach-churning, breathtaking, fun-filled ride.

I HAVE FUN AT ALL TYPES OF AMUSEMENT PARKS.

SEPTEMBER 29

"Life is made of ever so many partings welded together."
— writer Charles Dickens

PARTING IS SWEET SORROW

One experience that's particularly difficult to go through—but which can become more frequent as you grow older—is loss. You lose your job because of a layoff or forced retirement; you lose your close friend or neighbor through relocation; you lose your personal possessions in a fire or theft; you lose your loved one through separation, divorce, or death; you lose your ability to take care of yourself.

Any loss can leave a vacuum in your life—a space and time that was once pleasantly filled but which now feels empty and meaningless. You may feel that it's nearly impossible to perform even the simplest routines, to concentrate on anything, or to accept that life must go on. You may even feel as if your life is over and that you have nothing to live for.

Everyone faces loss; some, more than others. But life gives you the permission to know loss; what this means is that life is naturally filled with loss that needs to be dealt with. You need to grieve your loss, let go of it, and then take action by recommitting to life and by being alive. You must go on and continue to raise your children, find a new relationship or friends, replace your possessions, look for work or a pastime that will occupy your time, or enlist the help of caretakers.

From this moment on, resolve to force yourself back into the swing of living—as hard as that may be. Think about some things you can do that will make you feel vital and alive again. Motivate yourself by saying, "I can get through this loss." And then believe that, over time, the sorrow will lessen and you'll eventually feel good again.

I RESPOND TO LOSS WITH HOPE FOR THE FUTURE.

SEPTEMBER 30

"I believe that only one person in a thousand knows the trick of really living in the present. Most of us spend 59 minutes an hour living in the past, with regret for lost joys, or shame for things badly done (both utterly useless and weakening)—or in the future, which we either long for or dread. Yet the past is gone beyond prayer....There is only one world, the world pressing against you at this minute. There is only one minute in which you are alive, this minute—here and now."

— writer Storm Jameson

HERE AND NOW

Do you always see each day as a new beginning—one that's fresh and clean and full of possibilities for the future—or do you sometimes begin a day by looking back and thinking about all the things you could have or should have done differently?

Beginning a day with thoughts about a day or a time gone by is like writing on a chalkboard that hasn't been washed since the start of a school year. Your new message is going to be hard to distinguish among all the other faded messages on the dusty surface. Chalky, ghostly images of minutes, hours, and days gone by make it hard to focus on the activities of the present time or to even look ahead and see into your future—whether that future is one minute from now or one year from now.

The best way to start today is to treat it as if it were a clean slate. Tell yourself, "All I can do with my life I can do only at this very moment—in the here and now. So I'd better get on with my life by participating in each minute of each hour." You can certainly apply what you learned yesterday to today, but you can't relive it, regret it, or revise it.

❧ ❧ ❧

I LIVE FOR TODAY.

OCTOBER 1

SLOWING DOWN, NATURALLY

Fall impels bears to hibernate, frogs to burrow deep into the mud at the bottom of ponds, birds to wing south, and trees to decelerate their growth with a final burst of glorious color. Fall induces most creatures to either shut down, slow down, or leave their spring and summer homes in preparation for the cold, dark end of the year.

Do you find that you, too, shut down, slow down, and want to leave? With the approach of colder weather, upcoming holidays, and a time change that advances darkness, you may find yourself feeling lethargic and a bit disinterested in life. Yet it's only natural that you, too, are experiencing a slowing-down similar to that of nature's, for you're part of nature's cycles of ebb and flow, high energy and dormancy, renewal and decline.

At times like this, staying in touch with nature can help you feel better. Rather than focus on your problems or stresses, you can look outside your window and see the changing colors of nature in the trees—some still boast bright reds, oranges, and yellows, while others display colors that are muted or browned. You can watch the leaves cascade to the ground like feathers from a torn down pillow. You can listen to the songs of the birds and rustle of the wind as it stirs up the fallen leaves. At this time of year, there's really so much more to focus on than early darkness, each day's duties, the problems of the world, preholiday pressures, and other stresses.

I AM PART OF THE PHENOMENON OF NATURE.

OCTOBER 2

"Old age puts more wrinkles in our minds than on our faces."
— essayist Michel de Montaigne

SATORI

Have you ever experienced a time in your life when you suddenly felt that the world was clear to you—a time when you somehow knew or could see deeply into the universe, into something that was much bigger than you, quite out of the reach of your stores of knowledge and experience, but which, at that moment, was as clear and comprehensible to you as the answer to the simplest math problem?

If you've experimented with recreational drugs in the past, if you're a runner who has experienced a "runner's high," or if you know how to meditate, you may already be familiar with this feeling—as if you're integrally connected in "cosmic ways" with everything around you. Spiritualists refer to this state of mindfulness as *satori,* which describes a sudden experience of clarification—almost like a turning over of the mind—usually after a period of contemplation. One spiritualist described satori in this way: "You are sitting on the earth and you realize that this earth deserves you and you deserve this earth. You are there—fully, personally, genuinely." Others have described satori as the doors of perception being opened, a state of "Itness" in which they are It and It is them, an "Ah-ha!"-like lightning bolt of sudden realization that forces arousal from a deep sleep, a feeling of illuminating "Wholeness," the state of enlightenment, a consciousness that occurs when the individual ego can no longer be separated from all things, a sense of inner abandonment, or an infinite reality.

To find satori, open your mind and senses; the level of wisdom that can be attained through satori is worth more than all the book learning you could ever absorb.

❀   ❀   ❀

I SEEK TO REALIZE; I SEEK SATORI.

OCTOBER 3

"One touch of nature makes the whole world kin."

— William Shakespeare

THE "KING PENGUIN"

Richard Tory Peterson, who died in 1996, made birdwatching and wildlife appreciation a national hobby. The nature that touched him—in the form of an injured flicker "I thought...was dead....Then, suddenly it exploded into life, and I was hooked"—entranced him since he was 11 years old. Later on, in the seventh grade, his science teacher encouraged him to draw birds and to apply his talents for meticulous detail. He was soon drawing and photographing every bird in sight. Many he drew from memory when there were no models available.

The first edition of his *A Field Guide to the Birds Including All Species Found in Eastern North America* went to print with an initial 2,000-book press run. The copies sold out in three weeks. Today more than four million copies of the book and its three subsequent editions are now in print.

In his later years, the six-foot-tall Peterson, whose status among serious birders was something approaching the awe of peasants for a monarch, was never better exhibited than when a rare bird, a Ross's gull, made a totally unexpected appearance in Newburyport, Massachusetts. The bird, which lives and breeds in Siberia and occasionally flies over western Alaska, attracted some 5,000 birders to the small seacoast town. But rather than sightings of the bird, the most exciting news for the birders was the arrival of Peterson. "He's here," they whispered to one another in low voices, and suddenly their "life list" of personal bird sightings included one of the rarest and most memorable of all—the man, nicknamed the "King Penguin," who gave millions the gift of birding.

I ENJOY THE GIFTS SO MANY OTHERS HAVE GIVEN
ME TO ENJOY TODAY.

OCTOBER 4

*"Be life long or short, its completeness depends on
what it was lived for."*
— biologist/educator David Starr Jordan

A LIFE WORTH LIVING

Cicely Courtneidge and Jack Hulbert were household names in Britain during the 1930s, '40s, and '50s, when they starred in plays, revues, and films. Often paired in such shows, they shared and held on to their mutual love of the theater until late in their lives. When they were both in their late seventies, they toured South Africa and then returned to Britain to maintain a hectic schedule of guest appearances and play productions. They celebrated their diamond wedding anniversary in their mid-80s, toasting each other with champagne, and expressing both their never-ending love for one another, as well as for the life work they were able to share together.

Could you, too, raise a glass to toast your life today, to the life you've lived thus far? If you can't, then you may understand the words of French writer Charles Pierre Péguy, who once noted, "When a man lies dying, he does not die from the disease alone. He dies from his whole life." From this moment on, however, you have the opportunity to turn your life around—to make changes, to shift your focus, to set new goals, and to chart a new course that can lead you toward the life you've always wanted to live.

As she was growing older, writer George Eliot wrote, in a letter to a friend, "The years seem to rush by now, and I think of death as a fast approaching end of a journey—double and treble reasons for loving as well as working while it is day." As your journey in life speeds ahead, you need to decide whether you want to just go along for the ride, passively watching the scenery as it blurs by you, or if you want more from your journey—a chance to make some meaningful stops along the way.

I DESIRE TO MAKE MY LIFE WORTHWHILE.

OCTOBER 5

PROTECTING MEDICARE

Robert Scheer, contributing editor for the *Los Angeles Times,*
wrote a column in which he noted that there's nothing that
annoys younger taxpayers more than seniors who are doing all they
can to survive—exercising, dieting, and changing their lifestyles.
And, he notes, they're remaining politically active, protecting their
right to live with the care they deserve.

His article urged support for the country's Medicare program,
based on his personal experience of taking care of his aging mother.
She had worked for over 40 years in a union job; her Medicare
kicked in when she retired. Had it not, he noted, he would have had
trouble supporting her. Even when he began to earn more money, the
costs of supporting his own family were escalating and, without
Medicare, caring for his mother—who was afflicted with Parkinson's
disease and received plastic hips after she was mugged—would have
wiped out his kids' college funds and much more.

Until she was unable to walk, Scheer's mother "...picketed the
governor and legislators in Sacramento every time it looked as if
they might stick it to the old people." By the time she died, she
required round-the-clock care. After his experience, Scheer recommended to "...rapidly aging [yuppies]: Wire your Congresspersons
to keep their mitts off the programs that help seniors, or be prepared
to turn your snappy condo into an underfunded nursing home."

I STAY POLITICALLY ACTIVE TO PROTECT MY RIGHTS.

OCTOBER 6

"For as I like a young man in whom there is something of the old,
so I like an old man in whom there is something of the young; and
he who follows this maxim, in body will possibly be an old man,
but he will never be an old man in mind."

— Roman orator/philosopher Cicero

WHAT DO YOU BELIEVE?

A belief is something you hold on to because you think it's true. So a person who suffers from claustrophobia and walks into a party may immediately think, "This room is too small" or "There are far too many people here," and his body will respond in kind to the stimulus his mind is feeding him—to feel the fear.

Your beliefs about aging can have the same kind of power over you. For example, if you believe it's too painful to walk without a cane, then it will be too painful for you to walk without a cane. If you believe you're too old to participate in a sport, then you won't participate in the sport.

But when gerontologists at Tufts University challenged such beliefs with a select group of the frailest residents of a nursing home, the results were astounding. They put all the members of the group on a weight-training regimen; after eight weeks, some of the residents who had previously not been able to walk unaided could now get up by themselves and go to the bathroom in the middle of the night. What makes the results of this belief-challenging study so amazing is that the youngest member of the group was 87 years old; the oldest was 96!

In reality, all that had happened was that a belief had been changed; as a result, the way the people were aging changed. If you let limiting beliefs dominate how you live as you age, then your mind and your body will surely waste away. But if you believe that you can do anything you want to, then you will. It's that simple.

WHAT I BELIEVE KEEPS ME YOUNG IN MIND AND BODY.

OCTOBER 7

"If I were to name the three most precious resources of life, I should say books, friends, and nature....Nature we have always with us, an inexhaustible storehouse of that which moves the heart, appeals to the mind, and fires the imagination—health to the body, a stimulus to the intellect, and joy to the soul."
— writer/naturalist John Burroughs

NATURE'S LESSONS

Nature is as much a physical entity as it is a social one; in addition to the resources it provides for itself—for self-preservation—as well as for humankind—for enjoyment, use, and, sometimes, abuse—nature plays an important role in the daily life of human society. Nature is the starting point of all living things as well as their sustainer. Nature, therefore, is essential to humankind; referring to nature as "Mother Nature" is apt, for nature is humankind's nurturing protector.

In today's society, however, Mother Nature has been left with many empty nests. For, as most people grow older, they come to believe that nature isn't "where it's at." Where it's at, they discover, is in the city, in front of the computer, in the living room watching television, on the telephone, in the midst of a morning or evening commute, in the middle of a project, in the stresses of day-to-day living—in sum, in countless other pursuits, problems, and pastimes.

Nature has many valuable lessons to teach you—lessons of stability and tranquility, creation and imagination, beauty and harmony, growth and faith. They are lessons that can never be learned from books, from experts, or from the media. They are lessons that can only be learned from the fields, the sky, the woods, the river bank, the seashore, the animals, and the earth. By seeking the natural elements in your everyday life, you can strengthen your relationship with nature.

❊   ❊   ❊

I LEARN FROM AND LIVE WITH NATURE.

OCTOBER 8

*"We did not change as we grew older; we just became
more clearly ourselves."*

— writer Lynn Hall

VOYAGE OF DISCOVERY

Journalist May Sarton, at the age of 70, wrote, "I am more myself than ever before." Yet finding this self is not always easy. Too often you spend years defining yourself in relationship to other people, other places, other things. You're someone's wife or husband, another person's life partner, someone's child, or a child's parent. You're a student at a particular college or university or a resident of a community. You're an assistant to, a manager of, an owner of, a chairman of, a collector of, or a participant in.

In so defining yourself, you certainly answer the question of who you are through what roles you fulfill. But you don't even touch upon who you are by uncovering what's in your heart and soul. British author D.H. Lawrence once remarked, "The human being is a most curious creature. He thinks he has got one soul, and he has got dozens." What this means is that there's much more to you than meets the eye—the eyes of others as well as your own eyes. Finding out who you are then becomes a voyage of discovery—a voyage that may often take you far away from the familiar shorelines that once defined you, far out onto uncharted waters, for a challenging and eye-opening adventure into the unknown.

You set off on this voyage when you're able to let go of what you've always thought or expected of yourself and seek instead to find out the thoughts you've suppressed, the risks you've never taken, and the desires you've been unable to fulfill. Self-discovery is about discovering as well as recovering who you really are.

I UNFURL MY SAILS ON A VOYAGE OF SELF-DISCOVERY.

"As he lay there he had gone back over his life, and bit by bit, had extracted from it some of the hard lessons of experience. Each thing he learned was so simple and so obvious once he grasped it, that he wondered why he had not always known it."

— writer Thomas Wolfe

FINDING THE SIMPLE SOLUTIONS

Have you ever tried to outsmart a squirrel from stealing food from your bird feeders? As your wallet shrinks with the purchase of new and improved baffles, repellents, and "squirrel-proof" feeders, and as your blood pressure rises at the sight of the squirrel's latest successful assault on that feeder, you may feel as if you're in a head-to-head competition with the furry rodent. The more the squirrel thwarts your efforts, the more problematic the situation becomes. Suddenly, deterring the squirrel is no longer just your goal; it's an obsession that gets more and more complicated with each passing day.

Yet, you could simply fill the feeders for the birds and spread seed and nuts on the ground for the squirrel; by feeding both species—which you're doing anyway—you save time, money, and aggravation.

So many things in your life are made more complex when you strive to solve a problem or fulfill a desire in only one way. That's like having only one road available to travel into the nearest city—can you imagine how difficult that would be! There are many different solutions and options that are available to you that can help you resolve a problem or make a decision. Some are discovered after a great deal of thinking, some by trial and error, some through your own foolishness or stubbornness, some as a result of mistakes or wrong turns, and some that can be extracted from the hard lessons offered by life experiences.

❀ ❀ ❀

I SEEK SIMPLE SOLUTIONS TO MY PROBLEMS.

OCTOBER 10

"Ever since life appeared on earth it has been influencing the history of the earth's crust: shellfish live and die, live and die, and in time their empty shells build the [canyon wall]; a tree root pries open a fissure, and in time another rock falls. But these have been slow, random, undirected influences."

— hiker/writer Colin Fletcher

UNCONDITIONAL ACCEPTANCE

Accepting that your life has a beginning as well as an end, years of strength as well as years of weakness, and times of health as well as times of sickness, is not about fatalism, about being helpless or hopeless, about giving up in any way, or about being stagnant or inactive. It's about being sensible and being able to take correct action at the appropriate time. Like the farmer who experiences a drought, you know that to cry out in anger or frustration won't make the rain fall any quicker, so you don't waste your time with such actions.

Acceptance is a dynamic, life-giving, and life-affirming act. Acceptance is wisdom, knowing when to restore valuable energy and to regain strength. And, also, acceptance is letting go, trusting that what is lost can eventually be regained. As written in the book of Job 14:7-9:

> *"For there is hope for a tree,*
> *if it be cut down, that it will sprout again,*
> *and that its shoots will not cease.*
> *Though its roots grow old in the earth,*
> *and its stump die in the ground,*
> *yet at the scent of water it will bud*
> *and put forth branches like a young plant."*

I ACCEPT THE CONDITIONS OF MY LIFE AT THIS TIME.

OCTOBER 11

"Once in his lifetime a man ought to concentrate his mind upon the remembered earth. He ought to give himself up to a particular landscape in his experience; to look at it from as many angles as he can, to wonder upon it, to dwell upon it."
— writer N. Scott Momaday

FOND CHILDHOOD MEMORIES

Imagine that today the clock turns back in time to when you were a child. It's October 11, and you're in the sixth grade. School is cancelled for the day. What do you do? Close your eyes, and let your mind take you back in time. Remember what you could be doing on this day.

Perhaps you're outside playing with friends—tumbling about in great piles of colorful, fallen leaves; rolling down grassy hillsides or romping over wide fields; engaging in a game of hide-and-seek or kickball. Maybe you're riding your bicycle down a steep hill, the baseball cards you've clothes-pinned on to the spokes flapping loudly in the wind that rushes by you. Perhaps you're fishing at a nearby pond. As you allow such memories to filter through your mind, recall some of the other things you used to do outdoors, in all of nature's seasons. After all the leaves had fallen, you may have built snow forts in the backyard. The hushed sounds of freshly fallen snow and the occasional jingle of a horse's sleigh bell may have transported you back to a time in American history when fireplaces warmed the homes. The fishing pond may have become a skating pond in the wintertime.

Even though the childhood home, beloved backyard, and the cherished pond may no longer exist doesn't mean that you can never revisit them. All you need to do is close your eyes and remember. They are always there for you.

I GO BACK IN TIME WHENEVER I WANT TO KEEP MY
CHILDHOOD MEMORIES ALIVE.

OCTOBER 12

*"Live as if you expected to live a hundred years,
but might die tomorrow."*

— religious mystic Ann Lee

AYURVEDIC PRINCIPLES

In India, the term *Ayurveda* is derived from two Sanskrit roots, *Ayus*, or "life," and *Veda*, meaning "science" or "knowledge." This ancient "science of life" is usually referred to as India's traditional medicine, but the Ayurvedic program also has a deeper spiritual basis. The most famous verse from the ancient Ayurvedic texts translates into "Ayurveda is for immortality." According to Dr. Deepak Chopra in his book *Ageless Body, Timeless Mind*, "The meaning is two-fold: Ayurveda is for promoting longevity without limit, and it does this from a belief that life essentially is immortal." According to Ayurveda, life energies need to be kept in balance, which is similar to the growing Western belief in the connection between mind, body, and spirit.

To grow older and grow better, you can use the following Indian principles of longevity in your daily life:

- Maintain regularity—regular habits, mealtimes, and bedtimes.
- Stay warm—avoid extremes of hot and cold; enjoy sunshine.
- Nourish yourself—eat nutritionally balanced meals; drink plenty of water.
- Stay relaxed—get plenty of sleep, meditate.
- Maintain stability—keep home life, work life, and relationships stable.
- Stay calm—avoid stress, seek out moments of silence, attune with nature.
- Express emotions—release positive and negative feelings.
- Respect life—give thanks through prayer, avoid conflict, and be compassionate.

❧   ❧   ❧

I LIVE A LONG AND HEALTHY LIFE.

OCTOBER 13

LIFE'S ASPIRATIONS

Do you remember how, when you were growing up, you aspired to be certain things—a newspaper boy or girl, an altar boy, a member of the church choir, a Brownie, a school crossing guard? When you entered high school, perhaps you wanted to be a cheerleader, the class president, a member of the football team, a debater, or a member of the student council. If you went to college, then you had to look ahead to the future—to determine who you were going to be—by declaring your major, earning the required course credits, and interviewing with prospective employers for positions in your field of study.

Then, as an adult, you ventured forth into the world with lofty aspirations for who you were going to be. You may have had a career path mapped out or the desire to manage a home and family. With these aspirations in mind, you did all you could to move along each path and reach the goals you had set for yourself. Also, along the way, you may have also indulged your interests in a variety of pursuits and pastimes and found yourself setting aspirations for your professional affiliations, civic organizations, charities, and athletic endeavors.

Today, even though you may have attained most or all of the aspirations you've set for yourself, you can still set others. Your aspirations don't have to be lofty goals or even admirable desires. You can simply aspire to be the master of your own fate—in charge of your life and the decisions you need to make as you grow older—as well as the only master in your tennis group.

MY GOALS AND ASPIRATIONS GIVE MY LIFE
DIRECTION AND MEANING.

OCTOBER 14

"Life cannot be captured in a few axioms. And that is just what I keep trying to do. But it won't work, for life is full of endless nuances and cannot be captured in just a few formulae."
— mystic/writer Etty Hillesum

THE UNEXPECTED THINGS IN LIFE

Try predicting the weather. One way to do so is by studying the clouds, to learn how to read changing cloud patterns through the recognition of common cloud shapes and what they mean. For example, you can expect a storm if high, scattered puffy cumulus clouds or horizontally flattened stratus clouds get thicker, increase in number, or get low and dark in the sky. But no matter how closely you observe the most important signals for approaching weather—or even if you study meteorology yourself—what you'll soon discover is that the most predictable thing about the weather each day is that it's totally unpredictable.

So, too, is it with life. Like the weather, life is full of unpredictable, surprising moments that oftentimes catch you completely off-guard. Sometimes the unpredictability changes your life in marvelous ways—a chance meeting results in a long-term relationship; sometimes the unpredictability throws you an incredible challenge—a car accident requires months of tiring rehabilitation; sometimes the unpredictability forces you to give up something or someone you cherished—a grandchild succumbs to cancer.

Change abounds in life. Without change, life wouldn't exist. So rather than wish that life could be more predictable, stable, defined, and easier to understand, relish the experience of change that life gives you. For such change helps you to improve hopeless situations, encourages trust in the unknown, conquers fear and develops courage, urges taking positive action, and alters your vision of life.

LIFE ALWAYS HOLDS NEW AND EXCITING POSSIBILITIES.

OCTOBER 15

"Days have gone by. It must be October, mid-October I think, because the leaves are flying fast. The great maples are skeletons against the sky....Pansy, now the nights are cold, sometimes comes to sleep with me....The only time I weep is when she is there, purring beside me. I...can hardly bear the sweetness of that little rough tongue licking my hand."

— poet/diarist May Sarton

PET PARTNERSHIPS

At the moment you're reading this page, thousands of pets are providing not only comfort and companionship to their owners but, in many cases, are performing such duties as helping their owners to safely cross the street, reminding those who are sick to take their medication, retrieving money from automated teller machines, and even saving their owners' lives.

Take, for instance, the heroic story of Lyric, a trained medical dog whose owner's severe sleep apnea requires her to sleep with an oxygen machine. One night, Lyric was alerted by the siren on the oxygen machine. Lyric first tried to rouse her owner—scratches on the owner's arm prove this—but when this was unsuccessful, Lyric raced to the telephone in the kitchen, knocked the receiver off the hook, pressed a button that automatically dials 911, and barked furiously into the handset. The enhanced 911 system flashed the owner's address on the screen, along with her medical condition and the fact that she had a specially trained dog to help her in emergencies. Within minutes, paramedics were at her house, giving her oxygen.

Any kind of pet can be a lifesaver—a man with sleep apnea has a pet iguana that sleeps on his chest and wakes him whenever he stops breathing; cats have been known to awaken sleeping families to a fire in the house. Also, any pet can be a life-enhancer that will improve the quality of your day-today existence.

I ADOPT A PET PARTNER FROM AN ANIMAL SHELTER OR HUMANE SOCIETY.

OCTOBER 16

"Guard your tongue in youth, and in age you may mature a thought that will be of service to your people."

— Sioux proverb

WOMEN'S ROLE MODELS

Women can learn so much from the role models in their lives. Perhaps your mother and grandmother were or are women of strength and courage who served as positive role models for you. Maybe one of your teachers, a spiritual advisor, or a friend of the family may have shown you the positive sides of maturing when you were growing up. Perhaps you developed a large part of your confidence and self-esteem from those who were pioneers, inventors, or other notable women throughout history who achieved greatness. Or maybe your role models are your contemporaries— people of all ages who live today and are doing things you always dreamed of doing.

Strong female role models can decrease your fear of aging. Also, they can help you to deal with society's often negative image of older women as unproductive. Remember such positive role models as Elizabeth Cady Stanton and Susan B. Anthony, both of whom worked vigorously for women's rights until very late in their lives. And think, too, of Mother Jones, a heroic fighter for unions and the oppressed, who was 93 when she addressed a convention of the Farmer-Labor Party.

There are plenty of female role models in today's society who are challenging ageist and sexist barriers, and who are doing so at all ages. Yet you don't have to always look outside yourself for role models; you, too, can be a role model for a peer as well as for a younger woman. What you do can influence others to improve your life in the present and influence the lives of those in their futures.

MY ROLE MODELS GIVE ME STRENGTH TO BECOME
A ROLE MODEL MYSELF.

OCTOBER 17

"She had finally reached the age where she was more afraid of getting old than dying."

— film producer/director Julia Phillips

LIFE AS A HORROR FILM

There comes a time in every horror film when you know something bad is going to happen. Even though every scene, character interaction, and line of dialogue in the movie has directed you to this moment of tension and terror, even though you know it's only a movie, and even though you know you could get up from your seat and walk out of the theater, you remain in your seat, eyes riveted to the screen.

You may feel that same kind of fear when you ponder what the upcoming years have in store for you. You know that there will be no escaping the effects that aging will eventually have upon your mind, body, and spirit, no matter how well you take care of yourself. Like the scene in a horror film when the evil person lurks in a darkened room, lying in wait for the movie's hero or heroine to enter and so begin the struggle between life and death, so too do you advance in your life, knowing at any moment that some not very pleasant things may spring out at you.

But if you constantly act and react out of fear, tension, and stress over what may or may not happen to you in the years to come—for example, you may lose your eyesight, or you may not; you may have memory lapses, or you may not—then you're going to live your life in a way that convinces you that danger lurks around every corner, and terrible things are out to get you.

Consider, instead, how different your life could be if you enjoyed the romance in your life, the drama of your life, the beauty in your life, and the wonderful experiences of your life. The movie of your life can be a four-star, happy-ending classic—if you want it to be.

❦   ❦   ❦

I WATCH HORROR MOVIES INSTEAD OF LIVE THEM.

"...for in every adult there lurks a child—an eternal child, something that is always becoming, is never completed, calls for unceasing care, attention, and education. That is the part of the human personality that wants to develop and become whole."
— psychologist Carl Jung

YOUR INNER CHILD

When you were growing up, did you promise yourself that you were going to live a life that was different from that of your parents? Also, did you make up your mind that all of your needs that weren't respected or satisfied by your parents were never going to be ignored again in adulthood? Today you may still be struggling to make this happen in your life; you may still be the needy, unhappy, and unfulfilled child you were so many years ago.

The more severe the influences are from your long-lost past, the more determined you may be today to strive to achieve a different life—one in which your childhood needs are met in a way that they weren't in the past. Rising above poverty, a limited education, dysfunctional behaviors, language barriers, prejudice, divorce, or death can make you determined to live a life free from all those things. Even if you were raised in a home of wealth, unlimited educational opportunities, and healthy parents, you may still feel the need to live a different way of life.

While the phrase, "Never forget where you came from" is an apt thought to keep in mind from time to time, it doesn't have to be the pervading influence that makes you always honor your inner child first and your adult self last. While you can't make up for your childhood years, you can start now to be kind, patient, and gentle both to the child that still cries out for recognition and attention within you and the adult that longs to let go of your sometimes painful childhood memories.

I AM A LOVING PARENT TO MY INNER CHILD.

"Go—not knowing where. Bring—not knowing what.
The path is long, the way unknown."

— from a Russian fairy tale

TAKING PLEASURE IN THE PRESENT

There's a Chinese parable in which a wise man journeys to a small village in the mountains, gathers all the villagers, and tells them that if they care to join him, they can move a mountain together. He explains to them that moving the mountain will be a task to be accomplished over generations. "The truth that you must realize," the wise man tells the villagers, "is that for all the hard work you will do to move this mountain and the many, many hours of labor, in the end it will be as if you only moved a teaspoon of dirt and one small pebble. You will not live to see the finished product—the mountain moved—nor will you even be able to see, on a daily basis, the reward of your work—a mountain taking shape, a peak, a valley."

Rather than refuse to work or to try to devise ways to speed up the process of moving the mountain so the task could be finished and everyone could enjoy the fruits of their labors, the villagers who chose to participate in moving the mountain did so with a smile on their faces. They chose to live in the present moment and focused on the task of moving the mountain, bit by bit. In performing the task, time meant nothing to them, nor did attaining the actual goal of moving the mountain. Rather, it was the task itself, and the ability to focus on that task, that became most important to them.

Can you begin to live your life in such a way that you, too, can do something without the need of an outcome? Can you do something for the sheer pleasure of it, and live solely in the present moment and not in some past or future time?

❀   ❀   ❀

I LIVE IN THE PRESENT, AND IT GIVES
ME MUCH SATISFACTION.

OCTOBER 20

"There is one God looking down on us all. We are all children of one God. God is listening to me. The sun, the darkness, the winds, are all listening to what we now say."

— Geronimo

A DAILY PRAYER

Oh God, help me to trust in your judgment as my greatest Teacher so I am always open and receptive to the lessons you bring me each day. Encourage me to be patient with my ability to comprehend as well as to apply what knowledge you give me. Be strict with me so I might study not only what is in my head but also what is in my heart, so I might create a balanced mixture of intellect and feelings. Ensure that I participate in discussions with those around me. Remind me to offer my kind support to them as well as a keen attentiveness. Also, make sure that I am able to gather the strength I need to provide alternate points of view, even when such views go against what so many others may believe or may want me to believe.

Oh Great Teacher, I pray each day to you so I might never lose the lessons that I have already been taught. I pray, too, to be a teacher myself who can spread this knowledge to others, much as a gardener might spread seeds in a garden. Help me to know that it is not enough to speak from facts but to offer experience, for it is the experience that truly nourishes the seedlings of tiny truths and helps them to grow into strong stalks of understanding.

Dear Lord, I ask that I always foster a love of learning from You. Although sometimes the lessons you give me are hard and are fraught with many difficult questions to answer and tests of physical, emotional, and mental endurance, know that I strive always to be your good student.

❖   ❖   ❖

I ASK FOR DAILY SPIRITUAL HELP FROM MY
ALL-KNOWING TEACHER.

OCTOBER 21

"Life does not accommodate you, it shatters you. It is meant to, and it couldn't do it better. Every seed destroys its container or else there would be no fruition."

— writer Florida Scott-Maxwell

FACING LIFE'S CHALLENGES

Have you ever read or heard stories about those who have had to endure incredible pain, surmount unbelievable odds, or struggle twice as hard as the average person to attain something others take for granted? There are well-known people that fit such descriptions. The great role model Helen Keller grew up blind, deaf, and unable to speak in a world that commonly treated such individuals as less than human. Franklin Delano Roosevelt suffered with polio throughout his life, yet provided the country with strong leadership in a world that was torn apart. Eddie Rickenbacker floated aimlessly in a life raft for 21 days in the Pacific Ocean and lived to tell of his adventure.

There are others—strangers you come to know, whose stories fill magazines and newspaper columns—and there are those you personally know—a friend, family member, or acquaintance—who must struggle at this very minute for their next breath, to try to cope with the loss of someone dear, to deal with chronic pain, or to try to walk from one end of a hallway to another without assistance. Life is full of such struggles, big and small, challenges that are placed along the way that are meant to be overcome so you can become a stronger person. As Florida Scott-Maxwell wrote after eight decades of living, "When a new disability arrives, I look about to see if death has come, and I call quietly, 'Death, is that you? Are you there?' So far the disability has answered, 'Don't be silly, it's me.'"

❊ ❊ ❊

I USE ALL OF LIFE'S CHALLENGES
FOR POSITIVE GROWTH.

OCTOBER 22

"Our parents cast long shadows over our lives. When we grow up, we imagine that we can walk in the sun, free of them. We don't realize, until it's too late, that we have no choice in the matter; they're always ahead of us."

— writer Richard Eyre

PARENTAL INFLUENCES

When you were growing up, did you imagine living a way of life that was different from that of your parents? Ever since you left home, you may have tried as hard as you could to break free of the hold they had over you. For whatever reason, there was no way you wanted to replicate who they were or how they lived their lives.

But now, you may find yourself replicating your parents' ways of doing things. You may be preparing the same family recipes and setting the table the way your mother used to. You may have decorated your house or purchased furniture that mirrors the set-up and style you remember from your childhood home. You may find yourself humming tunes the way your mother often did when she was cooking. Or you may be stacking the logs and crumbling and stuffing sheets of newspaper between the wood in the fireplace just as your father did.

Imitating your parents' ways of doing things may be the only way you have of holding on to them as they age or remembering them since they've been gone. It's also probably the best tribute you can pay to them. But remember that whether you make a conscious or unconscious effort to keep them alive in your heart and mind, they're with you always. For, as writer James Baldwin has pointed out, "Children have never been very good at listening to their elders, but they have never failed to imitate them."

I KEEP MY PARENTS ALIVE BY THE THINGS I DO THAT
REMIND ME OF THEM.

OCTOBER 23

"It is so comic to call one's self old; even at ninety, I suppose!"

— diarist Alice James

JEANNE CALMENT, OLDEST LIVING PERSON

Jeanne Calment, believed to be the world's oldest person, celebrated her 121st birthday in 1996 with memories ranging from meeting the Dutch painter Vincent van Gogh and living under 20 French presidents, to her new career as a pop icon who is learning how to surf the Internet.

The frail, white-haired Frenchwoman, who married her late husband a century ago, was born on February 21, 1875, when Ulysses S. Grant occupied the White House, Queen Victoria sat on the throne of the British Empire, and emperors ruled Russia and Germany. On her 41st birthday, the bloodiest battle of World War I begun in Verdun, northern France. She reached 65 the year France was invaded by the Nazis in 1940, and was 70 when France allowed her to vote for the first time. Even though she uses a wheelchair and is blind and almost deaf, she's still lucid. In fact, despite the fact that she was born in a world before the invention of cars, planes, telephones, and the cinema, she recently signed a record contract and recorded a CD titled "Mistress of Time," in which she speaks to a backing of funk-rap, and techno and dance music. If the CD is a hit, Calment plans to use the proceeds to buy a minibus for her companions at the Maison du Lac retirement home so they can enjoy the Provence countryside.

Calment says her smile is her way of staying youthful, but her longtime doctor, Victor Lebre, recounted a different secret for her longevity: "What she says is, 'In life the good people are those who don't complain'...and her motto is 'act, act, act.'"

I LIVE BY THE MOTTO: "ACT, ACT, ACT"!

OCTOBER 24

*"Nature gives to every time and season some beauties of its own;
and from morning to night, as from the cradle to the grave, is but
a succession of changes so gentle and easy that we can scarcely
mark their progress."*

— Charles Dickens

MEDITATING UPON NATURE

The eternal cycles of nature come and go without announcement and fanfare, without media coverage and hype, and, unfortunately at times, without your notice. When was the last time you heard the wind as it gently stirred long blades of grass, the sound of gentle rain caressing a lake, or the call of geese flying overhead? When was the last time you watched the sun awaken, spotted a hawk circling lazily overhead, or truly noticed the color of a leaf? As long as you pay more attention to the visual and aural stimulations of the world that swirl around you and blow through your mind, the true progress of the natural world will be just a fleeting shadow that tiptoes silently out of your sight.

Nature teaches you about silence in the stillness of a forest, a quiet lake, a rugged mountainside, a squirrel foraging for food, a flock of geese floating on a pond, a field of wildflowers, puffy clouds in the sky, and the moon illuminating a blanket of snow. But while such natural locales may not always be accessible to you, you can seek such stillness from within.

Indian spiritual leader Mahatma Ghandi sought out periods of silence by setting aside a day of silence a week. Could you set aside a few minutes to be still? Establish a regular time for meditation in which you "go within"—to places beyond the noise and surface chatter of everyday life, to places within the natural world. Visualize yourself on a mountaintop, on the seashore, in a field of wildflowers, or in a forest. Then "listen" to the soothing progress that nature makes.

❀ ❀ ❀

I GO OUT TO NATURE BY GOING WITHIN.

OCTOBER 25

"My grandmother died four years ago at 104, and my mother, last year. For more than 30 years, I was the third-generation mother and daughter in my family. We were a club sandwich with my grandmother and children the slices of bread, and my mother and I the turkey and tomato."

— writer Anne Mazick Levin

THE SANDWICH OF LIFE

When you're in middle age, you're also in the middle of the generations of your family—like being the filling in a sandwich. Initially, this can be enjoyable; for example, when you're young, you're sandwiched between parents and grandparents. Anne Mazick Levin describes this as a time when "...the two upper layers covered us like a warm quilt, offering hugs and humor, soup and cookies."

But then, as you grow older, you become the one who's holding the sandwich together. If you've brought children into the world, then your parents and grandparents comprise one layer of bread and your children the other. Your children need your care, as do your parents. Even without children, your parents and grandparents still need your care as do your career, home, partner, pet, and anything and anyone else that needs your time and attention. As Levin remarked when her mother was rushed into the hospital, "Suddenly my role in the middle of the sandwich expanded. It's not easy to juggle a child's concert rehearsals, a parent's hospitalization, and the well-being of the rest of the family, not to mention a job."

Although being in the middle and trying to hold the sandwich together can be a difficult experience, it's one that anyone in middle age needs to go through. However, remember that you won't always be in the middle—there will come a time when you'll be one of the layers of bread, and someone else will be in the middle!

IN THE SANDWICH OF LIFE, I AM THE BEST FILLING.

OCTOBER 26

MALE SEXUAL ACTIVITY

Men as well as women undergo changes in their sexuality as they age. Lower testosterone levels may sometimes result in loss of sexual interest in some men. Middle-age and older men may experience changes in orgasm; they may not ejaculate during every sexual experience or have an orgasm every time they make love. Because sexual responses may slow down, older men may need a longer time of stimulation before they can attain a full erection; also, they may need a longer time to renew sexual energy after an orgasm. The likelihood of male impotence rises after the age of 50, although many men who once were able to maintain regular sexual activity can overcome incidences of impotence through sex therapy.

Also, worries about work, retirement, relocation, or finances; illness or chronic pain; tiredness, fatigue from overexertion, or over-training for an athletic activity; and excessive weight or poor body image all contribute to impotence as well as waning sexual interest. The mental fatigue experienced by older men, according to sex therapists Masters and Johnson, is quite different from that of younger men, which really translates into the side effects of long-term stress. Also, fear of failure is so dominant in males that any differences in their sexual activity and performance from when they were younger can make them withdraw from sexual experience.

Finally, social stereotypes that men are supposed to have stronger sex drives than women can make men feel that there's something wrong with them when, in reality, they're merely undergoing normal hormonal changes and shifts in their sex drive.

❊ ❊ ❊

I AM SENSITIVE TO THE FACT THAT THE
MALE SEX DRIVE CHANGES.

OCTOBER 27

"And it may have been that his only happy moments were these at dawn, when he went with his dog over the known ways, freeing his bronchial tubes of the catarrh that had oppressed his night, and watching as color gradually emerged from the indistinct gray among the field rows and the olive branches, and recognizing the song of the morning birds one by one."

— writer Italo Calvino

THE IMMORTAL SOULS OF ANIMALS

Ask pet owners if they think that their animals have immortal souls, and they will probably answer with a resounding "Yes!" What you, too, as a pet owner may know is that your animal is capable of compassion, sympathy, and perhaps even altruism. You can look into your pet's eyes and see boundless love. Take a walk or chat with your dog, and you feel the bond you share. You know that your life has been greatly enriched by the experience of loving and being loved by your pet. But try to explain that you believe your pet has an immortal soul—an ability to enjoy an afterlife and perhaps to "meet up" with you when you die—and your response will probably be met by raised eyebrows.

In the early 1900s, Anatole France wrote a story about a missionary who was shipwrecked on an island. The missionary, whose eyes were nearly swollen shut after his ordeal in the sea, baptizes the babbling inhabitants of the island, not realizing that they were penguins. This causes a great controversy in heaven. God assembles clerics and doctors, while St. Augustine participates in a great debate and summarizes that the penguins must go to hell when they die. St. Catherine of Alexandria is then consulted; she advises granting the penguins an immortal soul, but of a very small size. In the end, however, God turns the penguins into men who will "...commit sins they would not have committed as penguins."

❉   ❉   ❉

I USE MY FAITH TO UNDERSTAND THE SOULS OF ANIMALS.

OCTOBER 28

"When we are chafed and fretted by small cares, a look at the stars will show us the littleness of our own interests."

— astronomer Maria Mitchell

PERSPECTIVES ON PROBLEM-SOLVING

Have you ever become lost in a city or felt overwhelmed while trying to negotiate the complexity of such congested areas? When you're surrounded by tall buildings, being jostled about on crowded sidewalks while attempting to read a street map, or becoming more and more confused dealing with one-way streets and traffic rotaries, the city may seem like an endless maze of confusing twists and turns, an area of haphazard building construction and placement.

Yet if you were to view an aerial photograph of the same city, what you'd see would be an impressive display of orderliness and much forethought given to planning. Suddenly, there are no confusing twists and turns, but neat blocks; the placement of buildings makes perfect sense.

When you feel similarly lost in your life or muddled by a particular circumstance, viewing things from a different perspective can help you feel that your life is in order and that any troubling puzzle or problem can be resolved. As American humorist Garrison Keillor points out in viewing the world from space, "Out there in the Milky Way and the world without end, Amen, America was a tiny speck of a country, a nickel tossed into the Grand Canyon, and American culture the amount of the Pacific Ocean you bring home in your swimsuit."

What this means is that when you can view your life, your home, yourself, and your circumstances from a distance, you can see the boundlessness rather than the limitations, the new rather than the old, the way out rather than no way at all.

I REMEMBER THAT A VIEW FROM ABOVE CAN
CLEAR MY HEAD.

"Old age transforms or fossilizes."
— writer Marie von Ebner-Eschenbach

A COMMUNITY HEALTH PLAN

A little over 100 years ago, a small band of Italians left Roseto Val Fortore, a village in the foothills of the Apennines, and journeyed to America. They longed to achieve a better life in the slate quarries of eastern Pennsylvaniaa. They named their new village Roseto and recreated the strong community ties they knew how to form and nurture from their Italian heritage.

Most of the residents of Roseto lived in three-generational households. They centered their lives around family. They even built their houses so close together that neighbors could easily chat with one another as they sat on rocking chairs on their own front porches.

In the 1960s, with interest level high on communal-style living, researchers who studied the close-knit community of generations realized that while Roseto shared the same water supply and many other services with nearby communities, the town had only 40 percent as many deaths from heart attacks. "At first," Judy Foreman writes in her article on Roseto, "researchers thought the Rosetans might carry some special, protective genes. But this was not the case, for Rosetans who moved away—even to the nearby village of Bangor—lost whatever magic the town possessed against heart disease."

The effect was dubbed "The Roseto Effect," and the "magic" was simple: by maintaining close, strong family ties; by passing down family traditions from generation to generation; and by living in an atmosphere of familial and familiar love, support, and acceptance, the people lived longer, healthier lives.

❀   ❀   ❀

I CREATE 'THE ROSETO EFFECT' IN MY COMMUNITY.

"The dead might as well try to speak to the living as the old to the young."

— writer Willa Cather

BRIDGING THE GENERATION GAP

In the radical '60s, students walked through their universities with placards that proclaimed, "Down with the establishment!" What the young people were really saying was, "Never trust anyone over 30."

But today, you and others from your generation may as well be walking around with a sign that advises, "Never trust anyone under 30." Generation gaps today are like chasms; the younger generation is no more understanding of your generation than you are of them. In the early 1930s, younger generations were lauded for their fortitude. In the '40s, it was the youth who were the most patriotic and sacrificial. In the '50s, corporations bragged about their brilliant young technicians. In the '60s, youth protests gave birth to today's activism and environmental concerns. In the '70s, the youth were seen as the "new explorers," engaged in enviable adventures of self-discovery.

But today's youth evokes blank stares and images of, according to Neil Howe and Bill Strauss, authors of *13th Gen,* "...an eraser-headed kid with reflective shades, a backwards ball cap, and high-top sneakers, his Walkman tuned to heavy metal....That 13er is our manchild of the '80s. He, all grown up, is the future we fear."

Yet, you need to be supportive of the younger generation. There's much that they're doing to improve the quality of their future lives. Many are providing youthful entrepreneurships, working hard to save scarce global resources, and striving to live by the motto "Life, liberty, and the pursuit of happiness."

I SUPPORT THE EFFORTS OF THE YOUNGER GENERATION.

"No man was ever so completely skilled in the conduct of life, as not to receive new information from age and experience."
— Roman dramatist Terence

A NEW LIFE EXPERIENCE

Growing older gives you the time to travel, to learn, and to explore new areas of your life. Whereas growing older in the past signaled a time to altruistically live for children or grandchildren, today you can live in ways that help you to seek your own fulfillment rather than theirs. And whereas during the time of the Industrial Revolution a desire was created for attaining material possessions in maturity—cars, housing, clothing, and new and improved gadgetry—today the quest is for unique life experiences. According to Dr. James Ogilvy, past director of research for Values and Lifestyle Study at the Stanford Research Institute, "The growth of our economy is no longer driven by the desires of consumers to accumulate goods. It is driven by the consumer's quest for vivid experiences. The experience industry cultivates through education, broadens through travel, allows escape through entertainment, heals through psychotherapy, numbs through drugs and alcohol, edifies through religion, informs through reading, and enraptures through art."

What new experience would you like to enjoy? The "golden time" of your life is made even richer by a certain level of self-indulgence. Whether your choice of new experience involves something as elaborate as a sail-around-the-world adventure program, as rugged as a week-long hike along the Appalachian Trail, as mind-expanding as learning a new language, or as pampering as a retreat to a spa, let your new experience enhance your personal enjoyment of life.

❧ ❧ ❧

I SEEK SELF-FULFILLMENT FROM A MATURE
LIFE EXPERIENCE.

NOVEMBER 1

"Love doesn't just sit there, like a stone; it has to be made, like bread, remade all the time, made new."

— writer Ursula K. Leguin

THE NEW DATING GAME

The new dating game for single older people finds Club Med, which initially marketed its "swinging singles" resorts to men and women in their twenties, with the median age of its guests today fast approaching forty. Social groups, dances, and nightclubs are being redesigned to attract those in late adulthood who are looking for first-time or second-chance romances. And newspaper personals are beginning to advertise for desired partners who are sometimes middle-aged or older, as in the following ad:

> "If you are 60+ SWF [single white female], enjoy life, including music, dancing, camping, beach strolling, quiet dinners by firesides, I would be happy to hear from you. Write Box..."

In addition, marriage and family counseling practices, along with clinical social workers and psychotherapists, are focusing on helping middle-aged and older people make the oftentimes difficult transition from marriage to being single (because of death and divorce). This transition involves welcoming love in the second half of life in ways that help redevelop intimacy and affection with another partner and possibly even lead back to marriage.

What this means is that love needs to be redefined in the minds of older men and women. While former partners may always remain, in a person's heart, the one true love, love can be reexperienced and made anew in a new companion. Because love improves the quality of life, gives it meaning, and provides pleasure, love in the second half of life can be as rewarding as love in the first half.

I DATE SO I MAY FALL IN LOVE AGAIN.

NOVEMBER 2

"We are here to witness the creation and to abet it. We are here to notice each thing so each thing gets noticed....We are here to bring to consciousness the beauty and power that are around us and to praise the people who are here with us. We witness our generation and our times. We watch the weather. Otherwise, the creation would be playing to an empty house."

— essayist/poet Annie Dillard

THE HERITAGE OF LIFE

Nature shows you that you have a place in the living heritage of life every time you look around you at the passion, the challenges, the grandeur, the beauty, the discipline, and the opportunities represented by all of nature's wonders. Each and every wonder is a part of you; you are as profound as the sea, as gentle as a summer breeze, as beautiful as the side of a mountain, as soft as the warm sand, as active as the environment in which you live.

Your heritage of being a member of humanity, too, gives you justification and validation for being here on this planet each day. Your heritage encourages you to be strong. Your heritage helps you to trust and have faith in yourself. Your heritage implores you to act. Your heritage urges you to sometimes abandon the search for security and reach out to the risk of living. Your heritage tells you to accept living and dying equally. Your heritage stretches your mind and body. Your heritage pushes you to go out often into the world—both the natural world and the world in which you oftentimes live elbow to elbow with others—to go out into the Great Unknown as well as the Great Known in order to know more about yourself and the world around you.

You can make your time on earth most worthwhile by becoming more conscious of it—by noticing, every day, the wonder of creation in all living things.

I AM HERE TO WITNESS THE CREATION.

NOVEMBER 3

"I am an idealist. I don't know where I'm going,
but I'm on my way."

— poet Carl Sandburg

SELF-TALK

It has often been said that one sure sign to tell if you're getting older is when you find yourself talking to yourself. But what are you saying to yourself?

Self-talk can be very powerful. On the one hand, it can develop a healthy ego, build self-esteem, create confidence, help you strengthen problem-solving skills, and encourage optimism and positive thinking. On the other hand, it can trigger ego deterioration, destroy self-esteem, lower confidence, create more problems in your life, and promote negativity. How can you communicate with yourself in ways that help you to create a strong, secure individual?

First, avoid asking yourself questions. Self-questioning can erode self-confidence and instill self-doubt. Rather than ask, "Do I really think I can do this?" or "Why do I always get myself in a jam?" say "I can handle this situation," and "I think sometimes I try too hard."

Second, replace negative words in your vocabulary with positive ones: *can* for *can't, will* for *won't, want* for *should.* Negative words encourage negative responses; positive words beget positive changes.

Third, use your self-talk not only to help you to be more of an optimist, but also to help you to be a more capable captain of your own ship. Give yourself encouragement through praise and congratulations. Offer guidance and advice as if you were your own best friend. Be gentle with yourself when you're feeling blue. Emphasize the power and potential you have within yourself, and there won't be anywhere that you can't go in this world.

I USE POSITIVE, AFFIRMING COMMENTS IN MY SELF-TALK.

NOVEMBER 4

"The remarkable thing is, we have a choice every day regarding the attitude we will embrace for that day. We cannot change our past. We cannot change the fact that people will act in a certain way. We cannot change the inevitable. The only thing we can do is play on the one string we have, and that is our attitude."

— Judge Charles Swindoll

GET OFF THE PITY POT

Poison can change food from a source of nourishment to a source of illness. So, too, can self-pity taint life, changing it from an exciting adventure you're free to engage in to a stiff prison sentence that keeps you confined in a dark, barren cell.

Self-pity is an attitude of ingratitude. Self-pity looks at what you can't do, what you don't have, what you've lost, and what you can't change. Self-pity is the perfect companion to sharing a miserable existence. Self-pity is self-absorbed and selfish, for self-pity says, "Hey, look at me. I'm old. I'm feeble. I have a heart condition. My family doesn't love me. I'm a burden...." On and on self-pity goes.

A positive attitude is the dreaded and hated enemy of self-pity; whenever a positive attitude walks into a room, self-pity leaves. A positive attitude focuses on what you can do, what you do have, what you haven't lost, and what you can change. A positive attitude is the perfect companion to living a physically, mentally, and spiritually fulfilling life. A positive attitude cares for your self as well as the selves of others.

Today, get off the pity pot! Remember, as Charles Swindoll said, that a positive attitude "...is more important than circumstances, than what other people think or say or do. It is more important than appearance, giftedness, or skill. It will make or break a company, a church, a home."

I FOSTER AN ATTITUDE OF GRATITUDE.

NOVEMBER 5

"I was 37, too old for a paper route, too young for Social Security and too tired for an affair."

— humorist/writer Erma Bombeck,
on why she started writing her newspaper column

ERMA BOMBECK

When it became known that Erma Bombeck was suffering from kidney failure, 30 of her readers offered to donate their kidneys to her. Such loyalty and devotion from fans she had never met provided convincing evidence that Erma Bombeck was more than a newspaper columnist to those who read her articles religiously. In many ways, she was their friend.

Erma Bombeck died in 1996, but she left behind a written legacy that chronicles a career that took off in midlife. She was an at-home mom when she started writing her humor columns for a neighborhood newspaper, but prior to that she had worked as a feature writer for the *Dayton* (Ohio) *Journal-Herald*. In 1965, less than a year after she started writing her column, it was picked up by that same newspaper, where it ran twice a week. Just a few weeks later, the column was syndicated and began appearing in 20 newspapers. By 1971, it ran in over 200 papers and had become something of a journalistic phenomenon. At the peak of her career, Bombeck's column ran regularly in as many as 900 newspapers.

Bombeck branched out into television (she was a regular commentator on "Good Morning America"), and she became a best-selling author. Even when she learned that she had breast cancer and underwent a mastectomy, even when a congenital kidney disease took its toll on her kidneys and necessitated that she undergo dialysis four times a day while waiting for a transplant, she kept on writing, her humor sharp and entertaining until the end of her life.

I ADMIRE THOSE WHO SMILE THROUGH THEIR TRIALS.

*"When a man is no longer anxious to do better than well,
he is done for."*

— artist Benjamin Haydon

BENEFICIAL GOAL-SETTING

Which do you think is worse: not reaching a goal that you've worked hard to attain, or not having any goal to reach at all? You might think that having no goals is better than falling short of a desired goal; without the need to fulfill a desire, you won't feel stress or pressure to succeed, and you certainly won't fail. Also, you may think that American society is far too goal-oriented, so having no goals will let you enjoy life more and take away the need to constantly compete with yourself and others.

But what exactly is a goal? A goal is simply a change you wish to bring about so that you can improve the overall quality of your life. Most goals begin with a desire that springs from a dream: a vision of how you could be, how things could turn out, or how you could be in tandem with the events in your life. If you don't acknowledge such a desire, dream a dream, or create a goal, nothing will ever change.

Writer Benjamin E. Mays once opined, "It must be borne in mind that the tragedy of life doesn't lie in not reaching your goal. The tragedy lies in having no goal to reach. It isn't a calamity to die with dreams unfulfilled, but it is a calamity not to dream. It is not a disgrace not to reach the stars, but it is a disgrace to have no stars to reach for." So what's worse is to have nothing to look forward to, nothing to strive for, nothing to reach, nothing to attain. Life is much more interesting when you can create new visions of what your life can be like and what you can be like when you achieve a goal.

I ENVISION A BETTER SELF AND A BETTER LIFE
THROUGH THE GOALS I SET.

NOVEMBER 7

LEARNING TO GROW YOUNGER

There's no secret of youth more powerful than that of learning. As long as new perceptions continue to enter your brain, no matter what your age, your body can respond in new ways. As one 80-year-old man once said, "People don't grow old. When they stop growing, they become old." You're only as old as the information that swirls through you; new knowledge, new skills, and new ways of looking at the world keep the mind as well as the body fresh and vibrant, full of life.

Greek philosopher and moralist Diogenes Laertius once advised, "Let no one be slow to seek wisdom when he is young, nor weary of the search thereof when he is grown old. For no age is too early or too late for the health of the soul." A vast array of special programs specifically geared for enhancing and expanding the knowledge of older people are being offered, not only at colleges and universities, but also at work sites, churches and synagogues, YMCAs and YWCAs, community centers, and adult education programs. Instructors who teach such programs love the liveliness of the classrooms—their students are eager to debate important points, ask penetrating questions, and even offer new perspectives from their own expertise—and students have enjoyed learning everything from how to carve linoleum to playing jazz piano to earning a degree in law.

Even refresher courses or more advanced levels of learning in an area in which you thought you knew most everything can help you to look at familiar information in a new way. What in youth you learned, in age you can better understand.

THE FOUNTAIN OF YOUTH IS KNOWLEDGE.

"The past should be a springboard, not a hammock."

— unknown

EMPTYING YOURSELF FOR FULFILLMENT

There's the story told about a visitor who traveled a great distance to consult with a wise Zen Master about her inability to feel good about herself and her life. When the Master greeted her, she immediately began to talk about her life. The Master silently prepared tea for them as she went on and on. Then the Master began to pour tea for the woman. The woman continued to talk as the Master poured, then suddenly stopped in mid-sentence. The Master had filled her cup and was continuing to pour the tea, which had now overflowed the cup and was spilling out onto the floor.

"Why do you continue to pour after the cup is full?" asked the visitor.

"To show you," replied the Master, "that you are like this cup: so full of your memories of the past that nothing can go into the cup in the present. You cannot experience happiness in the present until you have emptied your cup."

Can you treasure the way your life is now rather than continue to relive the memories of the past? In your mind is a multitude of stored memories. Some may not be so good or pleasurable to think about, but there are probably many positive, wonderful memories of the past that you hoard like gold because you wish they had never come to an end.

Yet, think of how many more wonderful memories you can create in the present by giving yourself an opportunity to live fully and completely in the here and now. What's past is past, what's done is done, what's over is over. It's that simple. But there's so much more to come.

I VALUE MY MEMORIES OF THE PAST AND THE MEMORIES
I CREATE IN THE PRESENT.

November 9

"It has begun to occur to me that life is a stage
I'm going through."

— writer Ellen Goodman

THE STAGES OF ADULTHOOD

Just as infancy, adolescence, your teenage years, and the young adulthood stage of youth have helped you to progress through life thus far, so too are there stages of maturity that help you to progress through adulthood.

In the infancy of your aging, you recognize the potential of the second half of your life and therefore explore ways to enhance your well-being by changing bad habits, dealing with weight issues, eating well, paying attention to your appearance, revising unhealthy lifestyles, and exercising and moving for health.

In the adolescence of your aging, you pay attention to your sexual needs, make decisions regarding childbearing, deepen the intimacy within your current relationship or look for a more committed interaction, explore career options and retirement, and analyze finances in order to save for the future.

In the teenage years of your aging, you may look into housing alternatives and living arrangements, experience hormonal changes, retire, and become a caregiver to aging parents and relatives.

In the adulthood stage of your aging, you face your own health issues, pay attention to decisions that affect the security of your future, cope with a changing society and generational issues, and confront dying and death.

Writer Maggie Kuhn defines aging as "...the term for a continuous process of growth through life." Each stage of young adulthood as well as maturing adulthood helps you to grow through the seasons of your life—birth, growth, decline, and death—in enriching ways so all the seasons of your life are precious.

I TAKE PLEASURE IN EACH SEASON OF MY LIFE.

NOVEMBER 10

"The point was not to find the gene. The point is to keep women from dying of breast cancer."

— genetic researcher Mary-Claire King

THE GENETICS OF BREAST CANCER

For 17 years, genetic researcher Mary-Claire King, who works out of her lab at the University of Washington in Seattle, struggled to confirm her belief that familial breast cancer could be blamed on a single gene. In 1990, she proved the existence of a mutated gene for early-onset breast cancer, which strikes before the age of 50 and kills thousands of women in America each year; in fact, breast-cancer incidence rises rapidly in women between 30 and 50—one in 14 women—then continues to rise, but more slowly, after the age of 50—dropping to one in 8 women.

But King had a problem with her research; she couldn't pinpoint the gene's precise location. So, she continued on. Discovery came about in 1994, when a competing research team located the gene, now known as BRCA1. How did King feel about not fulfilling her goal after two decades of diligent and determined work to find the gene that's carried by about 600,000 women in the United States? King remembers that her team responded at the time, 'Oh, my God, somebody else found the gene'....Then we went in the next morning and did the next experiment....You have to go right on." King's sense of purpose—she sees her life work as "solving breast cancer"—took her on a grueling crusade that continues to this day, no matter which lab has been credited with the discovery of the mutated gene. "I think there are two keys to success," King says. "One is not being daunted by one's fear of failure. The second is sheer perseverance."

I DO ALL I CAN TO HELP SOLVE THE BREAST
CANCER PROBLEM.

NOVEMBER 11

"Human beings are set apart from the animals. We have a spiritual self, a physical self and a conscience. Therefore, we can make choices and are responsible for the choices we make. We may choose order and peace, or confusion and chaos."

— civil rights activist Rosa Parks

ROSA PARKS

Rosa Parks was born in the South, 50 years after slavery, at a time when racial segregation was legally enforced. Her grandparents told her what it was like to be brought up as slave children; she knew first-hand of Ku Klux Klan activity in her own community. Her parents raised her to always feel racial pride and self-dignity, so she grew up determined to achieve the total freedom her grandparents and parents never really had—the freedom that was taught to her in history books, which was a worthy goal no matter what the sacrifice.

So when Rosa Parks refused to give up her seat on a city bus for a white person—when she stubbornly resisted being forced to the back of the bus with the other "colored people," she wasn't so much standing up for all African-Americans, but for her own pride and self-dignity. Yet her one simple, personal act helped to change the world for all people of color; her struggle for her own rights and freedoms sparked others to struggle for theirs.

Rosa Parks once said, "To this day I believe we are here on earth to live, grow up, and do what we can to make this world a better place for all people to enjoy freedom. Differences of race, nationality, or religion should not be used to deny any human being citizenship rights or privileges. Life is to be lived to its fullest so that death is another chapter. Memories of our lives, our works, and our deeds will continue with others."

❧   ❧   ❧

I PROTECT MY PRIDE AND SELF-DIGNITY.

November 12

"Perhaps middle age is, or should be, a period of shedding shells; the shell of ambition, the shell of material accumulations and possessions, the shell of the ego."
— writer Anne Morrow Lindbergh

RIGHTING WRONGS

As you grow older, you may find that what once seemed all-important to you shifts in relevance to your life. Suddenly, it's not so critical to get that promotion or to buy that fancy new car; you're not so serious about something that once made you passionate and excited; you're more relaxed about the people, places, or things that used to cause you stress.

Also, those things that may have seemed unimportant to you or had no significance in your life suddenly are all-important, are profoundly meaningful. This proved to be the case for Hans Frank, a New York City international tax attorney, as he grew older. In his forties, he fell back on his remembrances of exile from Hitler's Germany and began to use his legal expertise and idealism to lead Self-help, a group founded to assist Jewish refugees. He then expanded Self-help's mission to include home care for the elderly and, more recently, for AIDS patients. Today, at 85, he's busy guiding Self-help's attempts to recover Nazi-seized property in the former East Germany. He says, of this new focus of Self-help, that it's "a very fortuitous ending to my career that gives me great satisfaction."

Perhaps you, too, can find ways to refocus your time, energy, and passion from the "missions" that you may have adopted early on in life but which today leave you with the feeling that something more important, more vital, more meaningful to yourself and to others is missing from your life. Do you have a self-help mission upon which you can embark?

I HELP MYSELF AND OTHERS.

NOVEMBER 13

"And indeed, it is old age, rather than death, that is to be contrasted with life. Old age is life's parody, whereas death transforms life into a destiny."

— writer/philosopher Simone de Beauvoir

LIFETIME ACHIEVEMENTS

As grand as the biographies of past heros and heroines of history and society, politics and activism, the sciences, literature, the arts, and exploration and invention are portrayed in books and encyclopedias, one thing they all share in common—if they died at an old age—is that, in the end, they suffered from the same symptoms of aging as you do today. They may have had memory lapses, disabilities, diseases or illnesses, and frailties. They may have been termed, at the time, "doddering old fools." As they grew older, they probably found that they couldn't understand the younger generation. They most likely lost their mobility and their ability to take care of themselves. They moved slowly, found it hard to see and hear, and told the same stories over and over again.

Yet, death erased such signs of aging and, instead, left them with their lifetime achievements intact. So, too, can it be with you. What's most important for you to remember right now is the entire body of your life, not your body as it is at this moment. What's most significant is what you've learned and the experiences you've had, not all those things that you've forgotten. What's most meaningful are the relationships you've shared with friends and family members and the people who you've loved truly, madly, and deeply—not the loves you've lost.

I FOCUS LESS ON WHO I AM NOW AND MORE ON
WHO I'VE ALWAYS BEEN.

November 14

"I venerate old age, and I love not the man who can look without emotion upon the sunset of life, when the dusk of evening begins to gather over the watery eye, and the shadows of twilight grow broader and deeper upon the understanding."

— poet Henry Wadsworth Longfellow

END-OF-DAY VISUALIZATION

The reward at the end of every day of your life is sleep. Although as you get older it may become harder for you to fall asleep, you can make whatever amount of sleep you get more peaceful and relaxing, filled with pleasant thoughts and reflections.

To do so, set aside a few minutes before you turn off the lights to close your eyes and visualize walking down a pleasant, nature-filled path. Each step you take moves you farther away from the day's activities and the many tasks you did or have left undone. Look around you as you walk. Breathe deeply. See lakes and mountains and hear the soothing sounds of a babbling brook; watch the rise and fall of gentle ocean waves that reflect a glorious sunset; breathe deeply of the humid air in a tropical rain forest while being serenaded by an orchestra of jungle sounds. In the inner sanctuary you create in your mind, nothing is important—nothing except peace of mind and the hours ahead in which your mind will be gently stilled.

As you reach the end of your evening "nature walk," you may feel the tensions and pressures of the day fall from your shoulders. Your body may feel lighter. Your lips may be turned upwards to form a gentle smile. You may feel a yawn building in your chest. At this moment, you can remind yourself, "Today has been good. I appreciate the day I was given, received something good from experiencing it, and now can close my eyes and let the reward of sleep drift over me."

TONIGHT I'M SATISFIED WITH MY DAY AND MY LIFE.

NOVEMBER 15

*"People who grow up without a sense of how yesterday has
affected today are unlikely to have a strong sense of how today
affects tomorrow. It is only when we become conscious of the flow
of time that the consequences of action...become a consideration.
It is only when we have perspective on our lives that motives
besides immediate gratification can come into play."*

— writer Lynne V. Cheney

RESTORING HARMONY

What happens when the harmony of your world is disrupted?
Imagine your life to be a still pond; suddenly, a rock is
tossed into the pond. Ripples extend out from the rock's point of
entry, disturbing the surface of the water; over time, the pond's stillness will be restored.

So, too, it can be in your life. You may go along with the flow
of your life—the routines, the familiar people, the set way of doing
things—when suddenly a "rock" is thrown into your still pond: a
parent needs your care, you become ill, you face an important
career decision, an unexpected bill forces you to consider using
your retirement fund for payment. Because the harmony of your
life is disrupted, you may want to do something quickly to restore
the former balance. But the actions you take not only impact that
particular moment, but also all the moments thereafter.

For example, if you decide to move your parent into your
home, how will your life as well as your family's life be affected on
a day-to-day basis? If there are safe as well as risky options that can
help you cope with your illness, how will each of the options affect
the quality of your life? If you've reached a crossroads in your
career, what are the paths you can take and where will they lead?
And are there other financial options you can use instead of your
retirement fund?

I RESTORE HARMONY BY TAKING THE RIGHT ACTIONS.

NOVEMBER 16

"Her grandmother, as she gets older, is not fading but rather becoming more concentrated."

— writer Paulette Bates Alden

LESSONS IN DYING

Centuries ago in this nation's history, when it was not uncommon for up to three generations to be living together under the same roof, almost everybody expected to die in their homes, surrounded by their loved ones. Today death most often occurs in a hospital or nursing home, which not only deprives family members of the natural experience of death, but also prevents them from continuing to interact regularly with grandparents and parents and to share experiences with them that oftentimes reveal, even while dying, that the beloved elders continue to be "themselves"—to be lucid, entertaining, strong, feisty, fascinating, loving, and nurturing—the people you know and love.

Take, for example, the following memory a 57-year-old daughter had of her dying mother:

"Mom needed to be hostess and in charge in her home even while dying. She continued to direct and guide her children about her care. While we held a cup to her mouth, she would urge, 'Eat with me.' When she needed more care, we hired hospice workers. When I introduced my mom to the new worker, Mom was already in her 'withdrawal from the world stage.' But she drew herself together from her fetal position under the blankets to peek at this new person, and, in her weak, raspy voice, said, 'Welcome to my home.' These were her final words to the world. What a magnificent, feisty, independent woman this mother of mine was. Mom passed on as peacefully as possible considering her pain and weakness. She showed us how to live and how to die."

I RESPECT THE WISHES OF AN ELDER WHO WISHES
TO DIE AT HOME.

November 17

"Growing old is partly an inescapable process of accommodation and adjustment."

— sculptor Käthe Kollwitz

REDESIGNING AMERICA

The next time you're waiting in your car at a red and yellow traffic light watching pedestrians as they dash across the street, notice the amount of time allowed for safe crossing before the light changes. Now think about how much time an elderly person would need to safely cross the street before the light changed to green. The next time you board a city bus, notice the height of the steps on the bus. Would an older man or woman be able to climb aboard easily? The next time you race off to catch the incoming subway, pay attention to the path you have to take in order to reach the platform in time, which may involve several flights of stairs, a narrow and crowded corridor, and cranky turnstiles. Would your aging parent or grandparent be able to negotiate the obstacle course you just successfully completed?

The physical world that you easily moved through in youth and perhaps now in midlife may soon prove to be problematic. As you grow older, your individual differences from the "norm" of current design standards may make it difficult for you to continue to "fit" into your environment.

Yet shouldn't your environment be redesigned to "fit" you—and the millions of other aging Americans who are currently facing or will soon face similar difficulties? It's up to you to begin now to push for changes that will address such needs—more rampways for stores and other buildings to provide easy access; lower stairs or special lifting platforms on public buses, and "people movers" for subways; pedestrian street lights that allow more crossing time or mid-street traffic islands; and so on.

I PUSH TO REDESIGN AMERICA FOR ALL OF ITS CITIZENS, YOUNG AND OLD.

"Ah well, perhaps one has to be very old before one learns how to be amused rather than shocked."

— writer Pearl Buck

ANN LANDERS

At 77 years old, columnist Ann Landers has been dishing out her advice for 40 years, with a candor that sometimes gets her into trouble with those who disagree with her opinions. Dubbed "the queen of free advice," Landers has had a career that keeps her fingers pressed on the ever-changing American pulse. Where she once used to be in great demand to visit high schools and talk about sex in the 1970s, in her popular "Straight Talk About Sex" talks, today she shakes her head at how different sex in the '90s is. About cybersex, she comments, "It's trouble, and it's getting worse."

However, Landers is rarely shocked at the changes in society or the topics she has presented with in the over 2,000 letters she receives each day. Rather, she maintains a level of distanced amusement. "If I allowed the letters to get to me, I couldn't do the work," she explains. "The letters are somebody else's problem. I try to be objective. Stand away." After she had received, over the years, numerous bogus letters from Yale students, she went to Yale to address the issue. "They came to heckle and harangue me," she remembers, "but I told them they just came to see how old the old broad was." One of her pet "causes" for which she's most outspoken is the tobacco industry; she takes them on often in her columns. When asked how she thinks the CEOs of such influential corporations as R.J. Reynolds and Phillips Morris view her, she replies with a smile, "I think they think I'm a smart little old lady out in Chicago, and they'd better leave me alone."

I AM AMUSED RATHER THAN SHOCKED
BY SOCIAL CHANGES.

NOVEMBER 19

"The art of living is more like that of wrestling than of dancing; the main thing is to stand firm and be ready for an unforeseen attack."
— Marcus Aurelius Antoninus, Roman orator

KEEPING A JOURNAL

Wishing away the passage of years doesn't make them go away. Neither does avoiding them, walking away from them, or denying them. While it's human nature to want to stay as youthful, as energetic, and as vital as possible, such wishful thinking never stops time, nor does it even keep time at bay.

Also, wishing that some things would get easier rather than harder as you grow older is not always realistic. While some of the challenges you have to face now and in the future can readily be handled with your knowledge, experience, and capabilities, there may be other challenges that will be a bit more difficult to handle— and that will require you to be tougher.

Instead of wishing that things would be different or that time would stand still, you need to face the years by standing firm and being ready for all that they have in store for you. But knowing that you must face this situation and actually facing it are two very different things. One way to gently ease into the process of aging is to write down how you feel in a journal. A journal can help you explore why you're having such a hard time growing older and why it's hard for you to look forward to the future.

Set aside a time each day when you can be alone and unhurried with your thoughts. If you need help starting the writing process, you might write at the top of a blank page: *Things I Fear the Most About Growing Older.* Then, when you're finished writing, you can reread your thoughts, recognize how you truly feel, and ask, "How can I face the years to come with a little less anxiety and a little more confidence and acceptance?"

I WRITE IN A JOURNAL TO GET IN TOUCH
WITH MY FEELINGS.

NOVEMBER 20

"We in middle age require adventure."

— writer Amanda Cross

THE ADVENTURE OF A LIFETIME

Do you long to have a truly great adventure—an adventure of a lifetime?

The experimental pilots who were the inspiration for the book *The Right Stuff* were well known for their lack of fear and their desire to challenge both the limits of human beings and the boundaries of space. They were unafraid to fly higher, to travel faster, and to push themselves and their jets to the edge.

Within you is that same "edge," which defines the boundaries of your "comfort zone"—what you're truly comfortable with—which has been developing since you were in your mid-twenties. Your comfort zone is firmly defined by middle age, after you've had time to focus on the formation of family, parenting, and your career. When you become used to doing things over the years, such things become comfortable and familiar to you; continuing to do them keeps you within your comfort zone. But when you seek to transcend past performances, explore new capabilities, break out of the norm, take chances, and risk failure, then you long to leave your comfort zone.

How can you answer your urge for adventure and expand the edges of your comfort zone so you can take greater risks and try new things? Begin by taking small risks and achieving them first before you try to tackle bigger risks. Rather than quit your job to start a new business, for example, talk to other small business owners about their own experiences. Preparing yourself to take a risk, rather than taking it right away, will help you choose the right adventure—one that will truly satisfy your desire to shoot for the moon and reach for the stars.

I PREPARE TO TAKE THE ADVENTURE OF A LIFETIME.

NOVEMBER 21

"A graceful and honorable old age is the childhood of immortality."

— Greek philosopher Pindar

WHAT HOME IS BEST?

There are choices you need to face about your dignity, the quality of your health care, and the control over your life you'd like to maintain as you grow older. One of these choices involves your future living situation. When you're no longer capable of taking care of yourself without the part-time or full-time help of a qualified caregiver, then you may need to face the reality of your situation with grace. You may need to go into a nursing home.

You may make this choice because even though living in your own home, surrounded by familiar things and familiar smells, is comforting, living alone is too lonely, too frightening, too isolating. In a nursing home, you'll be with people your own age, you'll have things to do and talk about together, you won't wear yourself out trying to maintain your home and yard, and you'll have many of your needs taken care of. Also, you may wish to go into a nursing home because you'll feel like you belong there more than in a family member's home, where you may disrupt their schedule and will be cut off from the stimulation and understanding that would be provided by your peers in a nursing home.

Your home or your children's home may not always be the best place for you when you need a particular level of time, care, and attention. To maintain contact with your peers, to be able to participate in diversions especially suited to your age and, in particular, to be under constant medical supervision, a nursing home is a choice you can make that can enable you to take charge of yourself and your best interests.

I TAKE CHARGE OF MY LIFE AND MY CARE.

NOVEMBER 22

"Cherish youth, but trust old age."

— Pueblo proverb

TRUSTING IN THE DARKNESS

Have you ever been awakened in the middle of the night, out of a sound sleep, to an anxious moment? Maybe you had a bad dream. Perhaps the cat knocked something over or the dog began to bark. Maybe a loud storm roused you out of sleep. Or, perhaps a problem you need to resolve invaded your subconscious thoughts.

Whatever the reason, being wrenched out of a peaceful slumber can make you feel anxious, unsettled, and frightened. The fact that you're surrounded by darkness may not help either. "If only it was daylight!" you might moan. "In the light of day, things always seem better." So you get up, make yourself a cup of tea, and read a book or watch television until you see the first light of dawn and hear the birds singing their gentle morning song. Then, and only then, do you instantly feel at peace, calmed by the realization that nighttime is over, darkness is lifting, and the daylight will restore your feeling of safety and security in the world.

You may sometimes see your life as a similar vacillation between trust and fear. When you were younger, there may have been more you trusted in the world than you do now. You may have felt more relaxed because the things you took for granted were always there—and now they aren't. You may have felt stronger, more sure of yourself and your place in the world; now you may feel confused.

You develop trust when you look back on all the risks you took when you were younger and realize that you survived them. You develop trust by recognizing the supportive people in your life. You develop trust by doing your best. You develop trust by believing in yourself.

THE MORE I TRUST MYSELF, THE MORE I TRUST LIFE.

"Lamps make oil-spots, and candles need snuffing; it is only the light of heaven that shines pure and leaves no stain."

— poet/dramatist Johann Wolfgang von Goethe

GIVING SPIRITUAL THANKS

As you look forward to your enormous Thanksgiving meal, to the friends and family who may be spending the day with you, and to time away from work, school, and other obligations, are you also thinking about the people who will experience Thanksgiving day without a bountiful home-cooked feast to quiet their rumbling stomachs, without friends and family with whom to share in the closeness of the day, and without a place to go in their hearts that doesn't feel spiritually empty?

There are many senior citizens who are living alone or in private care facilities, as well as many older, homeless individuals for whom Thanksgiving will be far less physically, emotionally, and spiritually fulfilling than your own holiday. Why not extend the holiday to them? Arrange to bring a nursing-home resident to your home for a few hours, or organize an event for senior citizens at a local facility. Prepare extra pies and platters of food and deliver them to shut-ins or donate them to shelters that will be feeding the homeless.

Also, think ahead to upcoming holidays. Invite friends and relatives who you know will be alone to spend Christmas or Hanukkah with you and your family. Volunteer to shop for shut-ins, or offer transportation to those who can no longer drive so they can buy gifts for those who will give to them.

The spirit of Thanksgiving is more than just a time for you to give thanks for all the blessings in your life. It's a time for you to reach out and give—to light the candles of hope and thanksgiving in other people's lives.

☙ ☙ ☙

I NOURISH MY SPIRIT AND THE SPIRIT OF
OTHERS THIS THANKSGIVING.

"I have always felt that a woman has the right to treat the subject of her age with ambiguity until, perhaps, she passes into the realm of over ninety. Then it is better she be candid with herself and with the world."

— cosmetics company founder Helena Rubinstein

HOW OLD ARE YOU?

Are you guilty of ageism? Think of all the conscious as well as unconscious ways you may disparage aging. When someone who's older than you are tells their age, you may respond, "You're 75! You certainly don't look or act that old." You may try on outfits that you think will make you look younger; if a friend suggests an item, you may look at it and say, "Oh, that dress would make me look old." You may look away from the sight of an elderly person who is struggling to carry bags up a flight of stairs and think, That won't ever be me. When stuck behind an older driver who's tooling along well below the speed limit, you may say, "Old people just can't drive." Or, when asked about your age, you may lie or try to change the subject.

However, owning up to your age can be the most powerful blow you can strike against such ageist thinking. Do you remember what Gloria Steinem said to a reporter who commented she didn't look 40? "This is what forty looks like," she snapped. "How would you know? We've been hiding behind our age for so long." And when Maggie Kuhn, founder of the Gray Panthers, was introduced by President Gerald Ford as a "young lady," Kuhn reportedly stood up and said, "Mr. President, I am not a young lady. I've lived a long time. I'm an old lady."

Age is part of your identity. To deny it is to say that you're unacceptable, that growing older is unacceptable, and that being old is unacceptable. To deny it is to deny *you.*

❀   ❀   ❀

I PROUDLY DECLARE MY AGE.

NOVEMBER 25

*"We ought to think that we are one of the leaves of a tree,
and the tree is all humanity. We cannot live without the
others, without the tree."*
— musician/conductor/composer Pablo Casals

BUILDING A COMMUNITY

Throughout history, individuals have chosen to live in communities so they could structure their lives according to their beliefs with other like-minded individuals. From St. Francis of Assisi and religious communities of the Middle Ages, to the Puritan and Quaker settlements; from communes of the 1960s to gay-sensitive communities in San Francisco, Fire Island, Provincetown, and Key West; to New Age ventures and group collectives that follow a particular religious or political leader; and to retirement and "snowbird" communities, such separatism encourages people to believe that they're better off living with others who share their same philosophies or lifestyles.

Yet harmony with humanity means being able to be a separate individual as well as someone who can connect with the diversity of many. It's easy to cooperate, to resolve conflicts, and to interact in peaceful harmony when you're linked with others who think, feel, and act in similar ways. It becomes harder when you're divided by who each of you is individually and by each set of wants and needs.

You can create a community rich with diversity by thinking of friends, family members, and others you'd like in your community as different trees in a forest. You each have your own set of needs, different ways of growing, and varied appearances, yet you all can live in harmony, and nourish and nurture one another despite these differences. Draw together those with whom you share a common bond and with those whose differences can teach you something about them, about yourself, and about the world.

I BUILD A COMMUNITY FOR COMFORT AS WELL
AS FOR LEARNING.

NOVEMBER 26

*"Old age, especially an honored old age, has so great authority,
that this is of more value than all the pleasures of youth."*
— Roman orator/philosopher Cicero

BE A MENTOR

When you were growing up, was there an older person in your life who took you under their wing and became your mentor—someone who helped you, nurtured you, supported you, and encouraged you? What would your life be like today if you hadn't been taken under their wing and helped by their tutelage? Would you have advanced as far as you have or as quickly as you did in your career? Would you have been able to do the things that you do now so easily, like make home repairs, build furniture, bake a traditional family dish, or make a quilt? Would you have taken the same paths in life that you did, faced the same challenges, had the same successes, or taken the same risks?

In many ways, you are who you are today because of the valuable lessons, knowledge, and experiences you were given by that special older person. While this most influential older person in your life may have been a parent, more often than not the older person you benefited from the most—who became your mentor—was probably not even a family member; rather, your mentor was probably a coach, a boss, a den mother or troop leader, a teacher, a neighbor, or simply a stranger who became a close friend.

You now have the opportunity to keep alive this gift you were given, to pass on what you were given to another. It's time now for you to share your authority, wisdom, experience, and knowledge with a younger person. Make an everlasting, positive mark on another young life.

I CHOOSE A YOUNGER PERSON TO MENTOR.

NOVEMBER 27

"I did not know that I could scorn women at twenty and be charmed by them at seventy."

— sculptor Rodin

"SEXPERIMENTATION"

Today, many progressive older couples are resisting "tying the knot" and instead pursuing their interests in romance and companionship. In some cases, the older men and women are participating in exciting sexual adventures—"sexcapades" or "sexperimentation"—that challenge their lifetime patterns of traditional social and sexual behavior. For example, there are older-woman, younger-man liaisons. There are "share-a-man" relationships where, because there are five times as many widows and widowers in the country today, a single older man might meet the needs of several older women—needs that include helping out around the house with such "man" things as plumbing and wiring, fulfilling the role of escort to social events, providing companionship through close friendship, and acting upon sexual needs. There are same-sex relationships, particularly between women, where basic affection and intimacy needs may or may not be satisfied through sexual involvement by heterosexual women because of interest and desire, by women who wish to explore the freedom and greater number of available partners through bisexuality, or by woman who are finally comfortable being gay.

Such new freedoms and the availability of partners can enable you to focus less on the need to settle down, and more on the enjoyment and pleasure that can be derived from sexual, sensual expression. You can grow old and still fall in love, you can grow old and still be sexually active, you can grow old and still be a social butterfly, and you can grow old and still have a great time!

I AM OPEN TO NEW FORMS OF PARTNERSHIP.

NOVEMBER 28

"The horse, the horse! The symbol of surging potency and power of movement, of action in man."

— author D.H. Lawrence

TAKING OFF YOUR BLINDERS

Sometimes those who retire from their profession become depressed, are suddenly afflicted by illness or chronic pain, or even die. Because they define who they are by what they once did, the minute their professional role is taken away from them they feel lost, useless, directionless, and hopeless. Without a professional role to fulfill, they find it hard to seek out and enjoy other interests.

There are many roles in your life that you may have fulfilled up to this point in time—professional worker, full-time parent, member of a self-help group, leader in the community, graduate student. Now, one or more of these roles may have changed dramatically or even ended. Can you see beyond them? Or, do you wear these roles like costumes and now, without them, you feel naked and vulnerable?

Horses that draw buggies around cities or who are ridden by mounted police on their patrols wear blinders to prevent them from seeing more than what lies ahead of them. However, horses used for pleasure wear no blinders and can see all around them. When you live your life solely through the roles you fulfill, then you go through life wearing blinders. The city horse that follows the same route every day would see a very different route if its blinders were removed. You, too, can experience a very different life when you remove yourself from a familiar role, take off the blinders, and thus see that there's a whole world available to you.

Think about the roles that help identify who you are. How would you feel if these were taken away from you today without warning? From this moment on, resolve to nurture what's inside of you so you can see what's all around you.

I TAKE OFF THE BLINDERS AND SEE WHAT I'VE BEEN MISSING.

NOVEMBER 29

*"When you lose the rhythm of the drumbeat of God, you are lost
from the peace and rhythm of life."*

— Cheyenne proverb

"BURNING BOWL" CEREMONY

Traditions honoring the light and dark transitions of winter have been celebrated since the time that humans lived in tribes. Wise tribal heads, who understood the need for spiritual renewal when darkness came early, created rituals for encouraging the return of the sun, letting go of the mistakes of the past, and creating possibilities for the future.

In the glow of firelight, the tribe would gather in a circle around a blazing fire. Drums would beat steadily in the background. One at a time, members of the tribe would sing, chant, or speak to the tribe of a wish for the future, a desire for the present, or a memory from the past. Then they would take an object created for the ceremony and toss it into the fire. The voices of the tribe would join in as the object burned, while the speaker then prayed. The prayer asked what needed to be realized to make a hope come true, what new strengths could be developed to let go of a past memory, and what could be done in the present to reach a desire. After all the members of the tribe had contributed their words, tossed their objects into the fire, and offered their silent prayers, the tribe would dance in rhythm to the beat of the drums.

You, too, can perform this ritual. Write a brief description of your emotions, attitudes, behaviors, or self-imposed limitations you want to change on a piece of paper. Light a candle, then touch the flame to it and toss it into your "burning bowl." As you watch the paper burn, think of ways to replace what you're releasing. Pray to God or a Higher Power for guidance.

I PRAY FOR THE PERSONAL POWER TO CHANGE MY LIFE.

NOVEMBER 30

"Most people get married believing a myth—that marriage is a beautiful box full of all the things they have longed for: companionship, sexual fulfillment, intimacy, and friendship....A couple must learn the art and form the habit of giving, loving, serving, praising—keeping the box full. If you take out more than you put in, the box will empty."

— writer J. Allan Peterson

GIVE AND TAKE

When difficulties arise in your intimate relationship, are you able to communicate with caring, compromise, and concern so that both of you are heard, both sets of needs are addressed, and a mutual compromise is agreed upon? Or are you quick to try to take care of the person's feelings by blaming yourself for the problem? Are you unwilling to talk about topics that cause you discomfort? Are you afraid to say what you want or need? Are you afraid to hear that there are things you need to do to improve a situation? But the most important question to answer is this: How willing are you to participate in the give-and-take that's necessary in an intimate relationship to make it work?

True harmony in relationships doesn't just happen. Like two people who sit opposite one another on a seesaw, the actions of one person can't help but affect the other. In order to bring the seesaw into balance, you each need to adjust to one another and work together until you can still the board.

From now on, strive to restore harmony in your relationship. Be ready to discuss and then work toward a resolution that gives each person some of what he or she desires.

※　　※　　※

I PUT INTO A RELATIONSHIP WHAT I WANT TO
GET OUT OF IT.

DECEMBER 1

INNER STRENGTH

The parable about the bet the wind made with the sun provides a good example of the difference between power and strength. The wind bet the sun that it could make a man who was walking along the road remove his jacket. The wind blew furiously at and around the man, frantic to prove itself right and win the bet. But the man only pulled his coat tighter around him. Then the sun took its turn. The sun beat its warm rays down on the man, and soon the man willingly removed his coat.

Such is the lesson of the differences between a power from which you can attain infinite wisdom and a strength that strives to control and manipulate. Try as it might, the wind—infinitely stronger than the sun—was incapable of getting the man to remove his jacket while the sun could, merely by using its gentle caress of powerful warmth.

You may think that growing older means growing weaker and, in many ways, you would be right. Over the years your senses may weaken, your muscles become stiff, and your stamina and endurance shrink. But that doesn't mean that all of you is weaker. You can exercise your mind every day and develop a formidable strength. The wisdom you develop over the years can out-muscle even the strongest body builders. And your steadfast faith is more than you'll ever need to run a marathon. Focus on your strengths in your heart, mind, and spirit, and you'll grow stronger every day.

I AM OLDER, BUT I AM STRONGER.

DECEMBER 2

"Life is a child playing around your feet, a tool you hold firmly in your grip, a bench you sit down upon in the evening, in your garden..."

— writer Jean Anouilh

LIVING MINUTE BY MINUTE

The cat that stretches out contentedly in the sun thinks of nothing more than the sheer enjoyment of the present moment. Moments later, the cat may begin to clean itself, to hint at its hunger, or set off on a hunt for mice. But until the moment in which the cat stretches and rises from its glorious spot in the sun, the cat is free from anxiety, worry, and concern. The cat is one with the moment.

Can you, too, participate fully in such moments of pleasure, contentment, and happiness when they arise, and enjoy them to their fullest? Or are you partially in the moment and partially out of it, your mind wondering what to do next or worrying over what has past?

If you're like most people, you probably spend 59 minutes, 59 seconds every hour living in the past with regret, shame, guilt, longing, or the desire to escape; or in the future, which you may look forward to with anticipation or dread. Rare is the person who knows the trick of truly living in the present.

Writer Storm Jameson once wrote, "There is only one world, the world pressing in on you at this minute. There is only one minute in which you are alive, *this minute*—here and now. The only way to live is by accepting each minute as an unrepeatable miracle. Which is exactly what it is—a miracle and unrepeatable."

Today, live each minute. Enjoy all the simple pleasures that you're blessed to experience. You'll never be able to be in the same minute—or experience the same miracles in that minute—again.

I LIVE EACH MIRACULOUS MINUTE TO THE FULLEST.

DECEMBER 3

ANOTHER GIFT OF A DAY

Suffering from a terminal or chronic illness can be physically wearing as well as emotionally draining. You may often contemplate suicide, consider not taking life-saving medication, or become careless in how you take care of yourself in the hopes that such things will accelerate your death or alleviate your pain. You may believe that your friends and family are selfish—thinking only of themselves—when they pressure you to "keep hanging in there." You may want to scream at them, "Can't you see that I'm done for? Why don't you just leave me alone and let me go in peace?"

But even though some of the most debilitating diseases and conditions can rob you of your stamina, take away or dull one or more of your senses, deprive you of your independence, or even strip you of your dignity, you can still live for something or for someone; you can still get some good out of life a bit longer.

Rather than focus on the effects of your current condition on your life and the way you feel, consider instead what coping strategies might help you to not give up on yourself or your ability to enjoy more quality time. The effort you direct toward improving your physical condition, the beneficial changes you make in your lifestyle as a result of your condition, the positive thoughts you can generate, and the relationships you solidify as a result of your reaching out can enhance your overall well-being and help stabilize your condition so you can enjoy life a little bit longer.

I CHERISH A NEW SPACE OF TIME TO ENJOY.

DECEMBER 4

*"Old age is full of enjoyment if you know how to use it....
Life is most delightful when it is on the down slope but not
at the edge yet."*

— Roman writer/philosopher Seneca

THE NEED FOR SPEED

Last winter, at a championship event, Corneil Russell snared the silver in both the downhill and the slalom, as well as the gold in the giant slalom. What's interesting about her achievements is that they came after Russell took up ski racing only a decade earlier. What's most notable, however, is that Russell is one of the top competitors in her category—Women's Class 6—which means that she's between the ages of 50 and 54.

One thing that you might share in common with Russell is an ageless need for speed. Not only do you want to participate in a sport or activity, but you need to be the best at it. Oftentimes this means being the fastest—the fastest runner, the fastest swimmer, the fastest bicyclist, the fastest downhill racer.

Masters ski races are held throughout the United States, Canada, and Europe; they draw as many as 200 male and female participants per event. In the United States, there are regularly scheduled competitions in all eight major ski regions. Racers can compete in age classes separated by five-year intervals and can either specialize in one event or ski them all—slalom, giant slalom, super G, and downhill.

These masters competitions aren't for the faint-hearted or sometime-skier; the races are run on full-length, World Cup-style courses. At the end of the season, athletes from various locales can "ski-off" in regional and national championships. The only requirement, other than being over 25 years old and a member of the U.S. Ski Association, is a burning desire to go fast!

❀   ❀   ❀

I RACE TO SATISFY MY NEED FOR SPEED.

DECEMBER 5

MAKING A LIFE-ENHANCING COMMITMENT

Ruth Simmons was the great-great-granddaughter of slaves and the youngest of 12 children born to Texas sharecroppers. When she was accepted on scholarship to Dillard University in New Orleans, she had little more than her intelligence, her ambition, and the clothes on her back. As a student at Dillard and later at Harvard, she pursued a master's degree and a doctorate in the romance languages because she was afraid she wouldn't be able to get a job in her field. When she was asked to direct the African-American studies program at Princeton University, friends begged her not to because they felt she would be typecast within academia. She took the position anyway and brought in leading African-American teachers, including Nobel Prize-winning novelist Toni Morrison; her program became a model for other colleges.

As a divorced mother of two children, Simmons struggled to balance career and family. She made flexible hours a job requirement. "Define your terms," Simmons advises, "and try to end up in an environment that will allow you to work under those terms." Even though her commitment to her children impacted on her career—she chugged along in the slow track for longer than she would have like to—she became a pioneering woman in her field. Today, at age 50, Simmons is the president of Smith College—the first African-American woman in the United States to be at the helm of a top-ranked school.

❈   ❈   ❈

I COMMIT MYSELF TO WHAT I CAN OFFER TO
MYSELF AND OTHERS.

DECEMBER 6

"This moment, this being, is the thing. My life is all life in little. The moon, the planets, pass around my heart. The sun, now hidden by the round bulk of this earth, shines into me, and in me as well. The gods and the angels both good and bad are like the hairs of my own head, seemingly numberless, and growing from within. I people the cosmos from myself, it seems, yet what am I? A puff of dust, or a brief coughing spell, with emptiness and silence to follow."

— writer Alexander Eliot

THE THREE FORCES OF LIFE

There are three forces that guide life: creation, or birth; destruction, or death; and maintenance, or the interval between creation and destruction. All three forces are present not only in humans, but in all living things—the stars, trees, flowers, planets, seasons, galaxies, and cells. Even though your life follows the forces sequentially, all three forces exist simultaneously. As someone or something is being created, someone or something is being maintained, and someone or something else is being destroyed.

Accept that these three forces are, in a nutshell, your life, and you can then make the most of each moment of your life. How can you do this? Dr. Deepak Chopra suggests the following ways in his book *Ageless Body, Timeless Mind*:

- Create and enjoy periods of silence.
- Connect with and enjoy nature.
- Trust your feelings.
- Stay centered and focused even in the most stressful and chaotic situations.
- Be a child; enjoy fantasy and play.
- Trust yourself.
- Remain open to new possibilities.

I MAKE THE MOST OF EACH OF MY LIFE FORCES.

December 7

"Do you know that disease and death must needs overtake us, no matter what we are doing?...What do you wish to be doing when it overtakes you?...If you have anything better to be doing when you are so overtaken, get to work on that."

— Greek Stoic philosopher Epictetus

GETTING IN MOTION

Do you experience times of mental dullness or sometimes want to withdraw from all activity? You may have poor concentration or trouble making decisions, and so you ignore obligations. You may let the phone ring as you lie on the living room couch in front of the television. You may feel bored and restless, but don't have the motivation to channel your energy into something interesting or useful.

Creative inventor Leonardo da Vinci once said, "Iron rusts from disuse, water loses its purity from stagnation...even so does inaction sap the vigors of the mind." There are things you can do when you feel a lack of motivation, a foggy mind, and a lack of interest in life. You can eat healthfully, for starters. Stay away from sweets and snack foods, and get the basic protein, vitamins, and minerals into your body. With proper nourishment, you can enjoy more energy and clearer thinking.

Second, take a shower or bath so you can feel clean on the outside, even when your insides feel like sludge. Brush your teeth. Comb your hair. Shave or put on makeup, even if you're not going out.

Finally, get in motion! Physical activity is an extremely important part of getting into motion and clearing the mind. Exercise keeps the muscles toned and the blood moving, and pumps oxygen to the brain for sharper concentration. You don't have to run a marathon or pump iron to get moving. Simply take a walk. Walk at least ten minutes every day, and you'll get your rusty wheels in motion!

I LET MOTION OVERRIDE LOW ENERGY.

DECEMBER 8

"I look back on my life like a good day's work; it was done and I am satisfied with it."

— painter Grandma Moses

A SEASON OF JOYFUL FORGIVENESS

The fall and winter seasons are perfect times to reconnect with old friends and family members. Holidays provide the perfect excuses to send cheery cards and "catch-up" letters, to make telephone calls, and to extend invitations to others as well as to accept them.

But if you have any unresolved, loose ends in your life—a family feud that rages on, ongoing resentment or anger toward a parent or an ex-partner, or guilt over a hurt you inflicted upon someone else—it may be difficult for you to initiate contact with some people. But haven't you held on to grudges and refused to forgive yourself or others for too long? Perhaps this year you can seize the opportunity to try to make peace with some old hostilities or amend some past transgressions.

On the list of people to whom you usually send seasonal cards or letters, add the name of someone with whom you'd like to make a clean beginning or atone for the past—someone with whom you're not necessarily on good terms, with whom you may have quarreled, or with whom there's unfinished business. A simple greeting might be: "Sorry that we've lost touch. I'd like to forget whatever water has gone under the bridge between us and begin anew. If this isn't what you'd like, then please accept my blessings for good wishes, health, and happiness this season. If this is what you'd like, too, then I want you to know how much I look forward to hearing from you." Sometimes it takes extending a hand to being offered a hand.

I SEND A "FORGIVENESS CARD" TO SOMEONE WHOM I'D LIKE BACK IN MY LIFE.

DECEMBER 9

"It costs so much to be a full human being....One has to abandon altogether the search for security, and reach out to the risk of living with both arms. "

— writer Morris L. West

PROTESTING GOVERNMENT POLICIES

Should you expect the government to safeguard your finances? Should you demand that the government provide a secure future for your children and grandchildren?

The unknown poet who penned the following words offered a personal protest against government ineptitude and misguidance. Can you offer a more effective protest against government policies that ignore the needs of the aging?

Hymn to the Welfare State

The Government is my Shepherd,
Therefore I need not work.
It alloweth me to lie down on a good job
It leadeth me beside still factories
It destroyeth my initiative
It leadeth me in the path of a parasite for politic's sake.
Yea, though I walk through the valley of laziness and
　　deficit spending I will fear no evil, for the
　　Government is with me.
It prepareth an economic Utopia for me, by appropriating
　　the earnings of my own grandchildren.
It filleth my head with false security;
My inefficiency runneth over.
Surely the Government should care for me all the days of
　　my life!
And I shall dwell in a fool's paradise forever.

I PROTEST GOVERNMENT POLICIES TO PROTECT
MYSELF AND THE FUTURE.

DECEMBER 10

"Age seldom arrives smoothly or quickly. It's more often a succession of jerks."

— writer Jean Rhys

RESTORING YOUR FORMER LUSTER

Have you ever noticed what happens to an old car that's been kept outside and left inactive? Eventually it begins to rust and decompose in a process that can't reverse itself unless someone intervenes and spends some time working on the car to get it back into running shape.

By the same token, a body that's ignored over time will be similarly affected. Entropy is the aging body's worst enemy, but it's one of the most easily defeated. One of the simplest ways to prevent entropy is to give the body something to do. Entropy is opposed by work; without work, energy simply dissipates.

Everyone who's aging is susceptible to entropy. Perhaps you've noticed the signs in yourself or others: a decline in muscle mass; loss of strength in large and small muscle groups in the body; a drop in the basal metabolic rate, or the amount of calories the body needs to sustain itself; an increase in body fat to muscle ratio; decreased aerobic capacity; increased blood pressure; blood-sugar intolerance; higher cholesterol/HDL ratios; loss of bone density; and a decline in the ability of the body to regulate temperature.

To defeat entropy, keep in mind that the effects of these signs are reversible. An improved diet and good eating habits; an increase in exercise and activity; maintaining a regular schedule that balances work, rest, and play; healthy lifestyle choices (such as not smoking and drinking in moderation); and getting seven or eight hours of sleep a night will help keep your body shiny and new.

I RESTORE MYSELF SO I BECOME SHINY AND NEW.

DECEMBER 11

"As we grow older, our bodies get shorter and our anecdotes longer."

— Robert Quillen

RESPONDING TO FORGETFULNESS

Do you think your current forgetfulness is a sign of increasing senility or, worse yet, evidence of a brain disorder, dementia, or the onset of Alzheimer's Disease?

Throughout your entire life—not just in your middle and later years—forgetfulness can occur. Fatigue, anxiety, inattention, intense periods of concentration, pressures and stress, living at a fast pace, and depression can contribute to moments of memory lapse or periods of memory decline. As you grow older, such things can continue to impact your ability to remember from time to time; also, you may become vulnerable to changes in your social situation and emotional state in ways that also cause memory loss. Deaths of loved ones, for instance, relocation to unfamiliar places, or increased social isolation can trigger confusion, panic, forgetfulness, and disorientation.

Also, not increasing your knowledge base as you grow older can prevent you from learning new things and expanding your mind in ways that help you to create new memories and provide you with new topics of discussion so you can avoid the repetitious retelling of stories, or refrain from making the same comments, or asking the same questions over and over again.

When you can expand your world beyond what it is now and you can stay physically and mentally active throughout your life, then you may find that your memory may actually improve over time. Also, using relaxation techniques such as deep breathing, visualization, and meditating can help you to stay relax and clear-headed.

I USE EXERCISE AND RELAXATION TECHNIQUES TO
ENHANCE MY MENTAL FITNESS.

DECEMBER 12

SENSES OF THE SEASON

Are there smells that trigger a childhood memory for you at this time of year? The smell of freshly baked bread may remind you of the times you stood on a stool in your grandmother's kitchen, helping her sift the flour for her special holiday bread. You may have watched her strong hands knead the dough, then later marveled at how delicious the whole kitchen smelled. Whenever you breathe in the scent of freshly cut pine, you may remember your father's workshop in the basement and all the projects he enjoyed as he listened to the ball games on the radio and hammered, sanded, and stained.

Other senses can trigger memories, too—the sight of your childhood home as you turn into the driveway, the scent of your mother's perfume and the soft caress of the collar of her fur jacket as you embrace, the sound of a fire crackling in the fireplace, the taste of sugar cookies warm from the oven.

This upcoming holiday season may be a time in which your senses once again work overtime, constantly shifting you back and forth from present to past, past to present. It may be a time when you can close your eyes, breathe deeply of all the familiar fragrances, and remember the people, places, and things that have always made you feel warm and comforted.

❀   ❀   ❀

I CLOSE MY EYES AND SENSE WONDERFUL MEMORIES
FROM THE PAST.

"In the past few years I have made a thrilling discovery...that until one is over sixty one can never really learn the secret of living."
— writer Ellen Glasgow

LIVING IS NOW

Many learned men from all professions and at various ages in their lives have, over the years, pondered the meaning of life. French writer André Gide once said, quite simply, "life eludes logic." Former California governor Jerry Brown determined that "life just is. You have to flow with it. Give yourself to the moment. Let it happen." Writer Kurt Vonnegut decided that "life happens too fast for you to ever think about it. If you could just persuade people of this, but they insist on amassing information." Theologian Elbert Hubbard advised that "the best way to prepare for life is to begin to live." Philosopher Kierkegaard opined that "life is not a problem to be solved but a reality to be experienced." Film maker Frederico Fellini said, "There is no end. There is no beginning. There is only the infinite passion of life." And writer Havelock Ellis mused that "dreams are real while they last. Can we say more of life?"

But perhaps French writer Albert Camus gave the best advice when he surmised that "if there is a sin against life, it consists perhaps not so much in despairing of life as in hoping for another life and in eluding the implacable grandeur of this life." In reality, the only meaning to life that needs to concern you right now is the moment-by-moment existence you go through. It's the breath you take at this second, the blink of your eyes as you read this page, the finger that absent-mindedly scratches your nose, and the thoughts that float through the corridors of your mind. There is no secret to life or to living. Life is now. Living is now.

I LIVE TOTALLY IN THE PRESENT MOMENT.

DECEMBER 14

"I am luminous with age."

— writer/ historian Meridel Le Sueur

FINDING YOUR INNER GLOW

Have you ever met people who seemed to have a glow about them—a brightness, an ability to illuminate even the darkest times? Not only does it seem as if they themselves are lit up like a Christmas tree, all cheery and bright, but it's as if they light up everything and everyone who comes into contact with them. Animals gravitate towards them. The telephone is always ringing in their home. People are often stopping by to visit. A few projects are being juggled at the same time. And yet when it's time for you to visit one another, you're always made to feel welcome.

As you grow older, you can develop a similar light within you. All it requires is a shift in attitude from what you consider to be important in this world. Too often, when you're growing up, you become overly involved in things that really don't matter—petty arguments or silly conflicts, pointless causes, or worrying about things that no amount of worry can change. When you're young, you may not know how best to channel your energy, so you leave your energy scattered about. This dims the light within you, for it can't glow with the same intensity for everything and everyone in your life.

To restore this glow within you today, you need to slow down, take stock of your life, and focus on those things that are most important to you. Like a gardener who prunes his plants, you need to cut off those things that are taking valuable nourishment away from you and that may no longer valuable to you; also, you need to cut back on those things that may spread out your energy in unhealthy ways. You grow luminous with age by keeping your life light and free.

I LET THE GLOW WITHIN ME SHINE.

DECEMBER 15

"At one of the rare lulls during the Jackie O. auction—when the bidding for some White House bauble hit a reef and John Block, the animated gavel-master, had to goose up the bidding—he leaned over the podium and said, 'Small price for a dream, folks.'"
— writer Fred Kaplan

TREASURES FROM THE PAST

Sotheby's auction of Jacqueline Kennedy Onassis's worldly possessions in the spring of 1996 astonished many when inexpensive and seemingly worthless items were sold for astronomical prices. An explicitly fake pearl necklace, worth $700, was purchased by the Franklin Mint Company of Philadelphia for $211,500 because they were worn in a famous *Life* magazine photo, snapped as little John-John was tugging at the beads. John F. Kennedy's golf clubs went for $700,000—and that was just for the woods. The irons went for another $350,000, a single putter went for $57,500, and his stroke counter lured $25,000. "The idea that you can buy a piece of that era that was so special," sighed Ettagale Blauer, an auction specialist. "This isn't comparable to anything ever." Most of the bidders seemed to be in their fifties or sixties and were probably in high school or college when Kennedy was president. They were as much out to recapture a piece of their nation's history as they were their own lost history. As one woman commented, "I remember seeing Jackie Kennedy getting an ice cream in Cape Cod when I was there as a child. The feeling of that memory—whatever it is, it's still there."

There may be many memories and memorabilia in your history that are just as valuable to you because of what they mean to you and your life. Keeping such things can help you to treasure those times in your life so they'll always be special, meaningful, and precious.

I TREASURE THE MEMENTOS OF MY OWN HISTORY.

DECEMBER 16

"If you haven't any charity in your heart, you have the worst kind of heart trouble."

— Bob Hope

OPENING YOUR HEART

Every day there's at least one person in this world who could benefit from your help. You may think that this means an elderly parent who needs you to coordinate home care and make medical appointments, or a partner who needs your help managing your future finances. But such caregiving activities are the responsibilities of family members and partners who care for one another; the help you can provide that's truly beneficial is that which you willingly give to strangers.

Every day hungry and homeless men, women, and children wander America's streets and alleys searching garbage cans for scraps, line up outside crowded shelters and soup kitchens for a one-a-day meal, or panhandle. Every day an elderly person who's living on a limited budget is shut in and therefore shut out from the normal ebb and flow of daily living. Every day middle-aged men and women are battling against debilitating diseases. Every day a person with a disability faces numerous difficulties.

Can you share your abundance with those who may go to bed tonight with an empty stomach by donating a bag of groceries to a local food pantry? Can you deliver a meal or spend a little less than an hour a week having coffee and conversation with a shut-in? Can you raise money from pledge sheets and participate in road races and walks to benefit the research needed to fight life-threatening diseases? Can you provide financial support for a disabled person's companion dog or wheelchair, read to someone who's blind, or volunteer carpooling services to those who can't get around on their own?

I OPEN MY HEART AND GIVE TO OTHERS.

DECEMBER 17

*"While we exist as human beings, we are like tourists on holiday.
If we play havoc and cause disturbance, our visit is meaningless.
If during our short stay—100 years at most—we live peacefully,
help others and, at the very least, refrain from harming or
upsetting them, our visit is worthwhile."*
— Tibetan Buddhist spiritual leader The Dalai Lama

HOLIDAY PEACE AND JOY

Wouldn't it be nice if the warm glow, loving feelings, nurturing acceptance, laughter and lightness, and togetherness you feel with your loved ones during the holidays was like an eternal flame? That would mean that, from this holiday season on, no matter what circumstances occurred, every day would be filled with peace and joy.

Look outside of your family, too, to your friends, neighbors, co-workers—even strangers on the street. At this time of year, anger has been replaced by anticipation, frowns have been reversed by smiles, silence has been filled with greetings and pleasant conversation. All around you, the world is on holiday; don't you wish that the whole world, too, could get along with one another in such peace and harmony—not just during the holiday season, but every day of the year?

Such emotions and behaviors make holidays special, but they often provide only temporary respites from the tension and stresses of day-to-day living. That's why it's of utmost importance that you enjoy the respite for as long as it lasts and then willingly let it go, without a struggle, when—or if—it ends.

Delight in shared laughter, relax with the ease of hollered hellos and casual chatter, be excited by the multitude of hugs and tender embraces. Enjoy each special holiday moment as it occurs.

I ENJOY THE PEACE AND JOY OF THE HOLIDAYS AND
STRIVE TO LIVE AS PEACEFULLY AND JOYFULLY AS I CAN
THROUGHOUT THE YEAR.

DECEMBER 18

NIGHT, THE BELOVED

Just as each day is a new beginning, so too can each evening be a new start. The falling darkness and rising chill of a winter night needn't frighten you or make you feel sad or "blue"; rather, it can present you with a multitude of fresh, enjoyable, and energizing opportunities. Nighttime can be a time to start on a project you've been putting off or to concentrate your energy on a hobby. Nighttime can be the first night of an adult education class, a bowling league, quilting bee, book club discussion group, a support group meeting, or a volunteering opportunity. Nighttime can be when you take a courageous first step in getting to know someone new by having your first date after a divorce or the death of a long-time partner. Nighttime can be the evening that you try a new recipe, start reading a good book, meditate, or take in a first-run movie.

Each night gives you the chance to recharge yourself physically, emotionally, and spiritually. Each night presents you with endless opportunities to start anew on your goals, your growth, and your interests. Each night is a new beginning. As French writer Antoine de Saint-Exupéry once wrote, "Night, the beloved. Night, when words fade and things come alive. When the destructive analysis of the day is done, and all that is truly important becomes whole and sound again."

❊   ❊   ❊

I MAKE TONIGHT A NEW BEGINNING.

DECEMBER 19

*"At different stages of our lives, the signs of love may vary—
dependence, attraction, contentment, worry, loyalty, grief—but at
heart, the source is always the same. Human beings have the rare
capacity to connect with each other, against every odd."*

— writer Michael Dorris

LIBERATION AND LOVE

While attending a financial planning course at a community for older men and women to help them find new direction in their lives after retirement, a 78-year-old woman asked the teacher for a private conversation.

"When my husband and I signed up to take your course," the woman began, "we wanted to learn about financial planning. But when I heard the statistics about how much longer I could expect to live, I've decided to divorce my husband of 52 years. I just wanted to thank you for giving me the courage to get out of a marriage that hasn't made me happy for a long time. If I've got another 20 years left to live, then I want to spend it with someone I love and who loves me. And I haven't loved my husband nor he me for a long time."

For some people, late-in-life separation and divorce can be a nightmare. The pain of rejection after so many years of devotion can be tough to deal with, as is the transition that needs to be made from being a couple to being a single person.

But for others, it can be a blessing. Some people feel more alive and interested in life. Learning how to function on their own presents them with an exciting new opportunity because it may be something they've never done before. For those people, especially women, who have for years met the needs of their husbands while suppressing their own, separation and divorce is liberating and opens the doors to a whole new way of living, learning, and loving.

I LIBERATE MYSELF SO I LEARN TO LOVE MYSELF
AND OTHERS.

DECEMBER 20

"Happiness is not having what you want, but wanting what you have."

— Hyman Judah Schactel

PARENTAL ISSUES

Holidays focus on families. As a result, it may be hard to escape from old hurts or unhappy memories whenever you return to your childhood home or interact with your parents. It may be difficult not to fall back into feeling like you're an unhappy child all over again, and you may spend your holiday with them trying to once more get the love, attention, support, validation, or apologies you may not have gotten from them when you were growing up. In effect, you want your parents now to finally make you happy and to give you the happiness you believe they deprived you of in childhood.

But not only can't you expect someone to give you happiness, you also can't change your childhood. As someone once said, "When you finally go back to your old hometown, you find it wasn't the old home you missed, but your childhood." What you can strive to do as an adult, however, is to reconnect with your parents today so you can create a good relationship now—and possibly in the future.

To do so, keep in mind that your relationship today isn't parent to child—it's adult to adult. Instead of making demands on aging and perhaps still dysfunctional parents, expect less from them. Rather than carry old grudges and hurts with you when you go home for the holidays or when your parents come to visit you, take a moment to think about all the things you do appreciate about your parents. Even though it may be hard to find things that are wonderful and warm about them, at least there may be little things they've done for you or kind or considerate words they've said that can mean a lot to you right now.

I AM HAPPY WITH MY PARENTS TODAY.

December 21

A WORLD OF WONDER

What is wonder? The oldest English prose ever written, around A.D. 720 in *Beowulf*, uses the word *wonder* for the first time, translated from Old English verse to mean "marvel" or "miracle." But today, *wonder*, used as both a noun and a verb, has several different meanings, from "marvel" and "miracle" to "be filled with curiosity."

To wonder at the world in which you live is to see beyond the mere existence of something or to move beyond taking that something for granted (such as a snowflake in winter), and to look at it through different eyes.

You can live in this world on a day-to-day basis without ever questioning the existence of even the most obvious things. You can get by in this world by taking pleasure from knowing the responses to one-answer questions, such as "What is the capital of South Dakota?" Or you can consult encyclopedias and other reference books to learn the answers you don't know.

You can live in this world on a daily basis always questioning, always appreciating, always seeking to discover. Live with wonder, and your life will be wonder-filled!

❀   ❀   ❀

I MARVEL AT ALL THE WONDERS IN THE WORLD.

DECEMBER 22

"Never make your home in a place. Make a home for yourself inside your own head. You'll find what you need to furnish it— memory, friends you can trust, love of learning, and other such things. That way it will go with you wherever you journey."
— writer Tad Williams

"HOME IS WHERE THE HEART IS"

Imagine that your house is burning. Fire fighters can't save it; it will be totally destroyed. Now imagine that everyone inside has escaped from the flames, but you can venture back into the house one last time without getting hurt to bring out one thing. What would you choose?

Many people who were asked that question didn't want to retrieve their wallet, jewelry, furs, or even an automobile. The majority of those asked said they would go back for their photo albums. To them, the pictures of family, friends, spouses, long-lost loves, and even themselves at various stages of their lives were cherished possessions—eternal memorials forever frozen in time, remembrances of the way things once were and the people, places, and things in their lives.

As much as you may love your home, if you had to lose it or leave it, you could still create a home elsewhere. Even if a home is shared with other family members, even if a home is a retirement complex filled with other residents, and even if a home is a bed, half of a room, and a shared bathroom in a nursing home, you can still call such locales home. For home is a feeling deep within you; four walls, a roof, windows, and a couple of doors are just the parameters of where you live, not the essential components that help you to feel comforted and connected with the world. There's much truth in the saying, "Home is where the heart is," for wherever your heart is, that's where home can be.

WHERE IS THAT PLACE I CALL HOME?

DECEMBER 23

"Lord make us mindful of the little things that grow and blossom
in these days to make the world beautiful for us."
— writer/educator W.E.B. DuBois

A DAILY PRAYER

When do you make conscious contact with a Higher Power through prayer? Most people pray only when they're faced with an emotional or physical difficulty so they can make what's difficult a bit easier to bear. But can't you also pray as a way of giving thanks, as a way of recognizing the blessings that are all around you, or even as a way of "checking in" every day, when you don't need but rather want to communicate with your Higher Power?

Author Rumer Godden once wrote, "There is an Indian belief that everyone is a house of four rooms: a physical, a mental, an emotional, and a spiritual room. Most of us tend to live in one room most of the time, but unless we go into every room every day, even if only to keep it aired, we are not complete." At this moment, whether you need your Higher Power or not, you can open the door to your spiritual room and keep it open in order to maintain an ongoing spiritual dialogue.

There are many ways to welcome your Higher Power into your "house." You may wish to use a familiar prayer each night before you go to bed, perhaps one learned in childhood: "Our Father, who art in heaven..." "Now I lay me down to sleep..." or "The Lord is my Shepherd, I shall not want...." You may prefer to create your own prayer—one that addresses the particular areas of your life in which you feel you need spiritual guidance and wisdom. Or you may simply ask your Higher Power each morning to make you mindful of the beautiful, natural living things around you. Make such communication a part of your daily routine, and you'll be rewarded by a profound and more intimate relationship with your Higher Power.

I FIND TIME EVERY DAY TO PRAY.

DECEMBER 24

"To celebrate his 40th birthday, my boss, who is battling middle-age spread, bought a new convertible sports car. As a finishing touch, he put on a vanity plate with the inscription '18 Again.' The wind was let out of his sails, however, when a salesman entered our office the following week. 'Hey,' he called out, 'who owns the car with the plate 'I ate again?'"

— Cindy Gillis, in *Reader's Digest*

A WEIGHTY ISSUE

You have a unique size, shape, and body chemistry that's strongly determined by heredity. How much you weigh is a result of the energy you input (what you eat), the energy you use (your activity level), and the way your body uses energy (its metabolism). You may eat the same amount of food and exercise even more than someone your age and sex, and yet you may be heavier or thinner than that person.

Also, as you age you may find yourself craving foods you were never really interested in when you were younger. You may develop a sweet tooth as you grow older and find yourself focusing more on the dessert course of a meal than on the meat, potatoes, and vegetables. As a result, any holiday season may be a time in which you easily gain ten pounds or more in a relatively short period of time.

One weight rule that does hold true from person to person, however, is that as you age, your body's metabolism slows down. You simply don't burn up the calories as you once did when you were younger. This means that your eating habits today may be adding weight instead of helping you maintain it.

To keep your weight at a level that both you and your physician feel is most healthy, avoid diets that rely upon supplements, weight loss pills, or limited-food intake. Instead, listen to your body's feelings of hunger, eat balanced meals, and increase your physical activity.

I CREATE HEALTHY DIET HABITS FOR THE NEW YEAR.

DECEMBER 25

"Gratitude is riches. Complaining is poverty. Instead of complaining about what's wrong, be grateful for what's right."

— writer Zachery Fisher

EXPRESSIONS OF GRATITUDE

Perhaps the most wondrous gift you could give and receive today is that of gratitude—gratitude for the people in your life, gratitude for the health you've been given, gratitude for the experiences you've gone through, gratitude for the emotions you've been able to feel, gratitude for all the wonders of the world you've been able to see, and gratitude for your humanity towards others.

How do you define gratitude? Is it the thanks you give to those who have given you gifts today? Is it the pat on the back you gave to the person who helped you prepare the meal, clear the table, or do the dishes? Is it the smile you were given by a homeless stranger who held up a plate for food?

Perhaps the most wondrous gift you can give today to another is one that's given from your heart, not your wallet; from your time, not your haste; from your creativity, not your marketing ability; from your attention, not your intention; and from your caring, not your caretaking. The best gift you can give is to show your gratitude for all you've been given in very simple ways. Ask a member of your support group out for coffee. Organize a household donation to a worthwhile charity. Provide a home for an animal from a shelter. Or tell a story of hope to someone who feels down.

When you feel grateful, you can express such gratitude directly. As an unknown person once advised, "When you feel grateful for something others have done for you, why not tell them about it?"

I GIVE A GRATITUDE GIFT FROM MY HEART TODAY.

DECEMBER 26

TAKING A STAND

What legacy would you like to leave behind for younger people who will someday be your age and face some of the same challenges you're now facing? You can start work today to shift public policies for the aging and the elderly in society so the country moves in directions that don't neglect the needs of the aged now—and in the future. In doing so, you can continue to make your life worthwhile, continue to remain active, continue to make waves in the world around you, and continue to be a contributing, caring, and creative member of society.

To be able to be an interdependent individual—someone who can benefit from mutual help—you need to be somewhat independent, which is why it's so important to fight hard to safeguard the entitlements and social programs that maintain a person's dignity and to push for those that aren't already in place. Both fighting to protect your rights and benefits and working to create new forms of interdependency, or mutual help, are critical to improving the road to aging.

It doesn't matter whether or not you live long enough to see the world as a better place for those who are growing older. What matters is that you don't spend the remainder of your life ignoring the potholes, bumps, and soft shoulders that impede your ability to make progress down the road of life. Now is the time to take and make stands. Whether you chain yourself to a fence outside a corporation that refuses to hire older employees or walk hundreds of miles to benefit a worthy cause, make this time of your life truly count.

I PARTICIPATE IN PERSONAL AND GROUP ADVOCACY
FOR THE AGING.

*"It's not true that life is one damn thing after another—
it's one damn thing over and over."*
— poet Edna St. Vincent Millay

ELEANOR ROOSEVELT

Have you ever watched a gerbil on its exercise wheel? Day in and day out, the gerbil probably logs hundreds of miles of activity, but it never experiences a change of scenery.

Writer A.P. Herbert once noted, "Imagine how little good music there would be if, for example, a conductor refused to play *Beethoven's Fifth Symphony* on the grounds that his audience may have heard it before." In life, you need to position yourself somewhere between doing the same thing over and over again, and refusing to do something simply because you've done it before.

When Eleanor Roosevelt was first lady, she traveled extensively as the eyes and ears of her husband. She kept President Roosevelt informed of people's problems throughout the Depression. During World War II, her efforts spanned the globe as she visited with soldiers and heads of state. But in 1945, after FDR's death, Eleanor's time of service to the citizens of the United States ended. As she faced the dilemma of what to do next in her life, she was asked by President Truman to be a delegate to the United Nations, and she accepted. In 1952, when President Eisenhower failed to reappoint her as delegate, she began working as a U.N. volunteer. Nearly a decade later, she returned as a delegate when President Kennedy reappointed her.

Eleanor Roosevelt made numerous transitions in her life—some that kept her doing the same things, and some that enabled her to do something new. Can *you* accept the old as well as the new?

I WELCOME CHANGE, AND I ALSO APPRECIATE WHAT
STAYS THE SAME.

December 28

"As a man advances in life he gets what is better than admiration—judgment to estimate things at their own value."
— writer/lexicographer Samuel Johnson

MORE THAN A MODE OF TRANSPORTATION

What's a car worth to you? When you were growing up and saving for your first car, its purchase probably represented years of working hard at odd jobs—babysitting, cleaning out the garage, summer jobs, or even part-time jobs after school. At the time, a car was not only the most expensive item you could buy, but also the most coveted. With a vehicle, you became popular with your friends and with those who wanted to be your friend so they could get rides. With a vehicle, you no longer had to depend upon your parents to take you to movies, to stores, and to your friends' homes. And with a car, you learned responsibility by taking care of something.

Today, a vehicle may not be the most expensive item you've ever purchased or will ever purchase. You don't need to own a car to teach you responsibility; you learned that years ago by taking care of yourself, perhaps raising a family, holding a full-time job and fostering a career, and caring for a home.

Today you can estimate a car's worth—not by its sticker price but by its value in your life. Owning a car and being able to drive it may still make you "popular" with your peers—with those who can no longer drive and must therefore depend upon you to take them places—but it also ensures your independence; it allows you to come and go as you please. What other things are worth more to you in value and the quality of life that they ensure than the money they cost?

I VALUE THOSE THINGS THAT MONEY CAN AND
CANNOT BUY.

DECEMBER 29

"You can close your eyes to reality but not to memories."
— writer Stanislaw J. Lec

ACCEPTING YOUR AGING

Do you color your hair? According to surveys, most women and some men who dye their hair do so to cover the gray. This is most common among women in their forties and fifties; 45 percent of them choose to chase the gray away!

It may be hard to resist the temptation to alter your appearance, since advertising promotes a multitude of bottles, tubes, and jars that contain cosmetics designed to help you to look younger and more attractive. In fact, the cosmetics industry itself exists and thrives because it tells people that how they currently look pales in comparison to how they *could* look if they only used certain products. So not only should an older woman hide the gray in her hair, but she should also hide all the wrinkles on her face and hands and mask or alter other signs of aging.

How willing you are to accept your appearance as an aging person will dictate just how much of your hard-earned money you choose to spend on attempting to look like something you simply aren't anymore and never will be again—young. The reality is, you *are* growing older and, as such, you can't stop the wrinkling, sagging, graying, and other visible bodily changes that naturally occur. To reject such things about you is to reject yourself; to reject yourself makes growing older an uncomfortable experience.

But if you can take off all your clothes, spend several minutes looking at yourself in the mirror, and instead see someone who looks pretty good at his or her age, then growing older can be an experience in which you focus less on your appearance and more on the experience of life.

I ACCEPT HOW I LOOK SO I CAN JUST ENJOY THE
EXPERIENCE OF LIFE.

DECEMBER 30

"Don't be afraid to cry. It will free your mind of sorrowful things."
— Hopi proverb

SHOWING YOUR TEARS

Wouldn't it be wonderful if people could see your true feelings of grief and sadness and respond to them in ways that encouraged you rather than discouraged you from expressing such feelings? Most of the time, however, you may hide your sadness because whenever you've been caught with tears in your eyes, you've been told not to cry; been given a quick, obligatory hug or shoulder squeeze; or been asked, "Haven't you been feeling this way long enough?"

You know that it would be so much easier to get over your sorrow if you had someone with whom you could share your tears, with whom you could be held tightly for as long as you needed to sob, with whom you could say all the things you want to say to clear your mind of the sad feelings. But too many people reject sadness because they would rather see happiness. A smile poses no threat and requires no need for meaningful discussion or a caring exchange; tears, however, signal an emotional need that requires time, attention, and caring.

While a smile can be beautiful, it really says little about a person. Tears, on the other hand, speak volumes. The Minquass Indians have a proverb: "The soul would have no rainbow if the eyes had no tears." Tears are not only your way of opening your heart to your own feelings, but a way of opening yourself up to others. So it's important that you express this emotion. Share your sadness with another. Ask for help and for a hug if you need it. There will be some people in your life who will have the ears to listen and the arms to hold you. They can be there for you, but only if you choose to open the windows of your soul to them.

I SHOW MY TEARS TO A TRUSTED FRIEND OR
FAMILY MEMBER.

DECEMBER 31

"If I had my life to live over again, I'd dare to make more mistakes next time. I'd relax. I would limber up. I would be sillier than I have been this trip. I would take fewer things seriously. I would take more chances. I would take more trips. I would climb more mountains and swim more rivers. I would eat more ice cream and less beans. I would perhaps have more troubles, but I'd have fewer imaginary ones."

— writer Nadine Stair

TRAVELING INTO TOMORROW

The first step in your journey toward growing better as you grow older begins with words from the Tao: "A journey of a thousand miles starts with a single step." The remaining steps in your journey bring you closer to the courage you need to face, with dignity and independence, the challenges, changes, and risks life offers you; the serenity you need to live without regret and remorse so you can remember, instead, with fondness and reflection; and the maturity you need to look for the valuable lessons in life.

The journey toward growing better as you grow older is different for everyone—where you go is not necessarily where others will also travel. And, for the most part, your journey will lead you into unknown territory. You must sometimes leave well-traveled paths to venture on those that are less traveled, step from well-lit stairs to ones shrouded in darkness, or follow trails made difficult from the tangles of weeds and rocks that sometimes block your passage. Yet, your journey is always one of progress—of looking ahead.

Persevere on the path of life into the new year. Be strong, yet yielding. Be open to all things, yet let nothing disrupt your center. Be compassionate and kind. Seek harmony with nature and within yourself. Let peace fill the days of your life.

❄️   ❄️   ❄️

"IF I HAD IT DO AGAIN, I WOULD TRAVEL
LIGHTER THAN I HAVE."

INDEX

AARP   Mar. 18, May 23, July 2

Acceptance   Jan. 28, Apr. 8, Apr. 29, May 19, Aug. 10, Oct. 10, Dec. 6, Dec. 29

Aches and pains   Feb. 7, Feb. 15

Achievements   Mar. 3, May 13

Action/movement   May 30, June 24, Aug. 16, Aug. 21, Aug. 23, Sept. 26, Oct. 23, Nov. 15, Dec. 26

Activism   Feb. 1, Feb. 4, Apr. 20, May 23, Sept. 18, Oct. 5, Nov. 9, Nov. 11, Nov. 12, Dec. 29

Acupuncture   Mar. 6, Mar. 23

Adventure   Jan. 6, Mar. 26

Advocacy   Feb. 4

Age bias   July 2

Ageism   Jan. 6, Feb. 3, Feb. 17, Mar. 6, Mar. 24, May 23, Aug. 6, Aug. 11, Oct. 6, Oct. 16, Nov. 24

Ages   June 28

Alcohol   Apr. 25, July 6, July 30

Alzheimer's disease   Feb. 28, Dec. 11

Amusement/ theme parks   Sept. 28

Anger   Jan. 30, July 23

Anxiety/panic   Feb. 22, Feb. 28

Appearance   Feb. 2, Feb. 11, Mar. 29, Apr. 11, Apr. 13, July 18, Sept. 8, Oct. 26, Dec. 7, Dec. 29

Arthritis   Mar. 21, July 3, Aug. 11

Assistance   May 18

Atherosclerosis   Mar. 15

Athletes   Apr. 15

Attitude   Jan. 1, Jan. 2, Jan. 5, Jan. 12, Feb. 27, Apr. 29, May 23, Aug. 30, Sept. 3, Nov. 4

Awareness   July 1, Nov. 2, Dec. 13

Baby boomers   Jan. 15, June 29, July 2, July 29, Sept. 27, Oct. 11

Balance   Apr. 21, Apr. 24, May 9, May 10, May 30, June 8, June 13

Beauty   May 5, July 18, Aug. 14

Bicycling   July 19

Blame   Aug. 13

Blues   Jan. 8

Bodybuilding   Mar. 10

Boredom   Jan. 27, Apr. 30, June 20

Boundaries/limitations   Mar. 19

Brain   Feb. 13, Feb. 28, Mar. 23, May 20

Burnout   Aug. 29

Caffeine   Apr. 14, Apr. 25, Sept. 2

Calcium   Apr. 25

Cancer   Jan. 21, Apr. 9, May 16, July 6, July 31, Nov. 10

Careers/work	Mar. 14, May 6, May 7
Caregiving	Feb. 12, Mar. 25, Apr. 1, May 11, May 18, May 27, June 12, Aug. 24, Oct. 20, Oct. 25, Nov. 12, Nov. 15, Nov. 16, Nov. 21, Dec. 16
Celebration	Aug. 28
Centenarians	Jan. 2, May 15, June 1, Sept. 22, Oct. 23
Centering	Feb. 23, June 14
Challenge	May 6
Change	Jan. 20, May 3, June 20, Sept. 9, Oct. 14, Nov. 6, Nov. 9, Dec. 27
Childhood	Oct. 11, Oct. 18, Oct. 22, Dec. 20
Children	Feb. 19, Mar. 8, Apr. 2, June 22, Aug. 5, Aug. 24
Chiropractor	Mar. 6
Cholesterol	Dec. 10
Clothing	Apr. 11
Comfort	June 2
Community	June 30, Aug. 11, Oct. 29, Nov. 11, Nov. 25
Compassion	May 27
Competitiveness	Feb. 8, May 13, Nov. 6
Connection	May 29
Control	Apr. 23
Cooperation	Sept. 17
Creativity	Feb. 8, Apr. 28, June 3, July 24
Culture	Jan. 15
Cycles	Feb. 11, Aug. 7, Oct. 1
Dance	Feb. 26
Dating	Nov. 1
Death	Jan. 12, Jan. 13, Jan. 17, Jan. 25, Feb. 9, Feb. 12, Feb. 16, Mar. 9, Apr. 8, May 13, May 25, May 28, May 29, June 9, June 21, June 23, June 25, July 26, Aug. 10, Aug. 19, Sept. 14, Sept. 21, Sept. 23, Sept. 29, Oct. 4, Oct. 10, Oct. 18, Nov. 1, Nov. 13, Nov. 16, Dec. 6, Dec. 18
Dementia	Feb. 28, Dec. 11
Depression	Feb. 5, Feb. 20, Feb. 24, Feb. 27, Feb. 28, Apr. 3, Apr. 14, Apr. 30
Diabetes	Mar. 27
Diet	Jan. 10, Jan. 11, Feb. 10, Feb. 21, Feb. 29, Mar. 2, Mar. 15, Apr. 4, Apr. 14, Apr. 25, May 1, July 30, Oct. 5, Oct. 12, Dec. 7, Dec. 10, Dec. 24
Disability	Jan. 9, Jan. 14, Mar. 11, Mar. 19, May 18, July 31, Oct. 21, Dec. 16
Discrimination	Feb. 4, July 2
Disease	Jan. 21, Mar. 6, May 15, Dec. 3, Dec. 16
Divorce	June 23, Aug. 19, Sept. 29, Oct. 18, Oct. 30, Nov. 1, Dec. 18, Dec. 19
Dreams	June 16, Aug. 15, Sept. 26
Elder-culture	Jan. 29

Elder hero	Feb. 17
Elder hostel	Jan. 19
Emotions	Jan. 12, Sept. 18
"Empty nest"	June 22
Energy	Jan. 26, Mar. 31
Entropy	May 30, Dec. 10
Exercise	Jan. 3, Jan. 10, Jan. 14, Jan. 21, Jan. 26, Feb. 10, Feb. 15, Feb. 29, Mar. 10, Mar. 21, Apr. 6, May 6, May 18, May 30, June 7, July 19, Aug. 8, Aug. 27, Sept. 11, Dec. 7
Experience	Feb. 25
Eyes	Mar. 27
Face	Mar. 29
Faith	Dec. 1
Family	June 6, June 10, Oct. 29, Nov. 11, Dec. 20
Fashion	Aug. 14
Fear	Jan. 25, Jan. 31, Feb. 3, July 4, Aug. 21
Finances	Feb. 16, May 17, June 1, Sept. 22, Sept. 27, Dec. 9, Dec. 19, Dec. 28
Flexibility	Mar. 21, May 21
Flow	June 5, Aug. 21
Focus	Aug. 7
Forgiveness	Jan. 30, Dec. 8
Freedom	July 4, July 17, Nov. 11
Friends/friendship	Feb. 20, Feb. 25, May 1, May 31, June 6, July 29, Aug. 28, Dec. 22
Funeral	Sept. 21
Future	Dec. 31
Gay/lesbian	Jan. 16, Nov. 25, Nov. 27
Generations/ generation gap	Aug. 4, Aug. 13, Nov. 18
Gerontophobia	Sept. 3
Give and take	May 24, May 25, Sept. 22, Nov. 23, Nov. 26, Nov. 30, Dec. 16, Dec. 25
Glaucoma	Mar. 27
Goals	Jan. 26, Feb. 1, Feb. 17, Feb. 18, May 2, June 12, June 16, July 12, July 13, Aug. 26, Sept. 20, Oct. 4, Oct. 13, Nov. 6, Dec. 24
Gratitude	Dec. 25
Gray Panthers	Jan. 6, Feb. 4, Aug. 11, Sept. 26, Nov. 29
"Gray parks"	Sept. 28
Grief	Feb. 9, Feb. 24, Mar. 9, June 13, Dec. 30
Growth	Feb. 3, Apr. 3, June 11, July 9, July 20, Dec. 14
Habits	July 30, Sept. 2
Hair	Dec. 29
Happiness	Jan. 8, Jan. 13, Mar. 1, Apr. 1, June 10, June 15, July 4, July 13, July 31, Dec. 20
Harmony	May 29, Nov. 25, Nov. 30, Dec. 17

Health care	Jan. 17, Apr. 9, Oct. 29, Oct. 30
Hearing	May 9
Heart/heart disease	Feb. 29, Mar. 15, Mar. 21, Apr. 9, June 13, June 25, July 8, Oct. 29
Holidays	Nov. 23, Dec. 17, Dec. 20
Home	Dec. 22
Hope	Aug. 12
Hormones	Mar. 23, Oct. 26
Hot flashes	Mar. 23, May 9
Housing	Sept. 17
Humor/laughter	Feb. 9, Feb. 27, Mar. 24, May 15, May 16, Oct. 13
Hunger	Jan. 11, Sept. 7
Hypertension	Mar. 15
Identity	Jan. 20
Illness	Jan. 17, Feb. 9, Feb. 12, Feb. 26, Apr. 9, June 5, July 6, Dec. 3
Imagination	July 24, Aug. 15
Impotence	Apr. 27, Oct. 26
Independence	June 17, Dec. 28
Individuality	May 31, June 4, July 17, Aug. 6, Nov. 25
Infirmities	Feb. 5
Insomnia	Feb. 15, Mar. 13, Apr. 14, June 29
Joint	Mar. 21
Journal	Nov. 19
Joy	July 13
Karma	Apr. 17
Last words	Jan. 13
Learning	Jan. 19, Feb. 3, Apr. 6, Apr. 12, Apr. 26, Apr. 28, May 8, May 13, May 20, June 18, June 30, Aug. 5, Sept. 1, Sept. 24, Oct. 2, Oct. 20, Oct. 31, Nov. 7, Dec. 21, Dec. 22
Legacy	May 7, Dec. 26
Letting go	Apr. 23, May 12, May 28
Life energy	Mar. 2, May 4
Life's meaning/ purpose	June 14, June 29, Aug. 28, Dec. 6, Dec. 13
Limitations	June 3, July 22, Aug. 29, Oct. 28
Listening	June 2
Live for today	Mar. 7, Sept. 30, Dec. 13
Living will	Sept. 21, Sept. 23
Loneliness	Feb. 13, Mar. 13, Apr. 19, July 4, Oct. 28, Nov. 21
Longevity	Oct. 12, Oct. 23, Oct. 30
Loss	Sept. 29
Love	Jan. 9, Feb. 14, Mar. 8, Apr. 1, Apr. 7, Apr. 24, June 23, June 26, July 23, Sept. 10, Nov. 1, Dec. 19
Malnutrition	Jan. 11
Marketing	Jan. 22, May 23, July 7, July 19, Oct. 31, Nov. 17, Dec. 29
Maturity	Jan. 31, Feb. 6, June 22, July 5, July 17

Meals on Wheels	Jan. 7, Feb. 12
Medical issues	Mar. 6
Medicare	Oct. 5
Medication	Apr. 14
Meditation	Feb. 3, Feb. 26, Mar. 2, Apr. 8, Apr. 10, May 10, Sept. 16, Oct. 2, Oct. 12, Oct. 24, Nov. 14, Dec. 11
Memories	Jan. 8, Jan. 15, May 20, Aug. 2, Sept. 12, Dec. 12, Dec. 15
Memory/memory loss	Feb. 28, Nov. 13, Dec. 7, Dec. 11
Menopause	Feb. 11, Mar. 23, Apr. 27, May 9, July 16, Nov. 9
Mental alertness	Feb. 13
Mentor	Nov. 26
Midlife	Jan. 1, Jan. 14, Feb. 5, Feb. 19, Feb. 27, Mar. 4, Mar. 5, Mar. 14, Mar. 18, Mar. 24, Apr. 3, Apr. 27, May 1, May 3, June 12, June 24, June 28, June 29, July 2, July 12, July 14, July 19, Aug. 5, Aug. 9, Aug. 14, Aug. 30, Sept. 23, Sept. 25, Sept. 27, Oct. 5, Oct. 25, Oct. 26, Nov. 1, Nov. 5, Nov. 12, Nov. 17, Nov. 20, Dec. 5, Dec. 10, Dec. 15, Dec. 24
Mind	Apr. 6, May 20
Mobile home	Feb. 21
Mobility	Aug. 9
Money	Jan. 22, Jan. 24, Feb. 16
Movies	Jan. 15
Music	Jan. 15, Feb. 26
Myths	Jan. 29, Feb. 17, Mar. 22, Sept. 3, Oct. 6
Nature	Jan. 18, Feb. 3, Feb. 11, Feb. 18, Mar. 30, Apr. 20, May 14, May 21, June 8, June 13, July 21, July 22, July 28, Aug. 1, Aug. 7, Aug. 23, Sept. 17, Sept. 24, Oct. 1, Oct. 3, Oct. 7, Oct. 10, Oct. 21, Oct. 24, Nov. 2, Nov. 14, Dec. 6, Dec. 21
Network	Jan. 23
Nighttime	Dec. 18
Nursing home	Apr. 22, Oct. 6, Nov. 21
Older Women's League	Feb. 4
One day at a time	Mar. 7
Optimism/pessimism	Jan. 5, Jan. 8, Jan. 12, Mar. 17, May 15, June 19, June 20, June 21, July 11, July 15, Aug. 30, Nov. 3, Dec. 3
Osteoporosis	Jan. 21, Mar. 15, Apr. 25
Pace	Mar. 28, Apr. 21, June 7, Oct. 19
Pain	Mar. 6, Sept. 25
Parenting	Feb. 19, Aug. 5, Aug. 24
Parents	Mar. 25, June 22, Aug. 24, Oct. 22
Passion	May 22, May 27, June 24, June 26
Past	Jan. 8, Jan. 28, Jan. 30, May 19, Aug. 2, Sept. 13, Sept. 30, Nov. 8, Dec. 12
Patience	Aug. 7, Sept. 20
Peace Corps	Jan. 7

Perfectionism	May 12
Perspective	Oct. 19, Oct. 28
Pets	Jan. 20, Jan. 27, Feb. 21, Feb. 24, May 11, June 17, Sept. 14, Oct. 15, Oct. 20, Oct. 27
Play	Apr. 2, Apr. 4, Apr. 24, May 26
Politics	Mar. 17, Oct. 5, Dec. 9, Dec. 26
Power yoga	Sept. 25
Prayer	Jan. 31, Feb. 3, Feb. 25, Mar. 5, Mar. 9, Apr. 8, Apr. 10, June 9, July 8, Oct. 20, Dec. 23
Pregnancy	Feb. 19
Prejudice	Aug. 7
Present moment	Mar. 7, Mar. 9, Apr. 24, June 15, June 21, June 26, Aug. 2, Aug. 3, Sept. 12, Sept. 30, Oct. 19, Nov. 8, Dec. 2, Dec. 12, Dec. 13
Problem-solving	Sept. 26, Oct. 9, Oct. 28, Nov. 3
Productivity	Mar. 3
Prostate problems	May 9
Proverbs	July 27
Psychology	Feb. 6
Quality of life	Apr. 16
Recreation	Jan. 23, Jan. 26, Sept. 28
Regret	Jan. 28, Mar. 31
Relationships	Apr. 17, May 31, June 5, June 10, Nov. 30
Responsibility	June 22
Rest	May 30, Aug. 29, Sept. 16
Retirement	Jan. 4, Feb. 16, Feb. 21, Feb. 27, Mar. 1, Mar. 8, Apr. 15, Apr. 26, May 15, May 26, June 30, July 6, Aug. 5, Aug. 20, Aug. 29, Sept. 27, Sept. 29, Nov. 25, Nov. 28
Retirement community	Jan. 23
Risks	Jan. 20, Mar. 26, Apr. 18, June 1, Aug. 12, Aug. 17, Oct. 8, Nov. 20, Dec. 31
Rituals	Mar. 16
Role models	Feb. 17, May 26, June 20, June 24, July 10, July 21, July 28, Aug. 11, Aug. 14, Aug. 25, Sept. 4, Sept. 6, Sept. 20, Sept. 22, Oct. 3, Oct. 4, Oct. 16, Oct. 21, Nov. 5, Nov. 10, Nov. 11, Nov. 18, Dec. 4, Dec. 5, Nov. 24, Dec. 27
Romance	Feb. 14
Running	Jan. 3, Jan. 26, Feb. 15, Mar. 3, Mar. 26, June 24, Aug. 8, Sept. 5, Sept. 25, Oct. 2, Dec. 4
Sadness	June 5, Dec. 30
Salt	Mar. 15
Satori	Oct. 2
School	Jan. 19
Season	May 21
Self-confidence	July 21
Self-esteem	Feb. 1, Mar. 1, Apr. 13, Apr. 19, May 11, June 7, June 16, Aug. 13, Aug. 18, Oct. 8, Oct. 16, Nov. 3
Self-help groups	Mar. 2, Mar. 7

Self-image	Feb. 2, Apr. 11, Apr. 13, June 7
Self-pity	Feb. 16
Self-talk	Nov. 3
Sensuality	July 28
Sex	Jan. 9, Mar. 22, May 5, May 22, June 23, Oct. 26, Nov. 18, Nov. 27
Silence	May 10, Oct. 24
Simplicity	May 10, Oct. 9
Single	June 23, Aug. 19, Nov. 1
Skiing	Dec. 4
Skin	Mar. 29, July 3, Sept. 8
Sleep	Mar. 13, Apr. 24, Sept. 2, Sept. 13, Oct. 12, Nov. 14, Nov. 22, Dec. 10
Smoking	Feb. 29, Apr. 9, Apr. 14, Apr. 25, July 6, July 30, Sept. 13, Dec. 10
Snowbird	Feb. 21, Nov. 25
Socializing	Jan. 23, Feb. 13
Solitude	May 11
Spirituality	Jan. 10, Jan. 25, Feb. 3, Feb. 18, Feb. 23, Feb. 25, Mar. 2, Mar. 5, Mar. 9, Mar. 30, Apr. 8, Apr. 10, Apr. 24, June 9, July 4, July 16, July 25, July 30, Aug. 6, Aug. 27, Sept. 19, Oct. 12, Oct. 20, Oct. 22, Nov. 4, Nov. 23, Nov. 29
Stability	Mar. 16, June 8, Oct. 12
Strengths	June 19, July 5, Nov. 19, Dec. 1
Stress	Mar. 1, Mar. 28
Stroke	Feb. 29, Mar. 15
Success	June 19, Aug. 26, Sept. 6
Suffering	June 5
Suicide	Apr. 30, June 9, Dec. 3
Support	Jan. 23, Feb. 12, Feb. 16, May 23, May 26, June 18, July 6, July 14, Sept. 14, Sept. 15, Oct. 20, Oct. 30, Dec. 18
Tai Chi	Aug. 27
Time	Mar. 11, Mar. 20, Apr. 4, Apr. 5, Apr. 21, July 1, July 12, July 20, Aug. 3, Aug. 7, Sept. 11, Nov. 19
Travel	Feb. 21, Apr. 12, May 17, Oct. 31
Triumphs/victories	May 13
Trust	Apr. 4, July 21, Sept. 19, Oct. 14, Nov. 22
Truths	July 27
Vacations	May 17
Visualization	Feb. 26, Apr. 16, Dec. 11
Vitamins	Jan. 11
Volunteering	Jan. 7, Jan. 27, Feb. 4, Mar. 11, Apr. 13, Apr. 20, Sept. 4, Sept. 7, Sept. 18, Sept. 22, Dec. 16, Dec. 25
Weight	Feb. 10, Mar. 15, Oct. 26, Dec. 24
Weight lifting	Jan. 26
Wellness	July 30
Widow/widower	Aug. 19, Nov. 26

Wisdom	May 4, May 19, May 24, June 5, Aug. 22, Dec. 1
Women/men	Jan. 6, Mar. 12, Mar. 23, Mar. 29, Apr. 1, Apr. 3, Apr. 9, Apr. 13, Apr. 25, Apr. 27, May 5, Aug. 6, Aug. 19, Oct. 16, Oct. 26, Dec. 16
Wonder	Oct. 21
Work	Jan. 2, Jan. 4, Jan. 29, Feb. 4, Mar. 12, Mar. 14, Mar. 28, Apr. 6, Apr. 24, Apr. 26, May 26, July 2, July 12, July 15, Aug. 20, Aug. 25, Oct. 4, Nov. 20, Dec. 5
Worry	Apr. 14
Wrinkles	Sept. 8
Youth	Jan. 5, Jan. 29, Feb. 6, Feb. 8, Apr. 11, May 19, June 11, June 27, July 7, July 14, July 17, July 28, Aug. 3, Aug. 4, Aug. 6, Aug. 8, Sept. 3, Sept. 18, Oct. 16, Oct. 30, Nov. 7, Nov. 18, Dec. 12, Dec. 26